the **stupidity** paradox

About the authors

Mats Alvesson is Professor of Business Administration at the University of Lund, Sweden, University of Queensland and Cass Business School, City University, London. He has published extensively across a wide range of organisational behaviour topics and issues, is one of the most frequently cited European researchers in management and organisation studies and a sought-after speaker around the globe. He is the author of *The Triumph of Emptiness*, Oxford University Press and *Reflexive Leadership*, Sage (with Martin Blom and Stefan Sveningsson).

André Spicer is Professor of Organisational Behaviour at Cass Business School, City University, London, known for his research in the areas of the human side of work, leadership and ethics. He is widely published in both academic literature and the general business media and is a frequent commentator on sustainable business, behaviours at work and business culture. He is the author of *The Wellness Syndrome*, Polity Press (with Carl Cederström).

Two things are infinite: the universe and human stupidity;
and I'm not sure about the universe.

Albert Einstein

The whole problem with the world is that fools and fanatics
are always so certain of themselves, and wiser people so full of
doubts.

Bertrand Russell

To be stupid, selfish, and have good health are three
requirements for happiness, though if stupidity is lacking, all
is lost.

Gustave Flaubert

Contents

Preface

A few years ago, both of us were invited to an official dinner. We found a place at a table together, sat down and started to catch up. One of us described how his student had recently been doing an internship with a powerful government department. Over the period of three months, the student had to help write a report. This was not the kind of report that would be shelved at once and read by no one. This report would set out an entirely new policy area for the government. You might think this was a difficult job requiring a team of very experienced people doing in-depth research. Apparently not. The student worked largely on her own. Her manager was in his twenties. When she asked him what was the most important aspect of developing a really good report, he replied: One or two impressive PowerPoint slides. This struck both of us as really stupid. How could an important new government policy that would affect millions of people be based on a few PowerPoint slides created by an intern who was managed by a twenty-something?

Was this just a one-off case of stupidity, we asked, and began to swap stories from the dozens of organisations we have studied over the years. We talked about top executives who rely on consultants' PowerPoint shows rather than careful analysis, headmasters and teachers who spend their time

enthusiastically talking about vague but positive organisational values rather than educating students, managers who
try to be inspiring leaders even though their subordinates are
not interested and are capable of working on their own, senior
figures in the armed forces who prefer to run rebranding exercises rather than military exercises, engineers who overlook
fatal flaws, IT analysts who prefer to ignore problems so as not
to undermine the upbeat tone of their workplace, senior executives who keep on launching programmes for change yet have
no serious interest in the outcome, and newspaper editors who
are more interested in finding the perfect mixture of celebrity
gossip than in preparing themselves for profound changes in
their industry.

When we came to the topic of universities, we realised there were just too many kinds of stupidity to mention:
pointless rebranding exercises, ritualistic box-ticking, misguided attempts at visionary leadership, thoughtless pursuit
of rankings, to mention just a few. We were worried that all
this stupidity was detracting from the core purpose of our
institutions: to educate students, develop new knowledge and
contribute to the wider community.

As we piled up all these examples, we started to realise that
something was very wrong here. We are constantly told that
to be competitive we must be smart. We should be knowledge
workers employed by knowledge-intensive firms that trade in
the knowledge economy. Our governments spend billions on
trying to create knowledge economies, our firms brag about
their superior intelligence, and individuals spend decades of
their lives building up fine CVs. Yet all this collective intellect does not seem to be reflected in the many organisations
we studied. Much of what goes on in these organisations was
described – often by employees themselves – as being stupid.

Far from being 'knowledge-intensive', many of our most well-known chief organisations have become engines of stupidity. We have frequently seen otherwise smart people stop thinking and start doing stupid things. They stop asking questions. They give no reasons for their decisions. They pay no heed to what their actions cause. Instead of complex thought we get flimsy jargon, aggressive assertions or expert tunnel vision. Reflection, careful analysis and independent reflection decay. Idiotic ideas and practices are accepted as quite sane. People may harbour doubts, but their suspicions are cut short. What's more, they are rewarded for it. The upshot is that a lack of thought has entered the modus operandi of most organisations of today.

But one thing puzzled us: why was it that organisations which employed so many smart people could foster so much stupidity? After some discussion, we realised something: smart organisations and the smart people who work in them often do stupid things because they work – at least in the short term. By avoiding careful thinking, people are able to simply get on with their job. Asking too many questions is likely to upset others – and to distract yourself. Not thinking frees you up to fit in and get along. Sometimes it makes sense to be stupid. Perhaps we live in an age where a certain type of stupidity has triumphed.

But that was not the end of the story. As we talked more, we realised that while being stupid might work in the short term, it could lead to bigger problems in the long term. When people buy into baseless ideas it can create a nice feeling today, but lay traps for tomorrow. At the time, the global financial system was in turmoil. One of the reasons was that banks had bought financial products they didn't fully understand. In the short term this didn't matter, as the banks continued to make money from these products anyway. But when financial markets soured, this lack of comprehension sparked disaster.

If organisations create so much stupidity, what does that mean for the people who run them? The fact is, many managers try to ensure that smart people don't use their intellect. There are many tactics that are used to do this. Anyone who has spent even a few days in a large firm knows them well. But to us it seemed that within modern organisations there is just too much stupidity, and that what is needed is a concerted effort to minimise some pointless practices that we find all around us at work. As we reflected further on this problem, we started to identify some very practical steps that can be used to destupidify our organisations.

Our realisations during that dinner – that smart organisations encourage stupidity, that this pays off in the short term, but creates problems in the long term – led us to write this book. Welcome to the paradox of *functional stupidity*.

Mats Alvesson and André Spicer
Lund and London, February 2016

Introduction

Attack of the quants

At the dawn of the twenty-first century, one thing haunted the greatest scientific minds. It was not the promise of a theory of everything, threats like global warming, or even new areas of research. Scientists at the best-known institutions across the world were complaining about the career choices of their students.

In the past, we are told, top young scientists were inspired by their studies to pursue careers as researchers. This produced a stream of brilliant thinkers who would come up with Nobel prize-winning breakthroughs. But this had stopped happening. Many of the brightest graduates had rejected careers in science. Instead they were flocking to banking.

The world of finance offered defectors from science many perks. The pay was much better, career prospects looked stellar, the plush offices full of attractive people were far more comfortable than dreary labs staffed with other nerds. Many of the skills that scientists developed during their training were in high demand in the financial markets. At the same time the long working hours and high levels of stress were familiar, and just like the lab, finance was still largely dominated by men.

Despite these strong similarities, there was one clear difference between the world of science and that of finance: the
culture. For many years, finance had been dominated by a
hard-driving culture of individual gain. Greed was good,
money was king and success was flaunted. In science the watch-
words were truth and discovery. People were proud of being
fairly indifferent to money. Intellectual challenges, developing
new knowledge and being recognised by the community were
much more important. The prospects of someone who had been
nurtured in the culture of science thriving in the showy world
of finance looked bleak.

However, the scientists who crossed over into finance did
not just survive – they began to thrive. The steady stream of
science graduates brought with them well-honed quantitative
skills. They were quickly put to work building highly abstract
models. Instead of trying to develop equations for tracking
the movement of stars, they were modelling the movements
of markets. These former scientists did not enter the rowdy
crush of the trading floor. They did their work in the hush of
air-conditioned offices. They did not see themselves as traders,
they were 'quants'. No longer scientists or bankers, they saw
themselves as members of a cutting-edge new field: financial
engineering.

As the number of quants employed by banks increased,
so their prestige and resources grew. Decisions about trading
strategies were no longer made in the heated cut and thrust of
deal-making. Instead, the abstract mathematical models took
over. Hundreds of billions of dollars quickly became dependent
on the models the quants devised. As the economy boomed,
untold wealth flooded into financial institutions. This mountain of money was placed under the purview of quants. What
had once been a fringe pursuit practised by a few geeks in

marginal institutions was now the axis of the modern financial system. The quants' confidence increased as their models generated exceptional returns. This in turn buoyed the confidence of the financial markets. Some grew so confident in financial engineering that they declared an end to boom and bust and the dawn of perpetual prosperity.

But at the very same time as confidence in financial engineering was increasing, the connection between the quants' clean abstract models and the messy realities of markets was beginning to fray. The fate of collateralised debt obligations (CDOs) is a perfect example. A CDO combines different kinds of debt. To create a CDO you might combine mortgages on houses in affluent neighbourhoods owed by prosperous families (a sure bet), car loans granted to people with modest means (a reasonable prospect, but some risk), and 'sub-prime' house loans made to so-called NINJAs – an acronym for people with 'No Income, No Job or Assets' (a sure loss). The trick was to assess this package of different types of debt only on the basis of the safest debt. So for instance a package of debt that was made up of sure bets, risky bets and sure losses was treated as if it contained only sure bets. The abstract models represented CDOs as one thing (a sure bet), while the reality was quite different (they were a messy mix of everything from sure bets to sure losses).

At this point you might ask: 'Why didn't someone stop and ask some hard questions?' The answer is: a few people actually did. A handful of people at all levels of the industry had pointed out some of the hidden problems in these financial models. However, these critics were a very small minority who were almost without exception ignored. Their old-fashioned messages of financial doom did not match the prevailing mood of optimism. But the major reason that bankers did not ask the tough questions about their increasingly fragile models was that they simply did not understand them. Financial markets had grown so complex that only a handful of quants could actually understand certain narrow aspects of what was going on. Senior managers of the largest banks had little idea what was happening in their own institutions. Regulators who were supposed to act as watchdogs either ignored problems or simply failed to grasp them. What is perhaps most shocking is that many quants admitted to not even understanding how their own models matched reality.[1]

This shared abyss of knowledge was fine as long as the market continued to rise, but serious problems emerged when markets started falling. When this happened, it became clear that many financial models were constructed on false assumptions. As this collective thoughtlessness grew more and more obvious, trust in these models evaporated. After all, banks were not even sure about the assumptions built into their own models. When this collective stupidity came to light, people stopped lending and trading with one another. The whole financial machine seized up. The result was a financial crisis with worldwide effects that are still being felt years later.

The financial crisis that began in 2008 is a testament to the stupidity lurking at the heart of knowledge-based societies. If we reflect on the crisis we can see an all too common story: banks appointed many extremely intelligent people. These smart people set about applying their impressive but narrowly focused skills. They developed complex models few people could understand. The glamour of financial engineering created a sense of hope and excitement throughout the whole industry, and investors began to believe in the power of the quants to work magic. They stopped asking tough questions and started to just believe. The upshot was a financial system that no one fully understood and no one was willing to question. As the gap grew between what models predicted and what markets did, problems built up, eventually to explode in the form of a global financial crisis.

The lead-up to the 2008 financial crisis shows us the stupidity paradox in action: smart people who end up doing stupid things at work. In the short term, this seemed to be a good thing because it helped to produce results. But in the longer term, it laid the foundations for a disaster.

Stuck in the silicon lagoon

Knowledge, learning, talent, wisdom, innovation, creativity: these words are all too common in business-school textbooks, consultants' reports and politicians' speeches. Organisations abound with 'chief knowledge officers', 'cognitive engineers', 'data alchemists' and 'innovation sherpas'. Even relatively low-level jobs have received the knowledge makeover: bin-men have become 'waste management and disposal technicians'; technical help-desk workers are 'investment development and research analysts'; secretaries are 'directors of first impressions'.

To find a place in this knowledge-intensive world, young people are advised to build their intellectual capital through years of more and more expensive education and a dizzying array of new experiences. Undergraduates now have CVs that boast of building wells in Ugandan villages ('entrepreneurship'), working in a café in Brooklyn ('service management'), making photocopies in London investment banks ('analysis'), and teaching children to ski in the Canadian Rockies ('leadership'). They hope this wide array of unrelated experience will win them a place in the supposedly lucrative 'creative class'.[2] This is of course a wonderfully elastic and seductive term which includes 30 per cent of the population in countries like the USA. Everyone from teachers to engineers fits in. The fantasy image of the knowledge worker is of a smart and amply rewarded free agent hanging out in an inner-city café and pushing their intellect to the limit. The reality is more likely to be someone working on a short-term contract in a data centre situated in an office park at the edge of a motorway. If asked (which is unlikely), they may well describe their job as dumb.

We are told that in order to 'win the war for talent' in a 'knowledge economy', organisations must craft smart strategies, build intelligent systems and nurture their intellectual capital. Nation states have been striving to become knowledge economies and attract highly skilled (and well paid) jobs. They sink millions into building 'knowledge clusters', 'science parks', 'innovation zones', 'talent corridors' and 'smart cities'. Most countries in the world have attempted to create their own 'unique' version of Silicon Valley. There is Silicon Alley (New York), Silicon Lagoon (Nigeria), Silicon Island (Japan), Silicon Oasis (Dubai) and Silicon Roundabout (UK).

This widespread zeal for smartness seems to be based on one single message: that the fate of our organisations, economy and working life hinges on our ability to be smart. Knowledge and intelligence are thought to be *the* key resources. But is being smart actually so important? Are knowledge workers really as smart as we would like to think? Do knowledge-intensive firms really act so shrewdly? Do nations have to nurture their intellect capital to thrive in the global economy?

It is time to question much of the hype about the knowledge economy, smart companies and brain workers. We think that most apparently knowledge-intensive organisations can be pretty stupid. Far from running a knowledge-based economy, most developed nations utilise most of their people to do low-level service work. Quick feet and hands combined with a friendly smile matter more for the economy than the intellect of a relatively small group of elite knowledge workers. Even if you possess some intellectual capital in the form of a university degree, there is a high likelihood you will end up working in a job that only really requires high-school qualifications. But in order to get there you need the credentials first.

If you scratch the shiny surface of almost any organisation claiming to be knowledge-intensive, you will find a quite different reality. Sure, there are often many well-educated smart people, but there is often little evidence that most of the corporate intelligentsia are fully using their intellect. Sometimes this is because many knowledge-intensive firms are packed with clever people working in jobs that are routine and uncomplicated. Think about your average market-research company. These knowledge-intensive firms typically hire well-mannered young people with decent degrees to do two things: call people while they are eating dinner to ask inane questions, or crunch the data that these phone calls yield. It is questionable just how much intellectual skill is required by either of these jobs. What they do require is a nice accent and thick skin. Small wonder that one call-centre operative described the job as 'an assembly line in the head'.[3]

Even when people do find themselves in a context where there is some scope to exercise their intellect, they often seem to avoid this. A recent study by psychologists at the University of Virginia found that over half of the people they tested would rather give themselves electric shocks than sit and just think for between 6 and 11 minutes.[4] This abhorrence of independent thinking is also common in the workplace. Managers often avoid having to think for themselves by becoming over-enthusiastic about showy ideas. For instance, following the financial crisis, senior executives at a large global bank started getting interested in 'authentic leadership'. They thought that by reconnecting with their 'inner values', it was possible to become more ethical *and* to increase their performance at the same time. The bank decided to send all its senior managers on training courses that would help them to locate their inner values. While this may have looked good on paper, many participants found the exercise to be either invasive, a waste of time, or both.

What is so striking is not just that bright people buy into stupid ideas. The real surprise is that by buying into these ideas, they can help organisations to function well and aid individuals in building their career. Baseless ideas can help organisations and the individuals working in them to look and feel good. By going along to an ethical training course, a senior banker will probably not change their values, but they might end up feeling a little bit better about themselves. In addition, people can be rewarded for having the right appearance, the right beliefs and the right attitudes. For instance, individuals who resisted going on the ethical training course were seen as being deviants who did not comply with the new more righteous tone at the bank. Indeed, the bank as a whole probably benefited from such training courses. It could show the media, politicians and the regulators that it was doing something (irrespective of how efficient or effective it was). It sent out a positive message to potential employees. Maybe it made existing employees more committed to the firm. What was much less certain was whether it actually achieved the putative aims. In many ways, this was completely incidental.

Shoot first, ask questions later

To understand why smart people buy into stupid ideas, and often get rewarded for doing so, we need to look at the role that *functional stupidity* plays. Functional stupidity is the inclination to reduce one's scope of thinking and focus only on the narrow, technical aspects of the job. You do the job correctly, but without reflecting on purpose or the wider context. Functional stupidity is an organised attempt to stop people from thinking seriously about what they do at work. When people are seized by functional stupidity, they remain capable of doing the job, but they stop asking searching questions about their work. In the place of rigorous reflection, they become obsessed with superficial appearances. Instead of asking questions, they start to obey commands. Rather than thinking about outcomes, they focus on the techniques for getting things done. And the thing to be done is often to create the right impression. Someone in the thrall of functional stupidity is great at doing things that look good. They tick boxes for management, please the clients and placate the authorities, but they also often do things that make little sense and that a sharp outside observer might find strange.

It is easy to suppose that people who do stupid things at work have a low IQ, poor education, a narrow mindset, or have been seduced by dogmatic ideas. And at times this is true. Most of us have encountered people in the workplace who have limited intellectual capacities, yet still seem to hold important positions. We have also probably worked alongside someone whose irrational prejudices and dogged fixations stop them from making rational decisions.

Most of the time, it is not imbeciles or bigots who do the most stupid things. Some of the most problematic things are done by some of the smartest people. A lot of these stupidities are not recognised as such. Instead they are treated as normal, and in many cases even applauded.

You need to be relatively intelligent to be functionally stupid. You need to use some of your cognitive capacity: even be analytically and technically sharp. But once in the grip of functional stupidity, you avoid thinking too much about exactly what you are doing, why you are doing it, and its potential implications. By following this tried and true recipe, you hope to avoid punishments and many worries that might come from deviation. You sidestep the burdens of having to think too much and upsetting others by asking difficult questions. What's more, you are usually rewarded for doing this.

Organisations encourage functional stupidity in many ways. Some have cultures that emphasise being action-oriented. 'Just do it' is no longer a catchy marketing slogan: it has become standard marching orders for the corporate nincompoop. As Michael Foley puts it in *The Age of Absurdity*: 'It is only our own impatient, greedy age that demands to be told how to live in a set of short bullet points.' Other firms have kindled an intense faith in leadership. As a result, practices that would not be out of place in a religious cult have become stock responses for managers in our largest companies. Many organisations foster a deep belief in the rationality of what are clearly irrational structures and systems. This means people cling to systems and structures that obviously do not yield the results they are meant to. Companies routinely talk about their brand as what makes them different, but if you take a careful look it seems to be same as in other companies. Firms often go out of their way to copy other organisations they think are successful, but often they have little or no idea of why they are copying them.

Our obsession with leadership, formal structures, brands and industry standards might seem sensible, but when taken to extremes – as it all too often is – it can shackle thinking. When people are obsessed with buying into success recipes and taking action, for instance, they are relieved of the burden of actually having to consider the tacit assumptions they act on, and the implications of their actions. It plays out as if they have learned that great military adage, shoot first, ask questions later.

The paradox of stupidity

Shutting off parts of your brain at work may seem like a bad idea, but it often comes with some big benefits. When functional stupidity kicks in, employees are spared from the taxing task of using all their intellectual resources. Instead, they can cognitively coast along and steer clear of irksome doubts. This can pay off for some individuals. They are not seen as troublemakers who ask too many awkward questions. They can display the kind of resolute certainty that singles out 'leadership material'. When they make authoritative claims that their company pursues 'excellence', their decisiveness and conviction will betray no signs of doubt.

Functional stupidity can have similar benefits for the entire organisation. By ignoring the many uncertainties, contradictions and downright illogical claims that are rife at work, people are able to ensure that things run relatively smoothly. We often value convenience over confronting the inconvenient truth.

Yet while stupidity can be convenient, it can also have major downsides. When people start ignoring contradictions, avoid careful reasoning and fail to ask probing questions, they also start to overlook problems. That way you may rest easy in the short term, but in the long term these problems will build up. As this happens, the gulf between rhetoric and reality becomes hard to deny. This triggers a profound sense of disappointment and disengagement on the part of employees. When this becomes overwhelming, it can easily spread to stakeholders like customers, communities, buyers and suppliers, regulators and investors. As a result, people stop trusting the organisation.

But there is an even more dangerous consequence of functional stupidity. As well as sapping trust, it can sometimes create the conditions for larger crises or disasters. This happens when minor problems build up, become connected, and create wicked problems that are impossible to ignore. The 2008 financial crisis we described at the start of this chapter is a case in point.

Functional stupidity is not just a one-way highroad to disaster. It can also sometimes spark more fundamental changes. When the costs of overlooking problems become too great, people usually start to reflect on their assumptions, ask questions about why they are doing things and consider the implications of their actions. As this starts to happen, they no longer engage in an elaborate dance of sidestepping difficult questions. Instead they face up to them. Rather than seeking safe consensus, people start to look for much more challenging and intellectually demanding dissensus. When this happens, the fog of collective thoughtlessness can start to lift.

Weeding out functional stupidity sounds like a great thing to do, but it always comes at a cost. Often this is huge. Constant questioning can create doubt, uncertainty and conflict. Too much time can be wasted thinking and debating. Toes might be stepped on. People might be embarrassed and hurt. Critical reflection can become an obstacle to creating compliance, motivating employees, implementing strategy and leading effectively. It can undermine authority and leadership. To nurture a positive image can be difficult if people think too much.

Occasionally in organisations there are flurries of critical reflection. This happened in one large US company when a vice president stunned a seminar room full of junior managers by suddenly asking why not a single member of the audience had pointed out the radical discrepancy between all the talk and how the company actually worked. The audience did not know what to say. They were perplexed by the brutal honesty – a virtue not common in a world where people prefer to believe what is preached rather than what is practised.[5] The intervention did open up some space to reflect on what was actually happening in the company, but such moments come rarely.

Functional stupidity is a paradox, simultaneously thoughtless and useful. It has good and bad sides. For instance, a compulsively optimistic outlook may mean that people in an organisation feel very positive and committed to their job. At the same time, it can mean that people overlook negative things, leading to costly mistakes. What was functional can prove to be disastrously stupid. In other instances, idiotic ideas can have some clearly positive effects. Steve Jobs was an expert at this. At some points of his career he had stupid ideas that came to grief. At other times these ludicrous ideas paid off.

The Marine Corps of the corporate world

'Like other meetings, this one was a ceremonial event. We marked it on our calendars many weeks in advance. Everyone wore the unofficial corporate uniform: a blue pin-striped suit, white shirt, and a sincere red tie. None of us would ever remove the jacket. We dressed and acted as if we were at a meeting of the board of directors.'[6]

This is John Sculley's description of a typical meeting at Pepsi-Cola's headquarters during the early 1980s. People entered the room in hierarchical order. First came the marketing consultants, clad in appropriate grey suits, sitting alongside the wall at the back of the room. Then the junior executives entered the room, and took a seat at the back. Only then did senior executives arrive, in a sequence dictated by rank. The chairman came last. They arranged themselves around the table in strict hierarchical order.

After this ritual was enacted, the meeting kicked into action. The main business was monitoring results, an often harsh business:

> These sessions weren't always euphoric. Often the tension in the room was suffocating. Eyes would fix on Kendall [the chairman] to capture his response at every gain or drop in every tenth of a market share ... An executive whose share was down had to stand and explain – fully – what he was going to do to fix it fast. Clearly in the dock, he knew that the next time he returned to that room, it had better be fixed ... Always, there was another executive in the room, ready to take your place.[7]

Pepsi is described as a place characterised by extreme, but fair, competition. Frequent, short-term, precise measurement of results based on market share meant that the contribution of each executive was easy to track. This was a workplace for the best and the brightest, but also the toughest. War metaphors were frequent. Managers described themselves as the Marine Corps of the business world. They were physically and mentally very fit. They hit the gym for frequent intensive workouts. During the 'Cola wars' of the 1980s – the competition between Coca-Cola and Pepsi over market leadership – there were many casualties, but people did not complain. Instead they lived up to an ideal of strong masculinity. According to Sculley, in this corporate Marine Corps, loyalty was vital.

When he decided to resign to move to Apple Computers, he was forced to break this bond of loyalty – an act that caused him a great deal of pain.

Sculley's story may help us to understand the success of Pepsi at that time. The Marine Corps culture meant that its executives felt under pressure to do their utmost. They focused intensely on results, worked very hard and gave little consideration to their life outside of work. Friends and family were often marginalised. The obsession with competition – both between and within the company – nurtured a rich martial vocabulary and combative rituals to match. This energised the executives by giving them a feeling that they were proving their worth through masculine rivalry: if you happen to be part of this group of company he-men, you belong to the best, the toughest and most capable corporate warriors who can handle the fiercest competition. In this corporate culture, men of true grit were selected and then promoted if they continued to deliver the goods by increasing sales, market shares and profits. This was all that mattered.

The culture Sculley describes was clearly functional. At the time, Pepsi moved from being a relatively marginal player in the market to challenging Coca-Cola's leading position. But it also had negative elements. The fierce competition obstructed cooperation. The company grew obsessed with short-term results and ignored the longer-term implications. For them, corporate life was like war. This meant they could do little else but fight and compete. There was not much room for reflection, careful thinking or critical analysis – beyond how to improve sales and market shares.

To fully embrace the idea that executives at Pepsi were the Marine Corps of the business world, some serious mindlessness was needed. After all, office workers in suits and ties sitting around in meetings and analysing numbers are not quite engaged in mortal combat. Intensive exercise at the gym and heated battles on the squash court would not change that. If they wanted to cling to the Marine Corps image, it was vital to suppress any reflection and exorcise any form of self-irony.

It is interesting how eagerly the executives of Pepsi embraced a militaristic identity. There seemed to be little reflection or doubt about the rigid rules of the (war) game inside the company. People appeared to be caught up in a quasi-totalitarian set of beliefs. Any personal sacrifice in the cause of increasing market share was celebrated. Sculley writes that he felt guilty if he had not done his utmost during the day and was not really tired when he went to bed. The rigid rituals, the militaristic language, the strong codes of physical appearance all came together to create a masculine, disciplined, performance- and career-fixated individual. Thoughtfulness was not a virtue during the Cola Wars.

Looking at this world from a safe distance, you might be puzzled. How was it that executives could summon up such energy and commitment? In fact, it is hard to imagine a scientist about to find a cure for cancer or a person in an aid organisation rescuing people from a disaster being more committed than Pepsi's warriors in the Cola wars. And for what? Selling sweetened water at a high price to teenagers? At the end of the day Pepsi's 'substantive' contribution to humankind is partly negative: the product is full of sugar which can endanger people's health.

In *Moby Dick*, Captain Ahab says 'All my means are sane, my motive and my object mad'.[8] This is the functionally stupid person in a nutshell. Narrowing your thinking can do wonders for the business and be great for your career, but it comes at a significant cost: stunted personalities, a complete imbalance between work and life, the myopic pursuit of questionable goals, and immersion in an unrealistic fantasy about yourself. To see just how ridiculous this is, try a brief thought experiment. Instead of seeing Pepsi as a Marine Corps, imagine if the situation was reversed and instead we saw the Marine Corps as the Pepsi of the US Armed Forces. If the US is in mortal danger, what should we do? Send in the Pepsi sales executives!

The road ahead
Our thesis in this book is that many organisations are caught in the stupidity paradox: they employ smart people who end up doing stupid things. This can produce good results in the short term, but can pave the way to disaster in the longer term.

Many organisations claim they rely on well-educated, reflective, bright people who are eager to learn. The sad reality is that they actually rely even more on almost the opposite: discipline, order, mindless enthusiasm, conformity, loyalty and a willingness to be seduced by the most ludicrous of ideas. Creating these characteristics can be tough. The solution that many organisations have hit upon, and many employees go for, is functional stupidity. How this works – and sometimes does not work – will be explored in depth in the rest of this book.

In Part One we look at the role stupidity plays in contemporary workplaces and professions. We begin by considering the myth of the knowledge economy. We question claims that developed countries have intelligent economies made up of smart organisations and even smarter workers. The reality is often the opposite. In chapter 2 we explore the thoughtlessness that characterises so much of organisational life today. We consider the role of cognitive biases, bounded rationality, ignorance and other intellectual traps in our working lives.

Chapter 3 outlines the concept of functional stupidity. We take a look at how functional stupidity works and what the consequences are.

In Part Two we will examine five kinds of functional stupidity which are common in organisations. The first is leadership-induced stupidity – this is when people develop an unquestioning faith in their own boss ('the leader') and the magical powers of leadership more generally. We look at structure-induced stupidity. This is what happens when people completely buy into processes and systems which they can see do not produce the result they hope for. Next we examine the kind of stupidity created by an untrammelled enthusiasm for brands and images. We then look at the stupidity created by imitating other organisations. And finally we look at how corporate culture can be a significant source of stupidity.

In Chapter 9 we ask what might be done about stupidity in organisations. We ask how stupidity can be managed. We outline some tactics that wily managers and savvy employees can use to turn functional stupidity to their own advantage. We also ask how it is possible to make organisations less thoughtless. We outline some interventions managers can make to drive down levels of stupidity in their firm. We conclude with a plea to make our organisations less stupid. By stopping all the talk about knowledge and starting to allow people to think again at work, we might be able to make our organisations, our working lives and our societies a little better for everyone.

Part One

Stupidity Today

1

The Knowledge Myth

The glorious age of the knowledge worker?

We live in an age of the knowledge worker, and have done so since at least 1962. That was the year the management thinker Peter Drucker was asked by *The New York Times* to write about what the economy would look like in 1980. One big change he foresaw was the rise of the new type of employee he called 'knowledge workers'.[1] They were not managers, shop-floor workers or professionals. Rather, their work was applying abstract knowledge to practical problems.

For Drucker, the rise of the knowledge worker had little to do with the changing nature of the economy. What had changed was the people doing the work. Following the Second World War, the general level of education in the US had risen. Expectations had risen too: these new more highly educated employees wanted to be treated as independent professionals, not skilled workers. In Drucker's view, the new class of knowledge workers 'expect to be "intellectuals". And they find that they are just "staff"'.[2] The mismatch between expectations and the jobs available meant that 'knowledge jobs have to be created'.[3] If they were not, he warned, 'it would present an infinitely more dangerous and more explosive problem than our racial ghettos'.[4] American companies listened to Drucker and took steps to resolve the problem. Corporate bosses opened campus-like environments, developed labs and installed open-plan workplaces, in the hope that these new workplaces would make staff who spent their days doing boring office jobs feel as if they were knowledge workers.

Across the Atlantic, a French sociologist was coming to a remarkably similar conclusion. Following the widespread social protests during May 1968, Alain Touraine was struck by profound changes taking place around him. Like Drucker, he was worried about highly educated younger people who wanted intellectually stimulating jobs but found themselves completely alienated at work. Touraine thought that the uprisings in Paris were an expression of this frustration. But the street protests indicated, he claimed, that greater social change was afoot. He saw a shift from an industrial society where one gained power by controlling the traditional factors of production (land, labour and capital) towards a post-industrial society where the real power lay in controlling information.[5] This was a society where 'economic progress depends more and more not only on the quantity of available labour and capital but on the ability to be innovative'.[6] It created an economic system where 'the treatment of information plays the same central role that the treatment of natural resources played at the beginning of industrialization'.[7]

Back on the other side of the Atlantic, the Harvard sociologist Daniel Bell was thinking about similar things. He too saw profound changes afoot. 'Post-industrial society is basically an information society,' he asserted. 'Exchange of information in various kinds of data processing, record keeping and market research is the foundation for most economic exchange.'[8] Instead of seeing the vanguard of this new economy as dissatisfied

students (as Touraine did), or overeducated and understimu-
lated office workers (as Drucker did), Bell looked to research
scientists staffing the labs of large corporations. Bell thought
these scientists were at the cutting edge of a profound shift in
how knowledge was used to create innovation. During industrialism, he argued, the most important innovations had been
based on 'random interventions' of talented craft workers who
dabbled in science. In contrast, recent innovations were based
on the direct and systematic application of scientific knowledge. According to Bell, this would not just give rise to new
industries, but to entirely new economic and social dynamics.
There would also be a shift in the dominant economic sector
from manufacturing to services. The central resource used
to drive the system would no longer be energy but information. The technology would no longer be mechanical hardware
such as the steam engine, but information technology such
as computer systems. The core skill base would no longer be
engineers and skilled workers in manufacturing, but those who
controlled abstract knowledge, such as scientists, professionals and other experts. Instead of using empirical procedures to
deal with ad hoc problems, this new dominant group would use
abstract models and principles.

Bell's ideas prompted a storm of reactions. Some agreed,
some did not. But the idea of post-industrialism captured the
imagination of corporate executives, management consultants
and business-school professors. There was a continual flow of
books, articles, papers, keynote presentations and strategic
reports lauding the role of knowledge for the contemporary
corporation. A vocabulary of largely interchangeable words
like learning, intelligence, wisdom and information came into
vogue. 'Knowledge workers', the 'knowledge economy', 'knowledge management' and 'knowledge-intensive firms' became the

leitmotif of contemporary capitalism. These ideas only inten-
sified during the mid-1990s as entirely new economic sectors
associated with the internet became fashionable. The bursting
of the dot.com bubble during 1999 did not deflate the collective
euphoria around these ideas. Today, it remains common for
people to preach the gospel of 'knowledge', 'innovation', 'creativity management' and 'the power of ideas'.

All this talk about the knowledge economy has generated
a new dogma. We are told that knowledge has become *the* key
resource, at least in advanced Western economies. Today it is
conventional wisdom that 'the foundation of industrial economies has shifted from natural resources to intellectual assets'.[9]
Researchers write: 'As the pace of change increases, knowledge
development among the members of the company becomes
the key to competitiveness, to remaining in the front line ...
Business has simply become more knowledge-intensive in all
companies, and corporate investment in education and training is more extensive than ever before'.[10]

To be competitive, we are told, organisations must harness
their intellectual capital. Knowledge is seen as 'the most strategically important of the firm's resources'.[11] 'The central
competitive dimension of what firms know how to do', write
Bruce Kogut and Udo Zander, 'is to create and transfer knowledge efficiently within an organizational context.'[12] Apparently
the most effective way for firms to remain competitive is to
'hire smart people and let them talk to one another'.[13]

The final article of faith is that organisations must employ
sophisticated knowledge workers. Even Marxists claim that
'the development of capitalism thus tends to create a working
class that is increasingly sophisticated. Workers' cognitive and
social capabilities are elements of the forces of production.'[14]
So-called symbolic analysts who do advanced thinking work

are now seen as the key figures in the workforce.[15] Instead of industrial workers who produce material goods, we now have knowledge workers who create 'immaterial products such as knowledge, communication, a relationship or an emotional response'.[16]

These articles of faith form the basis of what has become a remarkably resilient and widely shared dogma: that we live in a knowledge economy, dominated by knowledge-intensive firms which employ knowledge workers. A host of academics, consultants, executives and politicians have espoused this theme, and a vast body of writing on knowledge, information, competence, wisdom, talent and learning in organisations has emerged in recent decades. It seems that Peter Drucker's forecast in 1962 has proved to be remarkably accurate. Or has it?

The knowledge economy?

In 1996, the members of the OECD, the Organisation for Economic Co-operation and Development, were worried. Since its foundation, membership of this exclusive club had carried a certain clout. They are the richest countries in the world. However, by the mid-1990s their confidence was waning. Factories were closing in Europe and North America and opening in Asia. 'Developed' countries worried that they were being overtaken by 'developing' countries. OECD members faced an identity crisis. It had grown clear that they were no longer industrialised countries. What then were they becoming?

The answer was found in the idea of the knowledge economy: factories should be replaced with IT firms. Unemployed manufacturing workers could become computer programmers, consultants or personal fitness coaches. To transform into a knowledge economy, the OECD suggested that a nation needs to have a good education system, high levels of innovation, and lots of information and communications technology. Each of these things sounds reasonable – until you take a few moments to think about it.

One characteristic of a knowledge-intensive country is a good stock of 'human capital'. This means having a population who spend many years at school, with large proportions graduating from high school and university. Having an educated population is certainly a laudable aim, but simply to focus on increasing the time people spend in classrooms or lecture halls or the expansion of degrees is short-sighted.

Take the case of universities. The last few decades have witnessed an explosion of the university sector. By 2011, nearly 50 per cent of young people were entering higher education in the UK.[17] There is much to be said for extending access to higher education. It should create more informed citizens who are more capable of using their intellectual abilities. This, besides more occupational and technical knowledge acquisition, is the very reason we have higher education. However, reality is quite different. One recent US study of over 2,300 undergraduates at 29 colleges tested students when they started their programmes and then after two and four years. The researchers found that after the first two years, 45 per cent of students had shown no significant improvement in cognitive abilities.[18] After four years of study, 36 per cent of students had still made little or no measurable improvement in their ability to think and analyse problems. In other words, a large proportion of all students were as smart or as stupid as when they started. In some cases, attending university set students back. Business students performed worse in their first few years of university than they had done in high school. Perhaps it should not be surprising then that many students in today's universities seem to have little or no interest in the topics they are taught. And they don't learn that much. We have lived through a time of higher-education inflation: there is more of it, but it is questionable how much value is created in terms of true learning or credentials that really lead anywhere in the labour market.

For many students, attending lectures has become a chance to check Facebook.[19] Universities offer classes on subjects like Beyoncé, David Beckham, Zombies and *Star Wars*.[20] Entire fields of study have emerged around areas that were once learned on the job in a few days. Some universities have started offering degree-level courses in bartending or spa management. Of course, there are some institutions that have standards. Some of the traditional subject areas – natural science, engineering, medicine – are also less vulnerable to forces that lower quality. And according to the US study we mentioned above, about 60 per cent of students did develop intellectually. But on the whole, the university as a bastion of knowledge and learning has been replaced by mass education and lower demands. Customer orientation means that students should expect to have an easy life rather than struggle with learning. Rather than improving students' stock of human capital, it seems that the vast expansion of higher education may have the opposite effect: cultivating a taste for infotainment and the expectation of high grades for low effort. This is a typical experience of a contemporary university teacher: 'image triumphs over content, presentation over understanding, description over analysis'.[21]

Not only students, but also university management and other groups making decisions about the institutions, appear to have lost focus on what could be seen as their very reason for being. Most UK universities now comprise more administrators than faculty members.[22] This suggests that the purpose of higher education has become less about education and research and more about administering it.

On top of boosting education, extending innovation is also seen as an important part of a knowledge economy. One way to achieve this is to increase the amount of research that a country does. During the past decade, countries worldwide have pushed their scientists to publish more of their work in high-quality international journals. This has produced a flood of articles and an exponential growth in the number of journals. However, it is uncertain whether it has led to much in the way of fundamental advances. Within our own scholarly field of business studies, it is frequent to hear complaints that very few new ideas have been created since the late 1970s or early 1980s.[23] And this is despite a huge expansion in the number of researchers working in the area. As the numbers of researchers struggling to publish papers have exponentially increased, the insights from each published paper have likewise decreased. Mostly the results of all this research are next to useless for anyone beyond the pocket-size subfield the author is working in.

We thought this might just be a problem of our own intellectual ghetto. Sadly, it is not. A recent study of chemistry found that the great majority of researchers focus on relatively conservative questions that have little impact. They shun risky research strategies that could introduce fundamental innovations and have a wider importance. This is in the face of a massive expansion of knowledge about chemistry that should offer more opportunities for path-breaking innovations.[24] Boosting the number of high-profile journal articles may lead to increased knowledge, but in the best-case scenario it is likely to enthuse only a small group of specialists. Normally, papers pass quickly into obscurity and join the majority of scholarly articles that are not cited at all. The prevalence of journals online is actually making matters worse.[25] Today, we seem to face a situation in scholarly publication where, to parody the words of Winston Churchill: Never before in human history have so many had so little to say to so few.

The final plank of building a knowledge economy is heavy investment in information and communications technology (ICT). For policymakers this means plenty of telephone lines, computers and internet users. For the population to have access to computers and the online world is important, but just to assume that access to the internet can make a country knowledge-intensive is misguided. According to one survey, the most popular activities that North Americans practise on the internet are checking their emails, finding information with a search engine, accessing a map, looking up information related to a hobby or checking the weather.[26] People often use the internet at work to do non-work tasks like shopping, checking social media, reading the newspaper, monitoring sporting events or even viewing pornography.[27] One UK study found that employees spend an hour a day carrying out non-work-related tasks at their desk – mainly using the internet.[28] These are hardly the kind of knowledge-intensive activities that gurus of the knowledge economy had in mind. Arguably, the extension of internet access has not just given greater opportunities for sharing knowledge – it has also radically expanded the scope for people to engage in mindless activities like playing Candy Crush. Of course, the internet is used for all sorts of purposes – many of them in line with the idea of the knowledge economy. But the expansion of the internet has given ample opportunity for mindless cyber-drifting.

Most countries aspire to a knowledge economy. Nations around the world are pouring billions of taxpayer dollars into increasing their 'knowledge intensiveness'. They have invested heavily in innovation by raising participation in higher education, boosting the amount of scientific research they produce and extending access to information and communication technology. Worthy activities for sure, but in some cases these investments have backfired: more people attend university, but students appear to learn less; more research papers are produced, but fewer fundamental breakthroughs are made. The great spread of ICT has often just given users access to pictures of cats and celebrity gossip.

Perhaps it should not be so surprising that some have started to point out that far from experiencing a boom in innovation, we are actually witnessing declines.[29] Many fundamental innovations happened during the middle of the twentieth century, but since the 1970s we have actually seen a fall in the number of breakthroughs that fuel economic growth. The important innovations we have witnessed – such as the internet – were largely based on fundamental technologies developed earlier in the century. When innovation does happen today, it happens more slowly. The design and development of the first Boeing 747 (a radically new type of aircraft at the time) took five years. The design and development of the first Airbus A380 (a modest evolution) took fifteen years.

This should lead us to ask whether spending on the knowledge economy was more about public relations than producing innovation. Perhaps all this talk about knowledge is a way of creating an appealing image of an economy going places in order to avoid discussing the darker prospects that haunt de-industrialising countries around the world.

Knowledge-intensive firms?
While countries have tried to become 'knowledge economies', companies have sought to become 'knowledge-intensive firms'. Many of these are in the professional service field: accountants, management consultants, lawyers, communication specialists.

Some are in high technology. But more generally, there is an eagerness for firms to promote their 'knowledge-intensiveness'. Most organisations that like to stress that they are knowledge-intensive claim to have a unique knowledge base that is difficult to copy.[30] For instance, a legal firm might say it has expertise in an area competitors do not. The problem is that when you look carefully at what a firm does, it is hard to define and isolate exactly what is so special and unique about it. Sometimes what counts as 'knowledge' entails a piece of esoteric expertise, but what tends to matter more is the ability to mobilise extra labour power, be flexible and respond to client demands.

The role of very advanced knowledge is often more limited than claimed. Even when firms do have a unique form of knowledge, it is often not needed in the course of day-to-day operations. Most businesses rely on general skills and abilities that other firms in their sector also have. For instance, while an IT firm may have specialists who have an excellent knowledge of a particular system, much of the firm's day-to-day work is likely to be unrelated to this specific knowledge base. A person we interviewed had this experience. He held a PhD and had written his thesis on mergers and acquisitions. He then joined a large management consultancy firm and discovered, to his frustration, that after two years with the firm he had done no work within his area of expertise. Instead, the firm would assign people to projects where personnel were needed. Often it is the flexible use of disciplined and hardworking young people who can be plugged into any project that gives the edge to large management consultancy firms. Not their unique knowledge base.

It is no easy task to quantify and judge what knowledge-intensive firms produce. When a car breaks down, it's clear you have a problem. If it works after taking it to a mechanic, then the problem has been solved (although how well it has been solved is difficult to assess). It's far harder to know when an auditing report or piece of consulting advice is substandard. It is hard to gauge what knowledge-intensive firms do because they produce abstract things. Take a consultancy assignment. What exactly is produced? A report? A deck of PowerPoint slides? Meetings? The substance is tenuous. Often it amounts to little more than a feeling among senior managers that something has been done, and a sense of relief among middle managers that they are off the hook.

There is a yawning gap between the expertise of the people working in 'knowledge-intensive firms' and the people who consume their products and services. Usually clients of knowledge-intensive firms respond on the basis of faith: they have to believe what they get is high quality. And sometimes faith suffices: the fact that the client trusts the advice is what fixes the problem. Often 'solutions' provided by knowledge-intensive firms are little more than placebos. They make no concrete difference, but consumers feel relieved to have swallowed the pill.

Being a knowledge-intensive firm has very little to do with being knowledgeable. And even if you are knowledgeable, your clients may not care. So why do 'knowledge-intensive firms' bother to put on the charade? The answer is that it is more about creating an image. The real work of a knowledge-intensive firm is to persuade the client that it is smart. And in many ways this is OK: if the services a firm provides were measured by complex knowledge, then it is likely that clients would not get it.

Persuading people that your company is knowledge-intensive can earn big pay-offs. It creates a sense of community among members of the firm. To belong to a knowledge-intensive firm is much more appealing than being part of an average firm operating in 'the old economy'. Wielding the K word can turn a boring job filling in spreadsheets into a much smarter-sounding career in 'data analysis'. It can boost people's self-esteem and make them work harder. This is what happened when an internal IT service group in a large firm relabelled itself as an 'integrated services consultancy'. It was mainly doing internal consultancy and the work was more or less the same as before, but staff began to view themselves differently: they were now 'consultants', with 'clients' working with 'integrated services'. This much more grandiose title created a higher level of ambition.[31]

Knowledge-intensiveness can also foster an excellent external image of the company. If a firm is seen as having particular expertise, then it can help to convince clients that the often hefty price tag it charges is worth paying. Firms are much more likely to be willing to fork out big sums of money for 'deep expertise', 'cutting-edge knowledge' or 'thought leadership' rather than plain old advice.

The K word is often part of a confidence trick. A report from a highly reputable management consultancy is often respected because of the brand on the cover. Decision-makers and even the wider public accept the conclusions because the prestigious firm that produced it is thought to employ the best and the brightest. The reality is likely to be different: these same reports are usually produced by a handful of junior staff who have been working on the task for a matter of months. Senior people are always involved, but they are often busy selling services and interacting with clients. Their involvement in hands-on work is typically modest.

There is one final pay-off for firms that style themselves as knowledge-intensive: it can help to hide the many uncertainties at the heart of knowledge work. The advice that knowledge-intensive firms produce is usually presented as an authoritative final answer, but look behind the scenes and you discover that knowledge workers themselves are often very uncertain. They are not clear what the relevant information is, what the best criteria to solve the problem are, or even what the problem actually is. Knowledge workers might share their misgivings over a beer with their peers, but they are unlikely to admit to their client they don't know what they are doing or why they are doing it. Behind seemingly solid cases of 'best practice' we often find airbrushed descriptions of that practice. And what may be 'best' for one company is probably not relevant for another company.

But surely clients will know? Aren't clients rational actors with clear demands? No. Often, clients look for well-known brands, or a consultant they have personal contacts with. There is seldom any serious effort to learn from a consultancy project. After it is carried out or dropped, people in the client firms move on to other work. They are typically uninterested in careful assessment, feedback and learning.[32]

One of us studied an organisational change project involving a well-known management consultancy advising a large pharmaceutical firm. The project did not go so well. Little came out of it, partly because the client had too few people to undertake the change work. The lure of change and savings often looks promising on paper, but the project required significant resources to implement and ran into unexpected snags. When this happened, the consultants blamed the clients. They were slow, cautious, a bit too plump and spoiled. The clients blamed the consultants. They were young, raw, too abstract, and more interested in finding additional sales opportunities than doing 'real work'. The clients thought that the consultants were only good at doing one thing: PowerPoint presentations.

Fortunately, this was crucial for making everybody happy. A good PowerPoint show turned a failed project into a success in the eyes of top management. As often is the case, senior executives had no knowledge or no real interest in what was really going on. All they wanted was positive news and reassurance.[33] PowerPoint reality ruled.

The lack of interest senior managers took in this project makes more sense when you know that the market value of the client firm often rises when it publicly announces that it is hiring management consultants.[34] Whether these consultancies lead to concrete benefits for the client firm is not the issue: what counts is that the share price goes up.

Let us consider another example: IBM. This firm sells itself around the world as being a particularly smart firm, full of highly trained people tackling great global problems. It uses slogans like 'think', 'smart cities' and 'smarter plant'. One of the best-known 'members' of the firm is 'Watson', a supercomputer, which has competed in chess tournaments with grand masters and won a difficult quiz show on US television. The message from such PR stunts is clearly this: IBM is so smart it can build a computer that is smarter than the best experts in almost any field. For sure, IBM does spend a significant amount of money on research and development. It has a track record of creating some important technological breakthroughs such as the floppy disk drive, the automated teller machine and various computer programming languages. It has also hired some very intelligent people who are engaged in cutting-edge projects. But this is a tiny minority of the firm's global workforce. The reality is that most IBMers do far more run-of-the-mill activities such as sales, business process outsourcing, distribution, call-centre work and so on. The first thing on most IBM employees' minds is how they are going to make their quarterly results, not how they are going to live up to grand innovative challenges. But this does not square with ideas of 'smartness'. The firm uses some highly visible symbols of intelligence to create the right image. It helps those who work for the company to feel good about themselves. It is far nicer to say 'I work for IBM' than 'I work in a call centre.' It also helps IBM to win and retain clients. It gives their advice an air of authority. But perhaps most importantly, the image of being knowledge-intensive can help a firm like IBM cover up many of the uncertainties and ambiguities that go into getting the job done.

If we took all the talk about the knowledge-intensive firms too seriously, we would see only the brainy part of the picture. These parts exist – we don't deny it – but they are the spice, not the meal. These supposedly smart firms are not radically different from other organisations in the 'old economy'. They are prey to much the same follies that dog all organisations.[35] Often, their overwhelming belief in their own intellectual superiority blinds them to their own stupidities.

Knowledge workers?

One of the major ideas in any story about the knowledge economy is that during the past few decades, employees have downed tools and picked up laptops. We are told that a declining industrial labour force working in manufacturing jobs is being replaced by smart workers in the knowledge sector. This story has seized the hearts and minds of people across the political spectrum. Whether you are a committed libertarian or a postmodern neo-Marxist, knowledge work is already here. This is a brave and beautiful world that should make us all happy. The only problem is that no such world appears to have arrived.

A few years ago, Steven Sweets and Peter Meiksins decided

they wanted to track the changing nature of work in the new knowledge-intensive economy.[36] These two US labour sociologists assembled large-scale statistical databases as well as research reports from hundreds of workplaces. What they found surprised them. A new economy full of knowledge workers was nowhere to be found. The old economy was still there. Manufacturing still employed as many people as a couple of decades ago – although it was a slightly smaller percentage of the entire workforce, as the population had increased. The largest sector was distribution. The researchers summarised their unexpected finding this way: for every well-paid programmer working at a firm like Microsoft, there are three people flipping burgers at a restaurant like McDonald's. It seems that in the 'knowledge economy', low-level service jobs still dominate.

It might be tempting to ignore Sweets and Meiksins's unsettling findings as a freak one-off. The fact is that they are not. More and more researchers have started to see through the myth of knowledge work. For instance, Peter Fleming and colleagues took a close look at the labour statistics in Australia between 1986 and 2000 – a time when there was supposedly a boom in knowledge work.[37] Their account echoed Sweets and Meiksins's: far from an expansion of 'symbolic analysts', the increase in knowledge workers had actually come from a growing number of low-level information-handlers. For every software designer there were dozens of call-centre workers. A report by the US Bureau of Labor Statistics painted an even bleaker picture.[38] One third of the US workforce was made up of three occupational groups: office and administrative support, sales and related occupations, and food preparation and related work. Other occupations included construction labourer, security guard, child-care worker, janitor and cleaner, teaching assistant, non-construction labourer, home help aide and personal care aide. These are hardly well paid, highly skilled knowledge workers.

An article of faith in much of the talk about the knowledge economy is that to have the skills needed for the knowledge economy you need to have an advanced education: a bachelor's degree at the very least. Ideally you should have a master's degree or perhaps even a doctorate. This is a myth. Most jobs, even in the supposed 'knowledge economy', often require only the kinds of skills that you might get from a high-school-level education.[39] A report by the US Bureau of Labor in 2010 found that only 20 per cent of jobs in the US required a bachelor's degree, 43 per cent required a high-school diploma and 26 per cent did not even call for that.[40]

One study found that since 2000 there has been a decline in the demand for highly skilled knowledge workers.[41] This is despite the fact that there has been a dramatic growth in the number of people on the labour market who have higher levels of qualification. The upshot is that people who are highly educated do not take the managerial, professional and analytical roles they thought they were training for. Instead, they end up doing routine tasks that could easily be filled by people with lower skill levels. Not only does this lead to frustrated people with higher levels of education doing routine work, it also shifts people with lower skill levels further down the occupational hierarchy – and in some cases out of the labour market entirely.

Another favourite idea of promoters of the knowledge economy is that possessing superior cognitive abilities will get you off the hook of rising expectations and declining standards of employment. This does not seem to be the case. Even sectors which are particularly knowledge-intensive are being progressively deskilled. A recent report by a research unit at the University of Oxford found that 47 per cent of the 702 occupations they looked at were at high risk of being replaced by computerised processes.[42] Leading the way were supposedly 'knowledge-intensive' occupations such as insurance under-writers, auditors and credit analysts. The jobs that avoided the threat of automation often involved a highly interpersonal and situational aspect such as recreational therapy, social work and first-line supervision of firefighters.

Predictions about the displacement of knowledge workers by digital technologies and even robots have triggered much hype, but this is far from a new development.[43] Highly skilled human work has been replaced by machines for centuries. Eighty years ago, the economist John Maynard Keynes claimed that the rise of automation would free us from the drudgery of work.[44] It would allow us to work a twenty-hour week. We would have more time to devote to far more interesting things like leisure and hobbies. Today, Keynes's prediction seems like a bad joke. Ever greater parts of our lives are devoted to work.[45] Work has spilled over into all aspects of our waking hours. So much so, that the first thing most people do when they wake up is to check their smartphone (this is the first of the average of 150 times a day people check these devices). For many of us this means checking our work emails.

Instead of reducing work, automation has created more of it. But what kind of work has it created? The answer, accord-ing to the anthropologist David Graeber, is 'bullshit jobs'.[46] In a widely circulated essay, Graeber argues that while automation has reduced the amount of hours we need to work to get by, there has also been a simultaneous increase in work. But much of the work that has been created is essentially meaningless. Employ-ees working these 'bullshit jobs' suspect that society would be much better off if their job did not exist at all. As one HR direc-tor confessed to one of us: 'I now realise that much of what we are

doing has no significance whatever, and should not have either.'
While we might not be witnessing an explosion of meaningful 'knowledge-intensive work', we certainly seem to be living
through a growth in bullshit jobs. A recent survey of workers in
the UK found that 37 per cent of employees asked thought their
job made no meaningful contribution to the world at all.[47]

Knowledge cultures?

With the rise of modernism, science, education and democracy,
the stupefying effects of superstition, patriarchy and religious dogmatism have been cut back. Science, knowledge and
rationality have reduced the weight of tradition, religion and
totalitarianism. Sometimes, however, this journey has not been
so salutary. The literary theorist Avital Ronell has argued that
the growing stress on mastering the world through intelligence
prompts a widespread paranoia about avoiding stupidity.[48] The
increased stress on knowledge brings with it a widespread preoccupation with rooting out stupidity in others, and oneself.
In this sense, stupidity becomes the focus on intense work. We
are locked in a desperate quest to show that we are not stupid.
We do this by signalling our knowledge and intelligence. We
want to show everyone that we know. Not necessarily with hard
work to cultivate our knowledge and intellect – that is difficult
and demanding. Instead, we chase after various signs of being
educated, knowledgeable and intelligent.

But this war against stupidity can backfire. A fetishistic
interest in knowledge and intelligence can in some cases drive
ignorance and poor judgement. Decades of research by psychol-
ogist Carol Dweck shows that when people are afraid of looking
stupid they tend to miss opportunities to learn.[49] Intelligence
and reason are often discarded when some start to wax lyrical
about the knowledge society. All the talk of the knowledge

economy, knowledge work and knowledge-intensive firms can be seen as mantras being chanted in the quest to dispel the suspicion that stupidity remains a central part of life even in the most enlightened organisation. Some, such as the French philosopher Bernard Stiegler, suggest that matters may have got worse and that we could be entering into a new age of stupidity.[50] This kind of warning should make us wary of any heroic claims that we live in a culture where knowledge rules. After all, inflation in higher education does not produce a brighter population. Knowledge-intensive firms do not always do very smart things. Polished CVs or inflated titles do not certify greater competence.

A good illustration of the stupidity of trying to appear intelligent can be found in the commitment to information and knowledge asserted in many organisations. Some time ago, Martha Feldman and James G. March were struck by an fixation on 'information' in the firms they studied.[51] People required it, talked about it, had strategies and tactics related to it, and complained about shortages of it. Yet they felt there was too much of it. Most of the time people asked for more information, even though they did not use it. Feldman and March suggested that the preoccupation with information flourished due to the high cultural value attributed to it. Information symbolised reason, knowledge, reliability, security and even intelligence. Demanding information could be seen as a way of legitimating decisions you had already made: 'Using information, asking for information, and justifying decisions in terms of information have all come to be significant ways in which we symbolize that the process is legitimate, that we are good decision-makers, and that our organizations are well managed,' they write.[52]

A good example of this obsession with information is a project group that set out to make a decision for a new IT system. They worked hard, collected a wealth of information and embarked on a detailed and careful analysis. But in the end they were so exhausted by all this work, so overwhelmed by information, and so short on time, that they just decided to buy the system offered by the most pleasant sales representative.[53]

Paradoxically, it is the cultural value assigned to it that accounts for the overemphasis on information – an exorbitance that often prevents its practical use. While so strong a focus on information can give the impression of intelligence, it will also cause problems such as wasting time, and losing energy and focus for little real gain.

Another instance of how trying to be smart can result in plain stupidities is the online retailer Amazon. A recent in-depth investigation by *The New York Times* described how the company runs on the principle of 'purposeful Darwinism'.[54] The CEO insists that employees must work smarter, harder and longer. He says he does not accept two out of the three. To make this happen, Amazon recruits cohorts of smart and ambitious young people prepared to work extremely hard. They quickly find themselves working eighty hours or more a week. Staff will receive emails past midnight, followed up by text messages asking why they have not answered. In meetings people are relentlessly critical of each other's ideas. People are encouraged to 'disagree and commit'. When the time comes to assess their performance, a report of 50 or 60 pages of metrics faces each employee. They then have to sit in front of their manager and defend what they have done during the past year or so. In many cases, the manager would go into extreme levels of detail. Responses such as 'I'm not sure' would be dismissed as 'just stupid'. The upshot of these meetings was 'stack ranking', which ordered employees from the highest to the lowest performer. Those at the top gained promotions or additional benefits. Those at the bottom would soon leave the organisation.

This culture can drive high degrees of commitment. Marathon phone meetings would dominate holidays such as Easter or Thanksgiving – one employee reportedly spent her entire holidays working in a nearby Starbucks where she could get a wifi connection. However, there are others who find the relentless demands too much. Employees who had suffered personal bereavements or serious health issues, or who had to care for others – a stillborn baby, cancer, a dying father – were seen as unlikely to offer the requisite commitment. They were often managed out of the company, or left under their own volition. All in all, this extreme pressure meant that Amazon had a particularly high employee turnover rate. When former employees transferred to a new company, they would often take with them the grindingly critical work practices which they had learned at Amazon. As a result, they were often known as 'Amholes'.

The culture at Amazon encourages employees to be smart in a way that sometimes leads to the very opposite. They ask questions about everything and often neglect sociable manners. The president of Human Resources described how 'it would certainly be much easier and socially cohesive to just compromise and not debate, but that may lead to the wrong decision'. This constant critique might show that Amazon employees are intellectually switched on, but it leaves a vacuum of emotional intelligence, reflection and good judgement. The distress caused by these management practices is taken for granted. People crying at their desks are seen as a normal part of office life. Few moral questions are asked. Things that would signify failure in other organisations, such as extremely high turnover rates of employees, were taken as proof that the system was working effectively. Events that would normally prompt sympathy met with silence. What is perhaps most striking is that few people asked what the ultimate purpose of this harsh work culture actually was. The answer? To facilitate the high-speed delivery of Cocoa Crispies, selfie sticks and Elsa dolls. An overeagerness to celebrate intelligence here leads to its opposite. In trying to demonstrate how bright they are, Amazon people reveal thoughtlessness in terms of interpersonal relations and a disregard to what other uses such intelligence could more fruitfully be employed.

Conclusion: the stupid idea of the smart society

Since the late 1960s, commentators have been predicting the onset of a knowledge-based economy where knowledge-intensive firms compete to attract the smartest knowledge workers. We are still waiting. Some increase in the number of jobs that require advanced knowledge does not justify the hype around the idea of knowledge. Instead of a drastic boom in high-paid, knowledge-intensive jobs, we have witnessed a surge of low-paid, highly insecure, low-skilled service work. Although there is some growth of knowledge-intensive organisations using highly specialised knowledge, we have largely seen firms doing routine things but posing as if their roles were much more complex. Contemporary Western societies are full of grade, credit and title inflation. Institutions and people working in them try to beef themselves up to appear to be knowledgeable, creative and innovative. Rather than the boom of a knowledge economy, we have seen a series of policies being put in place which have backfired and actually reduced innovation.

No one would claim that knowledge is unimportant. Any number of professions call for skills, knowledge and seasoned judgement. Formal and symbolic knowledge probably matters more than ever. But this does not mean that a major part of the economy is about creative, intelligent people using sophisticated knowledge to create value. The problem is that the knowledge economy is more about alluring promise than hard realities. While it may give us a buzz to celebrate the 19,500 jobs created by the $15.8 billion of investment in the digital economy in the San Francisco bay area,[55] we pay little heed to the hundreds of thousands of jobs that are created every year in routine service work such as food preparation on the basis of much less investment.

The situation Peter Drucker described over fifty years ago has only got worse. There is a gap between the expansion of formal education and the facts of working life. The number of adults in the US attending colleges has quadrupled since 1970 (though this has come partly at the cost of lower quality and reduced learning). Yet the demand for employees with college-level education has not matched this rise. The result is more would-be knowledge workers and more frustration. There is now an army of people who want to flex their intellectual muscles at work, but find the only muscles they get to exercise are in their legs as they walk down the block to fetch the boss another latte.

The only solution that companies seem to have come up with to Drucker's question is this: convince your employees that they are knowledge workers employed by a knowledge-intensive firm that competes in the knowledge economy – even when they are not. This feat can be relatively easy: most of us like to feel that we are doing something smart. Label a job as knowledge-intensive, and the person who does it is apt to prize the label. It offers them the glow of being smart and at least occasionally doing smart things – even if they are not.

2
Not So Smart

Sleeping dogs

Sowing seeds, building sandboxes and encouraging artistry. These are hardly words that spring to mind when you think about writing software code. But this was how managers in the software division of Technovate, a hi-tech company, described how they dealt with engineers.[1] While managers emphasised creativity, they also said it was vital to maintain a 'firm grip' on the engineer's work. They wanted to make the work process more predictable, more controllable and more structured, while stressing too that all engineers are naturally creative – like artists. Believing that people are naturally motivated and creative then tracking their work in minute detail seems contradictory, but this did not trouble managers at Technovate. They easily toggled between claiming to encourage freedom and controlling their employees. But how did they deal with this glaring contradiction? The answer is straightforward: they ignored it.

Turning a blind eye to these tensions helped the middle managers get on with their day job, but it also created some problems. Engineers became confused. They were not sure exactly what their managers wanted from them – creativity or efficiency. They did their work but failed to come up with any particularly creative ideas.

There were a few moments when managers stumbled upon a process that seemed to actually work and stimulate their creativity. For instance, they found that having experts come and explain to the engineers how they developed their own patents was useful. However, this successful process was abandoned. As a consequence, little was achieved.

Various creativity initiatives were introduced and dropped without much heed to what worked and what did not. We might expect that such repeated failures would raise questions. The surprising thing is that the managers were not so troubled. When something failed, they just moved on to the next thing. If there were promising signs, they also moved on to the next thing. This turned out a string of mediocre results with little clear learning in between. When managers sensed problems, they elected not to stir up too much trouble. Better to let sleeping dogs lie. The lesson they learned was how to make their lives easier by turning a blind eye to things that did not bring positive feedback and not spending too much time exploring what happened and why. Making a show of creativity management seemed to count for more than actually doing something that seriously changed the way the engineers worked.

Knowledge is power, we are told. But at Technovation, knowledge was rather puny. In this firm, and many others like it, knowledge workers seemed to prefer to avoid being too knowledgeable. In some cases, downright ignorance was ideal. Although the hi-tech firm is just one organisation, it will be familiar to many people. The endless cycle of half-hearted managerial initiatives, flagrant contradiction, confusing ambiguity and a reluctance to learn is all too common. Having heads in the sand is probably more common than having eyes wide open. In this context, being knowledgeable can be a very dangerous thing indeed. Living a happy life in an organisation often requires a capacity to avoid trying to learn too much. Perhaps Friedrich Nietzsche was right when he wrote that 'we have contrived to retain our ignorance in order to enjoy an almost inconceivable freedom, thoughtlessness, imprudence, heartiness, and gaiety – in order to enjoy life!'[2]

Intelligence

Why is it that organisations can be so unknowledgeable? The easy answer would be that people running companies are stupid – they have low IQs or are uneducated . But this is not usually the case. Most knowledge-intensive companies go out of their way to select smart, well-educated people. Intelligence tests are a routine part of recruitment rounds. Many of the firms that claim to be the smartest in the world focus their recruitment on an extremely narrow set of elite universities. For instance, top US professional service firms target only a few Ivy League colleges (Harvard, Yale, Princeton and 'maybe Columbia') when recruiting new staff.[3] The irony is that it is precisely those firms that are packed with high IQs and degrees from the very best schools who do some very silly things. Enron was filled with people with degrees from elite universities who prided themselves on not just being smart but 'fucking smart' (as an ex-CEO put it in an interview). In the lead-up to the financial crisis of 2008, banks were crammed with high IQs and heavy-weight degrees. A colleague told one of us how she worked in a department of an elite investment bank that created one of the most toxic financial instruments involved in the recent crisis. The department was staffed almost exclusively by graduates of the French *École Polytechnique*, an elite school of science and engineering (motto: 'For the Homeland, Science and Glory') that prides itself on nurturing people with the best analytic abilities in the world.

Some suggest that our obsessive focus on analytical intelligence (the kind that IQ tests measure) and academic qualifications means we have overlooked other kinds of intelligence that actually make people successful. To deal with this problem, management gurus like Daniel Goleman have argued that we need to look at 'emotional intelligence' (EQ).[4] This is a rather broad and fluid concept that comprises a variety of different abilities and is hard to assess. Goleman and his many followers point out that while people in companies may be good at analysing a spreadsheet, they may be remarkably bad at dealing with emotions. Increasing emotional intelligence, we are told, is the road to career success and organisational flourishing. Despite the wave of enthusiasm around this idea, the evidence fails to support it. Having high emotional intelligence does not seem to make you much better at your job.[5] In many cases people get caught up in a therapeutic mentality and overstress the importance of fine-tuning the adaptation to and manipulation of people's emotions.[6]

Our obsession with IQ (and more recently EQ) has meant we have overlooked practical intelligence. This is the kind of everyday know-how that people use in order to get things done. When studying firefighters, Gary Klein noticed that the most skilled crew leaders had an uncanny 'feel for the situation'.[7] They made decisions under high levels of pressure without having all the information. What's more, these decisions would usually prove to be the right ones. One very experienced fire-crew leader talked of having 'extrasensory perception' and 'seeing around corners'. This seemed strange to Klein, but after spending lots of time with fire crews he realised that the 'extrasensory perception' came from repeated exposure to dangerous situations. After the fire chief had seen thousands of fires, he developed a sense of how a normal fire should look, feel, sound and smell. He also had an intuitive sense of what would happen next. The fire chief also knew when things did not look right. This deep on-site experience gave him a kind of muscle memory that seemed to bypass his brain. He knew when things felt right and when they did not. The big lesson for Klein was that relying too heavily on analytical intelligence measured by IQ tests can be a big mistake. If firefighters took time to do analytical problem-solving, they would be burned to a cinder. For a fire chief, being smart meant relying on your practical intuition.

Practical intelligence is easy to dismiss in corporate life. Quelling a fire is hard physical work requiring instant decisions that have life-and-death consequences. Most office work takes little physical prowess, beyond enduring boring meetings. Most decisions can wait for a long time. The outcomes of one's actions are often so remote that they are easy to forget entirely. Despite these stark differences, practical intelligence may be as important in an air-conditioned office as it does in a raging inferno. Richard Wagner and Robert Sternberg, North American psychologists, noticed that tacit knowledge was nearly twice as important as analytical intelligence in explaining why some managers succeeded and others did not.[8] Their conclusion: being analytically smart is important, but being street-smart often matters more. However, as with most other simple truths, things are not so straightforward.

People with deep expertise and repeated experience of situations have often developed deeply ingrained mental rules of thumb. These rules can be remarkably useful – they help those with such expertise to reach the right decisions quickly, as in the case of the firefighters. But these same rules of thumb can trip up the smartest and most experienced. The danger of street smarts is brilliantly demonstrated in a short experiment done by Daniel Isenberg.[9] He asked experienced general managers to solve a short business case of less than one page. The case was presented to them in short snippets on cards they were shown one by one. Isenberg noticed that the experienced managers relied on their hard-won mental rules of thumb. They began to solve the case and to offer courses of action before they had seen all the cards. They did not ask for further information: their experience helped them to get things done. But often they would ignore some crucial matter, and in many real-world situations, to jump into action before the facts are in can be fatal. Experience and street-smartness too can inculcate stupidity.

Where does all this lead us? The conclusion is that there is no easy way out of stupidity. People with a high IQ, EQ or excellent practical intelligence are not immune. The only way out of doing stupid things is critical thinking and reflection.

Cognitive biases

In the early 1970s, the question of why smart people, like the managers Isenberg studied, were so keen to avoid even the most basic protocols of rational analysis started to trouble two psychologists. Daniel Kahneman and Amos Tversky, suspected that smart people were often not particularly methodical and rational in their thinking. To test out their suspicion, they distributed questionnaires to a group of people who had high levels of intelligence, but were not particular experts in the area in question. They found that instead of relying on correct analytical procedures, they would use rules of thumb – something the researchers called heuristics. The outcome was often false results.

We might expect intelligent novices to make mistakes like this. What would experts do, Kahneman and Tversky asked, and they handed the same questionnaire to people who were experts in predicting probability – mathematical psychologists. What they found surprised them. This group of experts would make the same kind of mistakes that novices did. They relied on mental rules of thumb and avoided methodical rational thinking. This led Kahneman and Tversky to conclude that when 'making predictions and judgments under uncertainty, people do not appear to follow the calculus of chance or the statistical theory of prediction, ... they rely on a limited number of heuristics which sometimes yield reasonable judgments and sometimes lead to severe and systematic errors'.[10]

One common heuristic we use is anchoring. This happens when the first piece of information we are shown shapes our gauging of other information. For instance, in one experiment people were asked to spin a roulette 'wheel numbered 1 to 100 which, unbeknown to them, was designed to stop at either 10 or 65. After the rigged roulette wheel came to a stop, they were asked to estimate what percentage of nations in the United Nations were in Africa. The people whose spin of the wheel stopped at 10 estimated that 25 per cent of nations in the UN were African. Those whose spin stopped at 65 estimated that 45 per cent were African.[11] This showed how an irrelevant piece of information (the number a roulette wheel stopped on) could shape estimations made about a completely unrelated question (the number of African countries in the UN). Anchoring is by no means confined to the lab. Studies of negotiation have shown that the initial offer tabled – even if outrageously low or high – can have a big impact on the eventual terms people agree to.[12] This means if the starting price in the sale of a house is eyewateringly high, then the buyer often ends up paying over the odds.

A second heuristic that clouds analytical thinking is avail-ability. We make assessments about the likelihood of an event based on how easy it is to think about examples. For instance, if asked 'Is it more likely that a word randomly selected from the English language begins with the letter K, or that it has K as the third letter?', people tend to overestimate the prevalence of words beginning with K. In fact there are about three times more words in English that have K as their third letter than those that start with K. The misjudgement happens because people find it easier to call to mind words that begin with K than they do words where that letter comes third.

Similar processes have been found in business. For instance, when investors were asked how they thought the S&P 500 share-market index performed in 2009, 2010 and 2011, they tended to say that it was either flat or had fallen. In fact, the index had posted record gains during each of these years. Why were investors so off the mark? When they thought about these years, they recalled the financial crisis of 2008 and then assumed that shares would perform badly in subsequent years.[13] Similarly, when economic forecasters were asked to make predictions about the future state of the economy, they tended to ignore well-known dynamics such as business cycles and instead made their judgements based on the current state of the economy. So if the economy was doing well, they pre-dicted long-run growth; if it was doing poorly they had a much gloomier outlook.[14] Once again, well-paid analysts gave more attention to information that was at their fingertips and over-looked well-known patterns.

A third mental habit that clouds rational thinking is overconfidence. We overestimate our likelihood of success and underestimate the time it will take us to achieve it. For instance, when asked about their driving skills, 93 per cent of

US respondents and 69 per cent of Swedish respondents thought they were in the top 50 per cent.[15] A survey of faculty at the University of Nebraska found that 68 per cent of respondents rated themselves in the top quartile of teaching ability.[16] Ninety-three per cent of MBA students at the elite Wharton Business School thought they were in the top half of their group for academic performance.[17] When Americans go about remodelling their kitchens, on average they estimate that it will cost $18,658. In reality it ends up costing $38,796.[18] There are similar processes at work in organisations. When executives undertake a merger or acquisition, most report a high certainty that it will be a success. In reality, most mergers and acquisitions fail.[19] When people start a new business, they tend to judge their chance of success as very high. The reality of course is that most ventures fail.[20]

A fourth mental habit is relying on how information is framed. For instance, if we are asked whether we prefer a treatment that ensures that 90 per cent of patients will survive or one that means 10 per cent will die, most people go for the first treatment. The effectiveness of the treatment is exactly the same. The only difference is that the first sounds more positive: we tend to like options that emphasise surviving rather than dying. The business world shows similar effects. For instance, in one study different groups were given exactly the same task, but it was framed in different ways. Some groups were told that it would lead to a public good, while others were not. Those who were told it would lead to a public good tended to cooperate more than those who were not.[21] In another study, researchers found that a police squad in London which had been told it was engaged in 'terrorist prevention' (rather than 'routine surveillance') became much more likely to shoot and kill an innocent bystander.[22]

The final mental habit that clouds analytical thinking is that we are more influenced by losses than by gains. As a result we may often continue to invest in losing courses of action. For instance, gamblers will continue to put down money in the hope of 'winning back' their losses. The likely result is to end up losing more.[23] Similarly, companies that might be pursuing a losing strategy will invest even more in this strategy in the hope of making it work (which most of the time it does not).[24]

Each of these cognitive short cuts is common. Smart people frequently end up throwing good money after bad, making decisions on the basis of how they are framed, being overconfident about their own predictions, focusing only on the obvious, and making decisions on the basis of the first piece of information that comes their way. Possessing a high IQ and ample street smarts does not make you immune to cognitive biases. Indeed, it is likely to make you even more susceptible to doing stupid things.

Thoughtlessness by design

So far, we have reviewed some cognitive shortcomings that stem more or less from individual cognitive psychology. Looking at various forms of intelligence as well as cognitive biases tells us what can make individuals thoughtless. But thoughtlessness can be a collective function, virtually designed into organisations, and all the more powerful for it.

During the twentieth century, many jobs that had previously been complex and given workers scope to use their minds were dumbed down.[25] Tasks were broken down into ever smaller parts, a split effected between thinking work and doing work. This produced standardised products as well as standardised jobs. Henry Ford claimed that his great innovation was to create a work process that meant anyone – no matter their level of skill – could be involved in making a Model T Ford. Recent research in economic psychology has shown just how right Ford was.[26] If employees are put into 'foolproof jobs' (the kind that anyone can do because of a strict standard operating procedure), then their intelligence has little impact on their performance. You can have a whole factory full of people with low IQs and still churn out top-quality work at a very efficient rate. This is not the case for jobs that call for judgement and rely on intimate connections among the members of the production process. Here the average IQ level can make a big difference to performance. The moral of the story: if you don't want employee intelligence getting in the way of productivity, make jobs as foolproof as possible.

It might seem comforting to suppose that foolproof jobs are a product of twentieth-century industrialism, and now that we live in a knowledge society such jobs are drastically declining. However, as we saw in chapter 1, this is not so. If anything, there are now more foolproof jobs than ever. At the same time as there has been an expansion of knowledge-intensive work,[27] we have also seen the ongoing McDonaldisation of working life.[28] This process of specialisation and deskilling has continued apace. In place of workers on a production line we have delivery drivers who are guided by electronic systems. In place of secretaries working in typing pools we have call-centre workers saying the same few lines over and over again. In place of the highly specialised bureaucrat, we have consultants who have even more narrow specialities. While the quality of work might seem to have improved, many jobs remain as dumb as ever. The difference is that they have to be done with a smile.[29]

Bounded rationality
Stupidity is designed into many jobs in factories, call centres

and fast-food restaurants. However, there are many other jobs that give employees more discretion, enabling them to make choices about what they do, how they do it, and when. Yet despite the opportunity and encouragement to put their minds to work, the bulk of employees do not.

This is something that Herbert Simon realised over seventy years ago. Simon studied economics at the University of Chicago. His studies drummed into him the idea that humans are rational utility maximisers. As part of his undergraduate degree, Simon returned to his hometown of Milwaukee to study decision-making in the budget office of a municipal authority. The experience left him confused. 'My economics training showed me how to budget rationally. Simply compare the marginal utility of a proposed expenditure with its marginal cost, and approve it only if the utility exceeds the cost,' he wrote. But what he found in this Milwaukee office did not match the models he had been taught in Chicago:

> What I saw in Milwaukee didn't seem to be an application of this rule. I saw a lot of bargaining, of reference back to last year's budget, and incremental changes in it. If the word 'marginal' was ever spoken, I missed it. Moreover, which participants would support which items was quite predictable ... I could see a clear connection between people's positions on budget matters and the values and beliefs that prevailed in their sub-organizations.

Simon began to realise that decision-making in organisations was not perfectly rational. Nor was it completely irrational. Rather, the decision-making process was what he called 'boundedly rational'.

Simon used the term 'bounded rationality' to capture the

fact that while people in organisations often try their best to make rational decisions, they always face obstacles. People usually have limited access to the information involved, limited capacity to process it, and limited time to make decisions. As a result, decision-makers often do the best they can, rather than coming up with the perfectly rational solution. Simon called the process 'satisficing'. He won the Nobel Prize in economics for this idea. His work reminds us that far from being perfectly rational agents who are out to maximise utility, most of the time we simply do the best we can with the limited information, time and capacity we have. Most decisions made in organisations are about coming up with satisfactory outcomes, not optimal ones.

Since Simon formulated his idea of bounded rationality, much has changed. With the internet, almost anyone can tap into information that was not accessible to even the best-placed scientists or government officials in the past. The amazing advances in computing power mean that we can collect and process huge amounts of information very quickly. It might be tempting to think all this has helped us to overcome bounded rationality, but in fact it has made matters worse.[30] When making decisions today, we quickly find ourselves overwhelmed by information. To cope with overload, we fall back into satisficing behaviour. We try to do reasonably well, rather than strive for optimal solutions.

Mindlessness

One of the ways people manage their own intellectual limits is by following preset patterns. Bureaucrats working in the budget office Simon observed would plod through very familiar steps every year when developing a new budget. In the early 1970s, two psychologists noticed similar processes among the subjects in their lab. Ellen Langer and Robert Abelson realised that much of the time, we don't think too deeply about our own behaviour. Instead we quickly slip into pre-programmed patterns of behaviour that they called 'social scripts'. We are like actors who dutifully follow a script we have been handed which tells us what to do and what to say.

To test their ideas out, Langer and Abelson got one of their assistants to ask people coming into their lab for help.[31] Each request was the same apart from a few subtle changes. Half the time, the assistant seeking help presented themself as a victim by saying: 'My knee is killing me.' The other half of the time, the assistant simply said: 'Would you do something for me?' They found that when the assistant presented as a victim, they would be helped 75 per cent of the time. If they just asked for aid, they were only helped 42 per cent of the time. The reason why there was such a big difference in responses, Langer and Abelson thought, was that each request cued very different scripts. Complaining about a sore knee cued a victim script – and the associated moral obligation to help a victim out. When we are asked if we will do something for someone else, we consult a different script that is much more neutral. If we say no, we will not feel too bad. In both cases, the script does the thinking for us.

Langer and Abelson recognised that scripts have an influence on our lives that reaches far beyond whether we decide to help someone else out or not. Scripts drive all sorts of mindless behaviour. For instance, they found that the way a man in a film was first introduced would change how an audience of therapists saw him.[32] When the man concerned was introduced as a 'job applicant', the psychotherapists described him as 'candid and innovative', 'attractive and conventional-looking', and 'ordinary'. If the man was introduced as a 'patient', they described him as a 'passive, dependent type', with 'considerable hostility', and suffering 'conflict over homosexuality'. Changing the way the man in the film was labelled triggered different scripts. When he was a job applicant, the psychotherapists looked for signs that he was normal. When he was a 'patient', they looked for signs that he was abnormal.

The big insight that came from Langer and Abelson's work was that much of the time, we mindlessly follow scripts. Faced with a novel situation, we look for clues about what script to follow. Once we decide the scenario, we slip into mindless script-following. We also start to ignore contextual information. We grow rigid in our view of an issue, robotically adopting a familiar course of action.

Think about a routine service transaction. When you walk up and ask for help, the person behind the counter quickly tries to work out what script applies. Once they have figured this out, they are likely to grow more and more rigid about what they will and won't do. If you make any special requests, the person behind the counter is likely to bat them away.[33] It is not just routine service employees who follow established scripts. Large chunks of what goes on in organisations entail following scripts.[34] Meetings are highly scripted behaviour that we mindlessly work through. Job interviews also follow a script. So do emails. Much of this is sensible and necessary but can easily lead to mindless routine-following behaviour.

One of us studied managers who claimed to do leadership. They said that having coffee with their subordinates, listening to them or engaging them in small talk had a significant impact on them. They saw this as an exercise of leadership. If another person – say their secretary – had done the same thing, no one would have called it leadership, but the managers followed the scripts of leadership and saw trivial acts as full of impressive influencing activity.[35] The script then said: if managers are doing something (however trivial) in relationship to subordinates, it must be leadership. In fact, most of the tasks that make up the day of the average office-dweller are highly scripted. Scripts do the thinking, people rehearse them.

Mindlessly following scripts can have some big advantages. Scripts set staff pulling in the same direction. Script-following can also help make what people do look good to the outside world. But perhaps most importantly, script-following can help staff to conserve their cognitive resources. Going along with the script means you don't need to think too much. This can save time and effort.

Mindlessness also comes with some big dangers. Following scripts means that much of your work becomes about 'going through the motions'. This can easily go wrong, particularly in large organisations that keep a whole library of scripts. As people observe these, they risk ignoring contextual information, which means that they may become less vigilant. These small oversights can create ideal conditions for big mistakes. Mindless rule-following also impairs authenticity. If a person working in a service job just goes through the motions when talking with customers, the customers often feel the interaction is hollow. This can annoy the customer, but also create a sense of deep dissatisfaction in employees who are forced to spend their days speaking phoney lines. Mindless script-following can also lay the ground for some significant problems in the way that people make decisions. It can mean that decisions are made too quickly, crucial information is ignored, and the wrong lessons drawn from experience. Mindless script-following can contribute to getting things done, but it can also create some significant oversights and problems.

Skilled incompetence

Mindlessness is not a quality you would usually associate with experts, but people are experts because they follow well established scripts. They know each step so intimately that they can take it with their eyes closed. A medical doctor knows all the steps of examining a patient. They can do it without thinking. Often the hardest part of the job for an expert is to work out which script is involved. Once they identify the right one, they can go on autopilot.

As we saw in the previous section, engaging cognitive autopilot can offer significant upsides, but it also has downsides. The most pronounced of these is what Chris Argyris has called 'skilled incompetence'. Instead of facing up to problems, Argyris noticed, skilled managers would fall back into what he called 'defensive routines' – standard ways of behaviour that allowed them to 'avoid surprise, embarrassment or threat'. These routines gave smart managers a sense of comfort. They made them feel good even in the face of a situation that would normally make them feel bad, by acting to defer dealing with problems. But the same issue tended to surface again and again. Problems were never completely dealt with, they were just temporarily parked.

Argyris gives the example of a young entrepreneurial company he knew well, which had been growing fast for a few years. As with most thrusting new companies, the firm was flexible and fluid. However, the CEO thought it was time to make it more structured. The snag was that no one in the company knew how to do this. Staff would go away to management retreats, list all the issues, but then would jib at committing to concrete action. They kept postponing making a clear decision. When Argyris went along to some of the meetings, he saw these defensive routines in action. By avoiding making a decision, people felt good, but they also ducked the issue.

One of the big problems with this kind of skilled incompetence is that it stops people from learning. They become trapped in comforting routines that allow them to ignore troubling issues. By mindlessly going through the motions and asking for ever more analysis, the staff felt as if they were doing something when in fact they were not. Because these defensive routines made people feel good, they clung on to them. This was a natural response – breaking routine would bring them face-to-face with unsettling issues. But more disturbingly, it would mean that people would no longer feel skilful. Instead, they would have to face issues that made them feel incompetent.

Ignorance

Overlooking what is blindingly obvious can be a nasty side effect of professional obsessions. But there are also many cases when we ignore crucial information because it is in our best interests. The fact that we so often turn a blind eye to inconvenient facts can be seen in an experiment conducted by Joël van der Weele.[36] He got groups of German university students to play a game where it paid to collaborate. Economists use this kind of game all the time to test out how people make decisions about collaboration, but there were a few unusual twists to this experiment. First, one of the players could pick the rules. Second, they could choose to remain ignorant about whether it paid to collaborate. The researcher found that people were five times more likely to choose to remain ignorant when it was in their own interests. Further, he found that when people chose ignorance they were twice as likely to engage in selfish behaviour. The implication was clear: when it is in line with our own selfish interests, we often choose to remain ignorant, and when we pick ignorance we act selfishly.

This study was conducted in the rather artificial setting of a computer lab in a university department. We might not be so surprised that students studying economics are willing to overlook information when it is not in their interests and that they act selfishly. After all, economists are more inclined than others to maximize their self-interests.[37] However, the kind of behaviour that Van der Weele discovered in the lab can be seen all around us in everyday life. People at high risk of contracting an STD often avoid getting tested; wealthy people avoid driving through poor neighbourhoods; investors monitor their portfolios less when the market is declining.[38] We tend to go out of our way to ignore crucial information when the results might be disturbing or not in our best interests.

Consider the scandal at Volkswagen during 2015, when it was revealed that VW had installed 'defeat devices' into over 800,000 of its cars. These allowed the cars to pass increasingly stringent emissions tests through limiting the output of noxious gases only when the output was being tested. At other times the car would be up to five times more polluting. Senior executives at VW initially claimed that they had no knowledge of these devices.[39] Although this is a matter of debate, in many ways it was in their best interests to remain ignorant. By not knowing about the covert technology, executives were able to claim unabashed that the cars their company made were clean and green, cheap to produce and also had high levels of performance. When the bad news came out, they could also claim that he had no knowledge of these underhand means.

Usually we associate ignorance with having too little knowledge about a topic. Ignorance can be a great spur for unreasonable action. An excellent example of this is when senior managers adopt a new management technique such as TQM (total quality management). One study of the implementation of TQM found that managers were usually ignorant of the technical details. As a result, they have unrealistic expectations of its potential.[40] Because they have little idea about the outcome, they are all the more keen to give the ideas a try. This ignorance means most managements can charge headlong into implementing new fads and fashions that they don't understand.

Ignorance can be an important motivator. Often it is people who are ignorant of the potential chances of success who are the keenest to act. One of the more curious reasons for this is the 'Dunning–Kruger Effect'. This is the tendency of people with very low levels of skill to systematically and unreasonably overestimate their abilities. This effect was identified in 1999 by David Dunning and Justin Kruger, two psychologists working at Cornell University. They were inspired by the unfortunate case of McArthur Wheeler, a man who robbed two banks disguised only by lemon juice rubbed on his face. He believed this would make him invisible to security cameras. Dunning and Kruger wanted to know whether such delusions were unique to a few idiotic criminals or whether they were more common than we think. They conducted a series of experiments where they asked people to rate their own skill at some basic tasks like humour, grammar and logic. They also measured people's performances on each of these tasks. They found that 'participants scoring in the bottom quartile on tests of humor, grammar, and logic grossly overestimated their test performance and ability. Although test scores put them in the 12th percentile, they estimated themselves to be in the 62nd.'[41] In other words, the least skilled were not just bad at the tasks, they were also bad at recognising their own incompetence and poor at asking for help.

We might expect ignorance from incompetent amateurs; we would hope for more from professionals. But the University of Chicago sociologist Andrew Abbott thinks we might be too optimistic. In 2010 he examined research published in his own area of expertise: the sociology of the professions. He was struck by the amount of ignorance he found.[42] There were many pieces of work by amateurs who blundered into the debates and made claims that were either patently wrong or excruciatingly obvious. Any area of knowledge or expertise will always have chumps who think they have discovered a great insight when in fact they are repeating a mundane point. The hearer learns to smile and switch off when faced with such characters. What was more troubling for Abbott was a second kind of ignorance he detected among experts. He noticed that many people who should know better often overlooked vital or blindingly obvious points. It meant they were unable to see things that an outsider would readily perceive. It was often the experts' own expertise that blinded them. Trapped within what they knew, they missed the obvious.

All too often it is useful to be able to profess ignorance about awkward facts. Knowing what to know – but also what not to know – is a crucial skill that people working in any organisation pick up rather quickly. The sociologist Linsey McGoey has explored how this strategic ignorance works in a range of settings.[43] For instance, in the wake of the financial crisis, many of the senior managers of large banks pleaded that they had been ignorant about what their employees were doing. In organisations, there are often subtle procedures of ignorance, where people avoid informing senior people about problems. This is because senior managers do not want to face too many complicated issues. They also want to be able to claim ignorance when 'blame time' arrives. This can of course be a pure blame-avoidance tactic, but normally it is good to actually be ignorant. You have a clean conscience and you don't have to think about issues that go on under the radar. If things go wrong, it is difficult to prove that you really were told. There is a tricky relation between being informed about things that must be managed and being ignorant about issues that may go away or never come to light. Junior people are often faced with a difficult choice: should they inform senior people and risk being seen as someone disturbing the peace by telling them things they prefer to be ignorant about, or do they want to leave their superiors in blissful ignorance and risk being blamed for not having informed them about a problem that may escalate?[44]

If we return to the managers at Technovation whom we met at the start of this chapter, we find an interesting case of ignorance at work. The managers of the software development teams felt they had to support innovation and do 'creativity management'. However, it was not really something they were required to do. Their main goals were improving details of products and minimising errors. Seduced by the images of companies like Google and Apple, they wanted to emulate these firms by becoming more innovative and creative, but this turned out to be easier said than done. The various initiatives they tried did not always work very well, and rather than deal with these failures, managers largely ignored them. They silently dropped initiatives, without looking into whether they worked or not. Not learning from experiences helped these managers to concentrate on doing something new. Ignorance was bliss. Managerial ignorance can allow you to continue your work without the pesky pressure of having to think and reflect. Genuine learning sounds great, but it takes time and energy. It is tricky, complex and ambiguous work. It can also lead to hesitation, doubts and other costly downsides.

Conclusion

Many contemporary organisations claim to be knowledge-intensive firms, but such claims can be thoroughly misleading. For sure, there are organisations that rely on intelligent, well-educated and creative people. Some organisations have units staffed by people who specialise in sophisticated problem-solving, and there are those who do this, but these activities tend to be rare. But most organisations are actually hothouses of non-knowledge-intensive work. Of course a degree of competence is needed, and few jobs are entirely brainless, but supposedly knowledge-intensive organisations are often crowded with people with limited emotional and practical intelligence. These smart people may avoid careful analytical processes and instead rely on fast and frugal mental rules of thumb to get the job done. What's more, many firms actively encourage employees not to exert their intelligence overmuch. They push smart people into dumb jobs, swamp staff with information, enforce behavioural scripts that are followed mindlessly, encourage colleagues to avoid addressing tough questions, and incentivise experts and amateurs alike to be ignorant. As a result organisations can often help to encourage remarkably bright people to do stupid things. And people's inclinations to use their brains in narrow, unreflective ways lead to less wise decision-making and working practices.

We like to think that we as human beings are very intelligent creatures, but there is also overwhelming evidence that we make fundamental cognitive mistakes. We are often much poorer information-processors than we believe. We engage in wishful thinking, jump to conclusions, overestimate positive outcomes. We are often guided by emotions, fixed ideas or assumptions. Work life is often more comfortable if it is carried out mindlessly. Ignorance often is bliss. All this enables us to avoid difficult issues.

Human psychology and the organisation of work can be a big impediment to our cognitive functioning. It can mean we don't make full use of our intelligence, reach less than rational decisions, and even act in stupid ways. Normally we think that this is a bad thing, but it is only part of the picture. Being stupid has its upsides. In fact it is something that many organisations positively encourage. In the following chapters we ask how stupidity can be functional.

Functional Stupidity

Varieties of stupidity

When we think about stupidity at work, the image that comes to mind is of a thoughtless chump who leaves a trail of disasters in their wake. This kind of corporate klutzing is a stock theme of slapstick comedy. In Charlie Chaplin's classic portrayal of the factory, *Modern Times*, we follow a worker who is slowly driven mad by a production line that is relentlessly sped up. When Chaplin's character finally flips, he does all manner of stupid things, such as trying to tighten his co-workers' noses instead of tightening bolts. Naturally this riles his co-workers as well as his boss. This crazy behaviour causes the production line to seize up. Work grinds to a halt. Chaplin's portrait of stupidity at work is fictional, but there are many real-life stories of utterly stupid behaviour on company time. Ask anyone about stupidity in their workplace, and you will soon hear stories about the escapades of the departmental fool.

Tales of company klutzes stand out – their disasters are easily spotted but are, thankfully, infrequent. Most organisations have well developed systems and procedures for avoiding this. When disasters occur they are often the result of a combination of unfortunate circumstances and poor judgement rather than pure idiocy. The bulk of stupidity in the work-place does not spring from utter thoughtlessness. It is hardly abnormal, and it does not cause sheer havoc. Often stupidity is low-key, implicit, and has a mix of positive and negative out-comes. Sometimes it can go undetected for years. Often it is accepted and rewarded. Most stupidity in corporate life takes the form of functional stupidity. This involves narrow thinking rather than pure thoughtlessness, which is normal (in the sense of commonplace), and has functional consequences – at least in the short term.

Thoughtlessness

Sheer thoughtlessness is an important marker of common stu-pidity. Thoughtless individuals do not consider why they are doing something. They remain oblivious to the consequences. When disaster strikes, thought does not ensue.

Sometimes thoughtlessness is actually encouraged by com-panies. In an interview, the CEO of an auto-parts maker told the story of a water-cooler that made a huge mess in one of the company's factories. After he met his employees in the plant, one operator approached him and asked him to take a look at an invention he had made that would eliminate the mess. The CEO pointed out that 'for the first time, that fellow had begun to think about the efficient operation of the business. I asked him why he didn't think of this before. He said: "I didn't know I was supposed to think."'[1] In this case, the employee had been actively encouraged, even directly instructed, not to think. 'I asked him why he didn't bring the idea up before,' wrote the CEO. 'He said he did, but he was told to shut up and do his job.'[2]

This kind of total thoughtlessness is rare. More often than not, people are not completely thoughtless – they just are con-strained in their thinking. Managers and subordinates follow corporate cultures without paying much attention. Experts get obsessed with the detail and grow blind to the bigger picture. Followers willingly let their leaders do the thinking for them. Employees habitually avoid 'negative thinking' and look on the bright side. Professionals buy into systems that they suspect don't work. Employees follow rules that they know create more problems than they solve. In each of these cases, people are thinking – but only in the most narrow and circumscribed ways. Outside the box lies thoughtlessness.

Normality

A typical feature of pure stupidity is that it is abnormal. Being stupid is often seen as doing something that is out of the ordinary. It may be that someone with unusually low levels of intelligence has been hired. It may be that a staff member has personality quirks, a psychological disorder or strange ideological obsessions. There are many accounts of the dot-com crash and the financial bubble that show how extreme forms of stupidity were rampant. 'Normal' organisational processes and procedures were often abandoned. Extreme wishful thinking took over. Bizarre behaviour was rewarded. Failure eventually came, but it took some time. After the fact, people asked themselves: 'How could we have been so stupid?'

But stupidity is not always abnormal. It can often be a normal part of life at work. Consider one employee's account of his life in a recall department of the Ford motor company during the 1970s.[3] After training as an engineer and spending a few years as a campus radical, Dennis Gioia got a job with Ford in 1972. He clearly impressed the recruiters, as his file was marked with 'crown prince'. Gioia's job was to look at cars that had been recalled, scanning the files for any patterns. He was constantly asking himself whether the problems he saw in one returned car were also mirrored in other cars.

Part of investigating these cases involved going to what they called 'the chamber of horrors'. This was a warehouse a few miles from their office where burnt-out cars which had been involved in horrific incidents were sent. In 1973 he visited the chamber of horrors with one file containing a picture of a burned-out car. This is how he describes his visit: 'You have to imagine what it's like. Have you ever seen a burned-out – not a Pinto but anything? … It's awful. It's just awful. Especially if you use your imagination and remember that people were in it when it turned into that state. Everything's melted. All the plastic, and there's a lot of plastic. All of the wiring. Steering wheel is warped. I mean, it starts to rust in days. It's repulsive to see that kind of thing.' The sight of this burned-out car clearly shocked him. But this was stuff he saw every day, and he was trying to work out whether this was just a one-off problem or whether there was something more systematic going on. At the time, he said, 'I had bigger fish to fry … Bigger, more immediate problems to take care of.' And not much changed: 'The whole time I managed the Pinto file, I never got above five… In that context of everything else that's going on, it's that big.' He parted his thumb and forefinger.

When he returned to the office, Gioia registered some concern with colleagues. They didn't take it too seriously. 'I practically got laughed out of the office,' he said. Here is how he recalls the conversation that followed:

> Well, come on, Den. We're going to go in front of the executive panel with this evidence? What do you got? Two or three field reports? Why are we even discussing this?
>
> Well, I just came back from the depot. You should see what I saw.

Den. Come to your senses.

'So I came to my senses ... I realised, OK, first of all, I'd
done what I trained myself not to do, make decisions on the
basis of emotion. And, second, I realised, I had to prove it, and
I couldn't prove it.' By 'coming to his senses' and deciding not
to act to recall the car, he took a decision that probably con-
tributed to many more people dying before the Ford Pinto was
finally recalled in 1978.

This is not a clear case of sheer thoughtlessness. Gioia tried
to be observant and considered acting on his observations. He
talked about this with other people. But then he gave in and
neglected the issue. He adapted to the social norms: don't raise
problems and don't tell people bad news they do not want to
hear. This is standard in many companies.[4] If there is a chance
to avoid telling people bad news, people often take it. In this
case, thinking too much was abnormal. You 'came to your
senses' by putting the case aside and getting on with the job.
This kind of stupidity is a normal part of organisational life. It
is often widely backed in organisations – starting with the top
management and going all the way down the hierarchy.

Functionality

We usually assume that stupid people leave disasters in their
wake. Those who are truly stupid don't recognise the impact of
their behaviour. The stupid person is usually seen as someone
who bumbles into a situation they don't understand, sets about
doing all sorts of thoughtless things, creates a disaster and then
simply walks away with a shrug of the shoulders. This kind of
dysfunctional stupidity isn't limited to slapstick comedies. The
entire history of management is filled with people who create
problems and fail to learn from the last accident they created.

They think it is better to forget about it, hope others will not remember, and just move on. One is reminded of the cardinal rules that Robert Jackall uncovered among middle managers working for large US corporations – never stick around too long in one job, because something will inevitably go wrong, and it is better that someone else is blamed for it. 'Always try to outrun your mistakes,' one manager told Jackall.[5]

There are many cases where corporate stupidity can result in disastrous outcomes. These are the obvious instances of stupidity when something goes seriously wrong, and the consequences are there for all to see. But what is perhaps more surprising is the everyday forms of stupidity where people who act without thinking can create seemingly desirable consequences. After all, asking too many questions and spending too long reflecting on a situation can make you unpopular. Thoughtfulness can be seen as time-consuming and a waste of valuable resources. This is probably what happened when Dennis Gioia tried to talk with his colleagues about the problems with the Pinto. If you persist in asking tough questions, you are likely to cause problems for yourself. You will most likely upset the smooth workings of a group, threaten relationships with key people, and disturb existing power structures. All this could make being smart very costly indeed. Play dumb, and the status quo survives; team relationships continue unthreatened. All this allows you to focus on 'delivering the goods'.

There are many other instances we will look at in the following chapters where selective stupidity can have some good outcomes for firms and the people who work for them. The latest fashions produced by the leadership industries can seduce otherwise smart managers into believing in ideas that would not be out of place in a New Age commune. These ideas can give managers a sense of purpose and drive. Placing one's faith in structures can lead people to overlook senseless outcomes, but it can help to calm anxieties and worries. Copying other organisations can mean firms adopt processes and practices which are not right for them, but it also can give them a sheen of legitimacy. Focusing a firm's resources on brand-building and window-dressing can create unrealistic expectations, but it can also be a valuable self-esteem boost. Fostering a culture of relentless positivity can blind people to problems, but it can also help to hold people together. Sometimes, not using your full cognitive capacities can be a good idea.

A hint about how this process works can be found in a letter sent to *The Lancet*, an influential medical journal, by a Swedish medical researcher.[6] The letter, entitled 'Clever idiot', described how the correspondent had spent his working day and his leisure time reviewing a scientific paper. Being a diligent fellow, he read the paper a few times and then spent a couple of hours looking into the data. Eventually he was satisfied, and logged his review. Doing this kind of work was by no means out of the ordinary – he would write similar reviews about twice a month. Presumably most of his colleagues were doing much the same, so he did not give the purpose of his labours a second thought. That is until a few days later when he read an article about how the company that owned the journal he was reviewing for had a turnover of over a billion dollars and a profit margin of about 30 per cent. This got the researcher thinking – who benefited from all his hard work: reviewing papers as well as researching and writing for them? 'First the institution pays me to do research,' he wrote, 'then I give away the copyright of the results to the publisher, then the library of the institution buys the right to print my paper back from the publisher. I cannot avoid wondering how the management of such publishing companies view myself and others who do research and who also accept review commitments.' Clearly doing all this reviewing and research (paid for by the Swedish state and funding agencies) seemed to be the right thing – it helped him to progress in his career, and more generally improve the quality of scientific knowledge. Everyone else was doing it. But a little thought about the system revealed how idiotic it could be – it was a process that largely filled up space in journals but – more importantly – in the pockets of shareholders. Not thinking too much about these things helps the researcher get along with his job. It keeps his employers happy. It makes the publisher very profitable. The question that stays unanswered is whether it makes sense.

Functional stupidity

Spotting stupidity in corporate life can be both amusing and depressing. But before you start, we think it is vital to know what you are looking for. It is easy – if also quite rare – to find instances of pure stupidity in workplaces. These are the people whose utter thoughtlessness singles them out from their peers and creates dysfunctional outcomes. Or who simply make slips that better judgement would have avoided. Sometimes clever people do idiotic things. Corporate executives using company jets to fly themselves and their dogs to hunting resorts at the company's expense are one good example. When it emerged that senior executives at the Swedish company SCA had done this, there was predictable criticism from the mass media, shareholders and the public.[7] This exemplified the worst of business greed and selfishness. It also projected the image of a company that had low ethical standards. The errors are obvious and damaging.

We see this as an instance of pure stupidity. The fact that those who were involved were the elite of the Swedish business world, had fine educations and probably high IQs, did not help.

What are a lot more common, but possibly harder to spot, are instances of *functional stupidity*. This goes on when it is normal for people to be excessively narrow and focused in their thinking and when it leads to largely positive outcomes.

There are three telltale aspects of functional stupidity: not thinking about your assumptions (what we call reflexivity), not asking why you are doing something (justification), and not considering the consequences or wider meaning of your actions (substantive reasoning). Let's look at each of these in a little more depth.

The first aspect of stupidity is an *absence of reflexivity*. This happens when we stop asking questions about our assumptions. Put simply, it involves taking for granted what other people commonly think. We often fail to question dominant beliefs and expectations. We see rules, routines and norms as completely natural: they are just how things are. Members of the organisation don't question these deep-rooted assumptions – even if they think they are idiotic. An example can be found in Robert Jackall's study of life in large North American corporations.[8] After interviewing many middle managers, Jackall found that they often lived in a morally ambiguous universe. They did not reflect on assumptions that prevailed in their firms, even when they found them morally repugnant. It seemed that one of the hallmarks of an upwardly mobile executive was that they could stop thinking too deeply about issues and follow a few simple rules:

(1) You never go around your boss. (2) You tell your boss what he wants to hear, even when your boss claims that he wants dissenting views. (3) If your boss wants something dropped, you drop it. (4) You are sensitive to your boss's wishes so that you anticipate what he wants; you don't force

him, in other words, to act as boss. (5) Your job is not to report something that your boss does not want reported, but rather to cover it up. You do what your job requires, and you keep your mouth shut.[9]

Asking questions was clearly a dangerous occupation. One manager Jackall spoke with summed up the situation: 'What is right in the corporation is not what is right in a man's home or in his church. *What is right in the corporation is what the guy above you wants from you.*'[10]

A second aspect of stupidity is *not seeking cause or a good reason*. People stop asking 'why' at work. They do not ask for, or offer, reasons for their decisions and actions. A rule is a rule and it must be followed, even if no one is clear why it exists. Questions about why something should be done are either completely ignored, or dismissed with reference to rank ('The CEO wants it'), convention ('We've always done it this way') or taboos ('We could never do that'). This happened at every turn in the companies Robert Jackall studied. He noticed there was 'an amazing variety of organizational improvement programs' which were linked with 'the myriad of ideas generated by corporate staff, business consultants, academics and a host of others to improve corporate structures, sharpen decision making, raise morale, create a more humanistic workplace … and so on'. These initiatives were not important for their intellectual content. Nor did they matter because they led to real improvements in productivity (usually they did not). Rather, 'these programs become important when they are pushed from the top'. Privately, managers often thought the programmes were nonsense. One described them as 'elaborate rituals with no practical effect', another as 'waving a magic wand to make things wonderful again'. But publicly, managers asked no questions. They didn't want to know why these initiatives happened. Instead, 'managers on the way up adopt the program with great enthusiasm, participate in or run them with great enthusiasm, and then quietly drop them when the time is right'.

The third aspect of stupidity is a *lack of substantive reasoning*. People stop asking about the wider consequences of their actions and their broader meaning. Instead, they focus on very narrow issues of *how* something is to be done. Technical questions about the most efficient way to do something completely trump more basic questions, such as whether it should be done in the first place and what effects its practice might have. The way managers that Jackall studied did this was by focusing on what they called 'playing the game'. Successful managers who rose through the ranks were those who could duck big questions. Asking those questions came with the risk of career suicide. If you wanted to survive in the corporation, you needed to 'play the game'. Doing this involved 'saying one thing and meaning another'.

> [Y]ou have to come up with a culturally accepted verbalisation to explain why you are not doing what you are doing ... you say that we had to do what we did because it was inevitable, or because guys at the regulatory agency were dumb, you say you won when you really lost, you say we saved money when we squandered it, you say something's safe when it's potentially dangerous ... everyone knows that it's bullshit, but it's accepted. This is the game.

If we briefly return to Pepsi, we see functional stupidity in action. People assumed that competition and masculinity were superior values. They never raised questions about elaborate corporate rituals or rigid adherence to hierarchy and career-ism. Rather they saw these as set rules of the game. They never seemed to seriously consider the overall purpose of their work. Functional stupidity ruled.

To spot stupidity we need to step back and ask whether people are fully using their cognitive capacities. Do they have at least some awareness of the assumptions they are making (reflexivity), are they willing to ask for and give reasons for a course of action (justification), and do they show an aware-ness of the consequences or broader meaning of their actions (substantive reasoning)? If people are reflexive, ask for and give justifications, and engage in substantive reasoning, then stupidity is likely to be absent. If they routinely avoid asking questions about assumptions, don't seek justifications and give no thought to the consequences and meaning of their action, then stupidity threatens.

Forms of functional stupidity

Functional stupidity can come in different forms. Perhaps the most obvious is closing down *cognition*. People get locked into a mindset. Their objectives are set. They mistake modes of thought and intellectual frameworks for reality, stop looking past the boundaries of the models, and do not challenge them. Their patterns of thinking freeze and are hard to shed.

This happened to the quants that we met in the introduc-tion. Trapped in the models of the market they had devised, they started to confuse their models with the real world they described. This was fine when the financial markets were acting in step with the assumptions they built into their models, but it meant that they were blind to disparities. When financial markets outgrew their models, they baffled and overwhelmed the quants. Reality did not compute.

A second form of functional stupidity is *motivational* defects, in the shape of a lack of willingness to use one's cognitive capacities. Often this involves a lack of curiosity. Personality traits can play a role here. For instance, people who have low levels of 'openness to experience' (one of the five major personality traits according to most psychologists) are likely to find it difficult and disturbing to think about issues that are new to them. As well as traits, identities can also constrain people's motivation to think beyond a limited range. Their self-image as an 'organisation man' or a 'good professional' can stifle broader thinking, deter them from questioning issues or assumptions that might threaten their valued sense of who they are. Identity motivates us to consider certain things, but it can also demotivate us from making full use of our intellectual powers. We are more drawn to confirm our sense of self and our group affiliations than to reflect upon them.

At Pepsi-Cola we saw that the executives were attached to seeing themselves as part of the business Marine Corps. This prompted them not to perceive the more negative aspects of their culture. As tough and competitive individuals, they were not supposed to think about broader issues such as work–life balance, or whether indeed the task they were so committed to was actually a worthwhile one. Their shared identity blindfolded them. It stopped them from asking whether there were ways of acting beyond masculine competition.

A lack of *emotional* reasoning is a third aspect of functional stupidity. At the extreme, this means being unable to comprehend a range of emotions. More often, though, it involves a fixation on one particular emotion. If you are the proud developer of a product, then you may resist exploring its possible defects. Anxiety at work and personal insecurity may also reinforce non-thinking. Worries about the negative emotions created by thinking outside the box can induce stupidity. Of course, in many situations people will think, but they won't share their thoughts with others. You may consider something to be a problem, but you refrain from raising the issue or following the thought in your own actions. In many cases we tend to repress thoughts that lead to dilemmas. We often find it better to stop thinking rather than suffer a painful dilemma and the intense emotions that they bring.

One IT consulting firm that one of us studied set store by being upbeat, positive and optimistic. Don't mention negative things; try not to point at problems; frame topics to sound good. If they lost a client, then they would rationalise the event, even say things like 'Glad to get rid of them.' Within this can-do culture, its members drew a veil over anything that might disturb the general positive and upbeat mood. Most of the time this was OK, but it meant that anything that counted as bad news was ritually avoided. This had the effect of creating a false sense of positivity and unawareness of bad news. We will come back to this case in a later chapter.[11]

The final kind of functional stupidity is *moral* at base. This happens when attachment to a given ethos limits thinking. Those who are deeply committed to a moral scheme may resist or reject ideas that cut against it. If an organisation places a great value on loyalty, then people can avoid thinking for themselves. When loyalty is dominant, being a team player can be seen as a moral duty. The fear of deviation can fuel a moral compulsion not to think beyond the most narrow intellectual schemes.

An alternative media organisation that one of us studied was trapped by a strong moral scheme that centred on the value of 'autonomy'.[12] It celebrated non-hierarchical, fluid and 'horizontal' arrangement. Any attempt to instil arrangements that were seen as creating formal authority and bureaucracy was fervently resisted. This helped to hold the organisation together. It provided a sense of identity. But it meant that attempts to introduce formal systems that created some minimal hierarchies were completely ignored. People found it difficult to talk about the implicit hierarchical relationships that were lurking beneath the surface of the organisation. Ultimately, this taboo on hierarchy meant that members were unable to think about more formal and practically sensible mechanisms of organising. Eventually the organisation withered away.

These four aspects – cognitions, motivations, emotions and morals – are important for the understanding of functional stupidity. Many kinds of stupidity are less about cognitive shortcomings. Sometimes we can lack the motives to engage in thinking. At other times, our feelings take control. And our morals can trap us in exceedingly narrow patterns of thought. Much of the time, all four of these aspects of functional stupidity work together. For instance, when we lack the cognitive capacity, have little motivation, are not emotionally engaged, and face moral issues, we are likely to stop asking questions, even if we have the feeling something is amiss. But more frequently matters are a bit more complicated. For instance, we might have the cognitive capacities at our disposal, but we lack the motivation, the emotional drive and the moral inclination to put the serious question.

How does functional stupidity work?

Contemporary organisations are often engines of functional stupidity. It thrives in contexts where persuasion trumps substance. When playing with symbols is paramount, a gap can yawn between rhetoric and reality. In order to bridge it, organisations often foster functional stupidity. Adherence to managerial demands is rewarded, and criticism or reflection discouraged. Deterrents on thinking things through are embraced by employees themselves. They steer clear of awkward questions and focus instead on narrow ways of thinking. This can help to push doubts aside. Ambiguities are repressed and the resultant false sense of certainty can boost morale as people avoid conflict and focus on getting the job done. But it can also create some significant problems. People overlook small problems that can fester and propagate. Eventually these problems can spark crises, which may in turn fuel spells of self-reflection. This can have the effect of corroding stupidity, and opening people up to deeper thought and reflection.

Economies of persuasion

Developed economies have undergone an explosion of *economies of persuasion*. As the production of goods – and increasingly services – has moved offshore, developed countries have confronted the pressing question: how to keep their population busy. The answer has been to develop economies that manufacture images.[13] Large chunks of economies in many developed countries are now devoted to making things look good. According to one estimate, 30 per cent of the US economy now consists of persuasion activities.[14] Obvious examples include advertising, public relations and the media, but there are many other sectors that trade heavily in images. Creating a good appearance is crucial in the world of professional services.[15] People working in routine service work also have to put significant effort into presenting themselves in the right way.[16] Even in the public sector, organisations spend their precious resources nurturing the right brand. Non-profit organisations have also grown more and more consumed with image-polishing exercises. Saying the right things, speaking in the right way and dressing correctly are seen as crucial parts of many jobs and in particular, in senior, well paid, high status roles.

In an economy of persuasion, there is usually a huge over-supply of goods and services. People don't naturally want or need all the things that are churned out every day.[17] In the US, 40 per cent of the food is not even consumed.[18] On a global scale, between 30 and 50 per cent of food produced is just thrown away.[19] A recent survey in the UK found that the average piece of women's clothing is worn only seven times before being thrown away.[20] Two billion smartphones are sold every year.[21] To get rid of this growing stockpile of goods, people need to be convinced that they want all these things. Organisations must devote a large chunk of their resources to creating demand for the products and services they create. They do this by inflating expectations, creating seductive images and influencing con-sumers' desires. At first it was just the job of customer-facing employees like sales and marketing personnel to practise this image production, but slowly the logic of looking good has captured entire organisations. Work that is far removed from customers starts to be seen as part of a company's image-build-ing activities. Back-office administrators are encouraged to become 'brand ambassadors'. Shop-floor workers are prodded to 'delight the customer' while screwing in bolts on the produc-tion line. Even maintenance and cleaning staff are required to be 'on message' with the company's brand.

When looking good becomes job number one, the focus shifts from substance to image. Sometimes image-creation can be targeted externally: branding, marketing and public rela-tions become more significant than the core service or product the organisation creates. But often it is focused internally. Employees keep learning how great their employer is through employee branding initiatives, corporate culture programmes and CSR (corporate social responsibility) projects.[22] People in organisations rely on increasingly hollow status markers such as grand titles and impressive-sounding initiatives that are completely disconnected from their actual job.

Today, many schools have fallen victim to image obsession. In the past, teachers had relatively high levels of autonomy. They concentrated their energies on educating students. But as a result of constant educational reforms, schools are now more and more focused on various auditing exercises. In the UK, the event that most head teachers worry about is the periodic auditing exercise by the government schools inspector. When parents of prospective students visit a school, they are treated to lengthy PowerPoint shows with all sorts of tables detailing its performance in these auditing exercises. Schools spend time and resources working on the quality of leadership, how the school is branded, and its vision and strategy. Many window-dressing activities are set up to give an impression of 'excellence'. In Sweden, one of the overarching obsessions in many schools is getting their 'grounding values' right. These values always look impressive – but they are also very vague. Once they have got the values right, school leaders assume that success will follow. What the school looks like seems to count for more than the actual education. The people who run schools end up allotting less time and resources to teaching and learning, and more to image-polishing exercises. Schools become machines for persuading others that children are getting a good education, rather than institutions for educating children.

Stupidity management
In organisations where manipulating images is the most important concern, managers focus their efforts on shaping the mindsets of their employees.[23] This is nothing new. During

Henry Ford's reign, the Ford motor company put great effort into creating model employees. Ford wanted to give his employees a moral education. Sociologists were employed to study worker's lifestyles and redesign the communities they lived in. By minutely crafting the life of his employees, Ford hoped to encourage them to lead healthier and more moral lives, ultimately making them more productive.[24]

In today's image-obsessed organisations, executives also set out to manage their employees' lives, shaping the way employees think about themselves, how they feel, and what their moral judgements are. In her account of the life of investment bankers working on Wall Street, Alexandra Michel shows how the values of hard work and competitiveness were hammered into all employees.[25] In the first few years in the job, recruits were highly committed. They spent sixteen hours or more at the office. Their whole life became work. One young recruit described it as being 'like an artificial world. Instead of going home, after 5 pm people here just switch into leisure clothes, turn on the music, and the firm orders dinner for you. Ironically, you end up working a lot more because it is so convenient.' He thought it was 'like a psych experiment where the light is always on'. In this world, employees' sense of self was completely fused with the company. This got too much for many to bear after three or four years. Adapting to these conditions meant almost total surrender to a corporate regime with little heed paid to whether it made sense, even when employees were suffering from serious health or psychological issues triggered by the gruelling hours. They saw their sixteen-hour days as just how things were.

A central, but often unacknowledged, aspect of making a corporate culture work is what we call *stupidity management*. Here managers actively encourage their employees not to think too much. If they do happen to think, it is best not to voice what emerges. Employees are encouraged to stick within clear-cut parameters. Managers use subtle and not so subtle means to prod them not to ask too many tough questions, not to reflect too deeply on their assumptions, and not to consider the broader purpose of their work. Employees are nudged to just get on with the task. They are to look on the bright side, stay upbeat and push doubts and negative thoughts aside.

Sometimes stupidity management can be forceful and direct. In extreme cases employees are asked deliberately to cultivate their stupidity. For instance, the director of an advertising agency advised his copywriters never to visit the factories that produced the goods they were promoting: knowing that the truth about the manufacturing process and the products would make it difficult to write the kind of copy (by his own admission, often superficial nonsense) that needed to figure in adverts.[26] In an even more extreme example, the director of another advertising firm asked his employees to 'walk in stupid every morning'.[27]

Functional stupidity can also be encouraged in more subtle ways. For instance, managers can steer employees away from troublesome issues. We saw this happening at Ford when Dennis Gioia's colleagues encouraged him not to look too deeply into the causes of fires in a few Ford Pintos. Managers in large corporations who raise ethical issues are seen as having 'strange ideas' and hence not altogether to be trusted. Their views may be respected, but there is a stigma of lack of reliability. As a result, they are often given marginal roles and not awarded important tasks.[28] Similarly, junior staff in a management consultancy firm who talked negatively about extreme work pressure resulting from understaffing were seen as 'show-stoppers' who spoiled the whole working process.[29]

Stupidity management can also work through powerful

people setting the agenda so that awkward issues do not even feature in the first place. These are pre-emptive strikes within the field of stupidity management. For instance, corporate culture can encourage employees to have the 'right' outlook and attitude. Leaders can try to show others that it is wise to avoid being disloyal or deviant.

Ideology is also a weapon in the stupidity manager's arsenal. Often it is propagated purposefully. For instance, some organisations explicitly celebrate the value of being action-oriented.[30] In-depth analysis is frowned upon, quick and spontaneous action is celebrated, employees will be asked to follow the corporate cliché: 'Stop thinking about it and start doing it.' In one organisation enacting change programmes, careful consideration of their outcomes was discouraged. Employees were to focus their energy on showing that things were being done. This meant that changes were 'pushed through by managers trying to make a reputation and a career, who do not stay on to see them through'.[31] Of course, there are times when companies need to act quickly and decisively to deal with a clear and present danger. However, genuine emergencies are rare. Being action-oriented is usually driven less by a pressing situation and more by the ideological preferences of people in charge. And sometimes people respond to signals and act fast because it is easier than thinking issues through.

Self-stupidification

Smart people quickly learn when it pays not to think more broadly. When this happens, they start to engage in *stupidity self-management*. Doubts are cast aside. Critique is culled by the internal censor. Complexity, contradictions and ambiguity are denied, negative aspects of corporate life airbrushed out. A sense of faith and optimism is generated. People carefully nurture a sense that things are normal and acceptable. They avoid asking serious questions. Eventually individuals start to instinctively sidestep situations where doubts might be kindled, criticisms offered or justifications called for.

Self-stupidifying starts to happen when we censor our own internal conversation. As we go through our working day, we constantly try to give some sense to our often chaotic experiences. We do this by engaging in what some scholars call 'internal reflexivity'.[32] This is the constant stream of discussion that we have with ourselves. When self-stupidification takes over, we stop asking ourselves questions. Negative or contradictory lines of thinking are avoided. As a result, we start to feel aligned with the thoughtlessness we find around us. It is hard to be someone who thinks in an organisation that shuns it.

To avoid negative and disturbing thoughts, people often focus on the positive and 'safer' aspects of organisational life. They assume that the way things are done around them is natural. In some cases, they claim it is hard to imagine alternatives. The standard lines found in PowerPoint presentations, corporate strategy statements and CEO speeches become like intellectual comfort blankets. They help employees ensure that their own internal reflexivity does not radically clash with the party line. Being on board with what everyone else thinks gives them a sense of security. They can rest easy because they will not be the odd one out facing disapproval from authorities and peers. Instead, they are able to maintain a sense of being a good company woman or man.

Self-stupidification might seem like the easy path, but it often clashes with the realities of work. Work can be boring, harsh, unethical and unproductive. This hardly suits the positive working demeanour most companies favour. The clash between upbeat image and downbeat reality all too often

creates a sharp sense of dissonance. It can fuel doubt, aliena-
tion, cynicism and activism among employees. In some cases, it
can reduce people's motivation, damage their career ambitions
or even drive them out of the firm. However, dissonance does
not always light a revolutionary fuse. All too often, employees respond by growing more and more compliant. Stupidity
self-management comes to the fore. In order to self-stupidify,
employees try hard to ensure that the stories they tell themselves about work align with the positive tales that circulate
through official channels. They edit their own experiences so
that they match the optimistic vision promoted by others. By
mentally erasing negative experiences, employees are able to
maintain an affirmative worldview. This enables them to hold
on to the hollow ideas peddled by management.

Certainty and dissonance

Functional stupidity is a mixed blessing for organisations and
the people working in them. It can have positive results, but
also less desirable ones. Sometimes the positive aspects dominate, sometimes the negative. Often it is hard to assess how
much functionality rules, and how much stupidity. Both factors
will change over time.

On the upside, functional stupidity can provide a sense of
certainty and faith. Don't ask too many tricky questions, and
disruptions can be minimised. Employees can shed the burden
of doubt and sidestep the risk of overthinking things. Freed
from the weight of enervating thoughts, employees can plough
their energies into tackling the corporate greasy pole. Day-to-
day office life and building one's own career become much less
tricky. Functional stupidity also gives people a sense of certainty about who they are, what they want and the steps they
need to take in order to get on. If you are able to block out

experiences that trigger critical thinking, then you can avoid the vulnerability that comes with asking big questions.

Functional stupidity also provides a sense of community, certainty and order for organisations. Difficult questions are discouraged, as are requests for substantive reasons and broader justifications for actions. This can be helpful: asking questions can be costly. It swallows up time and resources and may squander social capital. Organisations that are frequently called on to justify their actions have to put sizeable resources into creating and articulating reasons for their decisions. This often means that people spend more time building a case for doing something than actually doing it. When the actions of a firm are hard to justify, it can breed doubt. This can undermine its perceived legitimacy and dissolve commitment among employees.[33]

By cultivating functional stupidity, organisations are able to avoid the costs of critical thinking. Sidestepping troublesome questions enables them to give their staff a sense of order, trust and predictability. For instance, by encouraging civil servants not to think too much about the possible problematic consequences of a proposed policy, a government department can get them focused on simply delivering the reforms.[34]

While functional stupidity is a key resource for an organisation, it can also do conspicuous harm. It can lead to meaningless and non-productive work being undertaken: writing plans, ticking boxes, endless meetings take over. Often there is a stark clash between the official version of events and the lived realities. For individuals, functional stupidity turns from a benefit into a bane when it reduces autonomy, narrows the range of choices or becomes a source of dissatisfaction. It may also throw doubt on the meaning and purposes of the individual's working life.

Reducing critical reflection may be reasonable sometimes, but at other times, glaring contradictions can be hard to ignore. When this happens, people are forced to face up to the question of whether they are willing to acknowledge these contradictions or whether they just want to continue to turn a blind eye.[35] Facing up to these tensions and trying to do something about them might be a sign of bravery, but as with any act of bravery, it comes at a cost. By pointing out blatant contradictions, individuals lay themselves open to penalties. They may be passed over for promotion, get less attractive assignments or find themselves the target of hostile comments. In some cases they may even be fired. This is a lesson many whistleblowers learn the hard way – speaking up about a problem has its risks. Even if they avoid obvious punishments, they are often ostracised.[36] People may admire whistleblowers at a distance, but within their own organisation or occupation, they can be seen as difficult, rigid and disloyal.

When functional stupidity takes root, it can create problems for the whole organisation. When thinking is cut short, small mistakes can be overlooked. Questionable ideas, practices and priorities can flourish. When this happens, it can instigate much bigger problems. For instance, one of the most palpable drivers of accidents is an organisational or occupational culture that encourages people to avoid asking difficult questions.[37] One of the drivers of the 2008 financial crisis was an unwillingness to raise doubts about risky investment strategies. This led many bankers to ignore increasingly large discrepancies between their models and the reality of the market. The consequence of this generalised stupidity was the collapse of many financial institutions and a broader systemic crisis.

To repeat: functional stupidity is a double-edged sword. For instance, the norm of being positive can lead to functional outcomes such as a good organisational climate. But it can also have negative outcomes such as suppressing the awareness of problems, reproducing received ideas and choking learning. Sometimes the positive aspects are more pronounced in the short run, while the risks are greater in the long term.

Self-reinforcing stupidity and reflexivity

Functional stupidity can become self-reinforcing. This happens when employees stop asking searching questions and are rewarded with a sense of (false) certainty. It happens when they are good team players, reliable followers and well adapted organisational members who do not threaten their managers or colleagues. It can create an optimistic narrative. People tell good-news stories. Sometimes there are rewards such as promotions, pay rises and pats on the back from people who matter. All this is taken as evidence that things are going well, and you should continue to follow the same course. This does not imply conservatism. More often than not, it means constant change and incessant trend-hopping.

There are times in organisations when the general positive vibe is threatened. This happens when hard-earned certainties are endangered. Naturally this preys on the mind of someone in thrall to functional stupidity. To protect themselves, they gradually learn to avoid thinking about disturbing things. This can be comforting, but it can also reinforce their faith in officially sponsored stories. By retreating into cosy beliefs, organisational members reaffirm the continued smooth functioning of the organisation as well as their own career paths within it. This creates a self-reinforcing loop: more functional stupidity begets more (illusory) certainty which in turn creates more functional stupidity. Intellectual laziness follows.

Functional stupidity isn't just a vicious circle with no escape.

There are some cases when widespread functional stupidity can create dysfunctional outcomes. Often these problems can be overlooked. However, there are times when they are so great that they become impossible to ignore. This prompts *reflexivity*. People start to ask deeper questions, search for justifications and engage in substantive reasoning. Sometimes this leads to the response: 'How could I have been so stupid?' But less drastic experiences are also common. For instance, professionals facing unemployment are often forced to ask difficult questions about their own futures.[38] Although such self-examination is painful, it can undermine functional stupidity. There are some cases where organisations actually encourage individual reflexivity. For example, in an attempt to recruit Pepsi's John Sculley, Steve Jobs at Apple asked him: 'Do you want to continue to sell sweetened water for the rest of your life?'[39] This shook Sculley's attachment to Pepsi. He started to ask himself what meaningful and important work actually is. Similarly, direct-selling companies recruit and motivate members by pushing them to reflect on the dissatisfying 'rut' that they experience in their everyday working life.[40] By doing this, they shake up people's existing commitments and spark a process of internal reflection.

Bad news can have profound implications for the whole organisation. Corporate disasters or financial improprieties sometimes prompt in-depth inquiries, and these in their turn can give rise to collective self-reflection, substantive questioning and the search for broader justifications. For instance, during an inquiry into changes in an Australian public broadcaster, senior people started asking questions about why the organisation existed, what its purpose was and how it should view itself.[41] However, inquiries can also become forums where groups avoid deeper and more searching questions, sidestep fundamentally systematic changes, and ensure a speedy return to 'business as usual'. For instance, government inquiries into the failures of the UK banking sector during the 2008 global financial crisis frequently revealed that leaders of financial institutions sought to avoid responsibility and self-reflection.[42] Public inquiries are by no means the only forums that can allow deeper collective self-reflexivity, the search for justification and substantive reasoning. There are many other spaces that can host stupidity-disturbing dialogue. These include social movements, insurgencies within organisations, the media exposing contentious issues to the wider public, and even leaders who are willing to encourage reflection on fundamental assumptions within an organisation.

Conclusion

We are frequently told that firms allow smart people to manufacture knowledge by using their superior intelligence. However, much of corporate life seems to be about manufacturing stupidity. If we take a look around nearly any workplace, we find that stupidity abounds. Although we are likely to focus on the most obvious instances of pure stupidity, many more such instances lurk in the shadows. These are cases of stupidity which entail excessively narrow thinking that is seen as normal and has functional outcomes.

Functional stupidity is so widespread in most organisations that it is simply seen as normal. There is much wishful thinking, following leaders without careful scrutiny, unreasoning zeal for fads and fashions, senseless imitation of others, change initiatives that lead nowhere, and use of clichés in place of careful analysis. When much of this is seen as 'best practice', spotting stupidity can be tough. But if you sharpen your senses and know what to look out for, it can happen. Important markers of functional stupidity include people being encouraged not to think about the assumptions they are making, not giving or asking for justifications of their actions, and not thinking of the wider implications or meaning of what they do.

Given the prevalence of functional stupidity, it is vital to understand how it works. We have argued that it is common in contexts where image trumps substance. In a small factory or on a farm, there is clear feedback about what works and what does not. An ad agency, a support department in a corporation or a government agency is likely to lack such direct feedback mechanisms. This is also the case in most work in large companies that are rife with complexities. Large parts of contemporary economies are short on clear links between work and 'substantive' outcomes. In these kinds of settings, people focus their energies on trying to make things look good rather than actually working on core tasks. Often this can open a huge gap between the rhetoric and the reality. The message might be great, but what actually happens underneath it all can be much less appealing. To convince people, managers spend valuable time and energy on stupidity management. They persuade otherwise intelligent people not to use their cognitive capacities outside prescribed frameworks. They refrain from taking moral responsibility to think through issues. To begin with this is a challenge, but fairly soon smart people start to self-stupidify. They stop asking the difficult questions and avoid deeper thinking. They realise that reflection is career-limiting and can lead to sleepless nights. The initial results can be positive: people avoid conflict and are able to get on with the job. But in the longer term, it can create the conditions for much more disturbing problems, and even disasters.

Part Two

Five Kinds of Functional Stupidity

4

Leadership-Induced Stupidity

The curious case of Benjamin Booker

Benjamin Booker was recently appointed as the CEO of a publishing company. In the past he had directed a newspaper. During his time there, he developed a reputation as an excellent leader. His subordinates said he was trustworthy and honest. He put effort into nurturing good relationships with the people he worked with. They thought he was great at understanding people. Unsurprisingly, he was well liked.

When asked about his own leadership style, Booker told us that 'you have to be authentic because people will see through you otherwise. If you're not authentic people see you as just playing, pretending, and then the leadership becomes wrong'. Booker thought that caring for his followers was a vital part of being an authentic leader. For him, it was important to do things like celebrate employees' birthdays. His often-repeated mantra was 'Faking yourself won't work'. 'You can create a positive corporate culture, but you have to be genuine,' he said. 'That's absolutely the most important thing, that you're honest'. He also celebrated his integrity and reliability. People can trust me, he claimed.

When Booker moved to his new role at the publisher, he

took his ideas about leadership with him. However these did not always go down so well in his new workplace. Someone who worked closely with him said: 'I think that Booker exaggerates. All this recognition of others, it's just a routine... there's no thought behind it, it's just shallow.' His attempts to be an authentic leader were often seen as false. Rather than seeing Booker as someone who was committed to strong principles, some colleagues felt he was a yes man: 'He can't do what he likes, the owners are keeping him on a tight leash. His wings are clipped,' a member of the management committee told us.

Booker saw himself as an authentic leader who focused on genuine relationships and staying true to his personal values. This seemed to work at the newspaper, but at the publisher it backfired. Many of his new subordinates thought he was a phoney. Despite these failures, he remained largely ignorant about how people saw him and resolutely committed to his approach to leadership.

Like so many other leaders, Booker celebrated a leadership style that might have worked in the past, but had run out of steam in his new workplace. He believed he was an authentic leader, yet many of his new staff thought he was a fake. Fortunately, Booker was able to conveniently overlook these contradictions and continue his work. By doing this, he could cling to a vision of himself that made him feel good. But this vision didn't necessarily match reality.[1]

Holding on to an image of oneself despite evidence to the contrary requires a healthy measure of stupidity. Leaders – sometimes very good ones – often stop themselves from asking difficult questions. They cling to an idealised notion of leadership that makes them feel good. They avoid looking too closely at their own assumptions and ideas about themselves. They overlook the evidence and buy into empty ideas. As a result they stay fixed on an ideal image of themselves as a leader – even when it is doing themselves, and others, harm.

The leadership delusion

It shouldn't be surprising that leaders are often deluded. Much of the talk about leadership propagates misleading ideas, and these have built a huge leadership industry.[2] Entry barriers are low and the opportunities high in this multi-billion-dollar sector. Business people, academics, consultants, mountain climbers, sport stars, horse trainers, sexologists, spiritual guides and individuals from almost every background are willing to offer their advice on leadership. This crew of self-styled experts bombard confused, desperate and bored middle managers with self-confident statements and recipes for success. They are often ready victims of the leadership industry that specialises in selling seductive images to managers and other leader-wannabes.

Most ideas produced by the leadership industries rely on flawed reasoning and pseudo-science.[3] 'Much of the oft-repeated conventional wisdom about leadership is based more on hope than reality, on wishes rather than data, on beliefs rather than science,' Jeffrey Pfeffer writes.[4] Sometimes ideas about leadership are harmless forms of corporate escapism. They allow stressed-out middle managers to feel like visionary world-changers or profound thinkers for a few hours. But all too often, ideas about leadership can be really problematic. According to McKinsey, companies in the US spend $14 billion every year on leadership development initiatives.[5] The results of all this effort are woeful. According to one report, 'there is scarcely any evidence that all this spending … is producing better leaders'.[6] We have spoken with many individuals who have devoted their careers to delusional ideas about leadership. We have heard employees talking about how their organisations have been decimated by leaders driven by misguided ideas.

The image of leadership that haunts the popular imagination is usually very attractive. Leaders, we are told, push people to think and develop their capacity. Leadership is supposed to be about influencing subordinates through superior vision, values, ideas and emotions. Management, by contrast, is more about nuts and bolts: planning, coordination and control. We are often led to think that leadership is sexy, management is boring. According to popular wisdom people obey managers while they are empowered by leaders. Those who manufacture ideas about management advise, the leadership industry preaches.

Sometimes the rhetoric of leadership matches reality. Leaders can motivate, transform and even serve their followers. But the great majority of leaders also cultivate stupidity. They can do this by encouraging the subordinate levels to deliberately dampen their thinking and eschew their autonomy. But perhaps most importantly, ideas about leadership can stop aspiring leaders themselves from thinking. It can encourage them to buy into persuasive ideas that are often based on little more than pseudo-science, or research guided by barely disguised ideology.

In this chapter, we want to challenge the common assumption that leadership is about mobilising superior intelligence, rationality or wisdom. Sometimes leaders are wise and exert valuable influence, but when they buy into ideas circulated by the leadership industries, they can stop themselves from asking broader questions, engaging in deeper reflection and considering the wider consequences of their actions. But what's more surprising is that all this non-thinking can now and then have useful consequences – at least in the short term.

Big leaders?

'Modern business leaders are knowledge workers of the highest order,' we are told.[7] We often assume that leaders have high IQs and great practical wisdom.[8] Leaders should also have high levels of emotional intelligence, superior self-insights, and know how to deal with the emotions of others.[9] They should be able to nurture their followers and help them to grow.[10] Leaders, we are told, should have the education, insightfulness and ability to see the bigger picture.

Wisdom, emotional intelligence, care and reflection are certainly desirable, but these qualities are not that common in the real world. All too often flesh-and-blood leaders fall short. Sometimes they are irrational and stupid – and convince their followers to be the same.[11] Many are a mix of positive and negative abilities. Great leaders like Churchill and Jobs could easily furnish a book with examples of how *not* to do leadership.[12] For every CEO who turns a company around there is another who has run a successful company into the ground. For every middle manager who inspires their team, there is another who alienates them. For every super-smart executive there is one with limited intelligence. But almost all attention goes to the heroic examples.

Over the past twenty years, we have followed dozens of leaders for extended periods of time. Most of these people were well educated, very experienced, and had great confidence. Many worked in knowledge-intensive companies. We expected to find smart people harnessing the intelligence of their followers. What we found was quite different.[13]

Consider the case of Bertram, a senior manager with a PhD working in a large pharmaceutical firm. When we asked him what he saw as the crucial component of leadership, he told us: 'My view is that it is teamwork and everyone is important, everyone is needed.' He then went on to point out that 'key scientists are important ... we must be prepared to reward them in a wholly new way as compared to what we've done.' If we look at these two views, we see a striking contradiction. On the one hand, Bertram thinks teamwork is important. On the other hand, he says that key scientists are vital. You may agree that both are important, but recognising and rewarding 'key scientists' could undermine an emphasis on the whole team. If some individuals are 'key', it's not clear that everyone is equally important. It seems that Bertram supports contradictory principles without noticing it.

Another example of these confusions and contradictions can be found in the story of Jen, a middle manager in a manufacturing company.[14] She has taken part in many leadership courses and read a lot about coaching. Needless to say, she likes to view herself as a coach. She sees her job as participation and delegation, and takes a dim view of managers who claim to know best. But when we observed Jen over a couple of weeks, we found no signs that she was practising what she preached. She spent her days attending meetings, and telling people what they should do in a rather non-coachly way.

Both of these managers – and the many others that we have studied – talk the leadership talk, but their leadership ideas and practice do not hang together. Bertram has inconsistent and confused ideas. Jen's ideal and practice moved in almost opposite directions.

Managers say they want to provide a vision, engage followers, and do many other great things. But they rarely walk the leadership walk. They often spend their days doing routine administration. Their jobs seem to be more about meetings and emails than setting great visions. This should not be so surprising. Managerial work is tough. Often organisational practice and the individual shortcomings of managers make it hard for ideals to be realised. But despite all this, most managers hold onto fantastic hopes about leadership – even despite so much evidence to the contrary.

Small followers?

A leader does not need to be completely superior, but on the whole we expect leaders to be 'better' than the people they lead. After all, why follow someone with lower intelligence, self-confidence, knowledge and creativity than you? When the person who is supposed to lead is much more experienced, better-educated and has a better overview of the task, then their leadership might make sense, but when you study leadership over a long time at close range, it is often not so clear that leaders are much better than their followers. Often people are promoted to managerial positions because of career interests, good contacts, political manoeuvring and seniority. Not because they have great potential as a leader. And even if the best are promoted, they may have been only marginally better than people around them.

To make managers with boring and stressful administrative jobs feel better about themselves, organisations go out of their way to accentuate hierarchy and status and boost their identity. This is what fancy titles, large office spaces, executive dress codes, formal meetings and special privileges are for. Managers are sent to expensive leadership-development programmes where facilitators do their best to help them feel like 'real leaders'. These little tricks help to create an impression that managers are superior and should be treated as leaders. But impressions can deceive.

A problem for leadership in practice is that people in

subordinate positions often don't see themselves as followers. Often, inexperienced and weak people are happy to follow. In very stressful situations, being a follower may also be convenient for experienced people. And most people feel the need for a certain degree of order, including well functioning administration and division of labour. But it's rare to find reasonably experienced people who really want to cultivate their followership. People prefer to see themselves as engineers, car mechanics, chefs, physicians and tax inspectors rather than followers. For instance, one junior manager told us about his unwillingness to be 'motivated' by would-be leaders. 'The managers I struggle with most are the "motivating" types,' he said. These were people 'who try to create energy and momentum, but only move back and forth without keeping a clear direction'. Another person we spoke with told us that 'my work has seldom received much leadership. Something which I appreciate! I have had pretty much carte blanche from the beginning. Sometimes this can be tricky, but mostly I find it stimulating. I am directed by goals and dislike being told what to do. So who or what should I say is leading me?'[15]

Managers trying to lead need followers, but much of the time their supposed followers don't feel that they need leadership. Managers are just as happy to view themselves as leaders as most other employees are unhappy to see themselves as followers. Non-managers like to have autonomy and work with people as peers. Often they are sceptical about high-profile leadership efforts. This often means there are leaders fired up by mythologies of leadership who anxiously roam the hallways of organisations, looking for followers.

Leadership as a source of stupidity

Of course all managers want their subordinates to do their work in a competent way. Very few like thoughtless people around them. Some leaders try to encourage their followers to use the full range of their cognitive capacities some of the time. But usually this isn't the case. All too often leadership involves the active cultivation of functional stupidity.

Leaders often encourage followers to avoid thinking too much. They ask them to buy into narrow assumptions, not ask too many questions and avoid reflecting on the broader meaning of their actions. By corralling followers' cognitive capacities, leaders try to limit how followers define, think and act. Encouraging stupidity through leadership can create functional outcomes – for followers, for leaders and for the organisation as a whole. It helps people avoid wider discussions and simply get on with the job. It can dampen conflict and create a shared sense of meaning. In this sense, selective thoughtlessness is the bedfellow of leadership.

The relationship between leadership and functional stupidity is complex. At one extreme are organisations that demand very high levels of compliance from their followers. In military organisations, the lower ranks have unthinking compliance drummed into them.[16] They learn not to think freely, avoid using their own judgement, and sidestep reflection. They learn to execute commands – no matter how stupid they seem. Sometimes, such unthinking compliance can lead to disasters, but it can also be absolutely central to the normal functioning of these organisations. Imagine an army in which the troops critically reflected on their orders before carrying them out.

At the other extreme are contemporary workplaces where leaders are encouraged to think about themselves as buddies, therapists or saints.[17] These forms of more humanistic leadership may displace some of the stupidities that come with command and control, but this does not necessarily mean the decline of stupidity per se. The assumption persists that leaders are morally, spiritually or socially superior to their followers. New forms of facilitative leadership emphasise dependence and lack of autonomy: the leader sets the path, creates enthusiasm, builds a feeling of belonging, provides employees with the right ideas and orchestrates personal growth. The follower is supposed to be a recipient of superior coaching from the leader. This creates an unequal relationship. The more leadership there is, the more subordinates are led. The more therapeutic the leader (scoring high on EQ), the more clientlike the follower is encouraged to become.

Sometimes acknowledging one's relative stupidity can be sensible. When there is a clear imbalance of ability, expertise and overview between leaders and followers, it is fine if the followers don't ask too many questions. But this can change. New circumstances may weaken a leader's authority. Subordinates can quickly grow out of being rookies. When this happens, stupidity can cease to be functional.

Continuing to believe in leadership when the circumstances don't warrant it may not be particularly wise. In many cases, a would-be leader may not be a head above their subordinates. When this is so, the very idea of a leader leading and followers following may be rather stupid. But it can still yield some positive outcomes: having a leader around (even if they are not so smart) can reassure people: It can give them a sense of order, someone to turn to when there are problems, and someone to blame when things go wrong.

Devoted to leadership

The idea of leadership has a devoted following. Millions of people around the world read books on how to enhance their leadership abilities. Organisations spend billions trying to develop leadership. Governments assume that any problem

– no matter how tricky or difficult – can be solved with more leadership. Thousands of courses on leadership are run around the world every day. Many business people love leadership. In many ways our faith in leadership has made it into a kind of secular religion.[18] This religious quality is obvious in the idea of servant leadership. Robert Greenleaf's foundational essay on the topic talks about 'prophecies', 'seekers', 'healing' and 'faith'. Leaders, Greenleaf claims, need to have almost divine qualities such as 'a sense of the unknowable' and the ability to 'foresee the unforeseeable'.

Transformational, charismatic and authentic leadership also has religious qualities.[19] Transformational leaders are said to be able to create 'conversion' experiences for their followers. Jesus Christ is frequently seen as an early archetype of a charismatic leader. Authentic leaders are encouraged to connect with their deepest beliefs and nurture their spiritual side.

The secular religion of leadership has many devotees. We suspect that the leadership industry has many more committed followers among managers than among their subordinates. This global community of believers shares a common faith in the innate goodness of leadership. The faithful are naturally eager to preserve some idealised notion of the leader. To do so, a measure of stupidity does not come amiss. It helps them overlook the contradictions and confusions, the vagueness and idealisations, the lack of evidence and the poor reasoning that is such a staple of many ideas about leadership. In particular the popular ones that make managers so keen.

Like religion, leadership promises moral order. It gives supplicants a sense of reassurance. Relatively mundane administrative activities come to be seen as genuinely heroic and meaningful actions. Managers start to think that their trivial acts may have important effects.

One devotee we met was called George. He was a middle manager in a hi-tech firm. Most of his days were spent doing mundane things, but he always tried to see them as very special. When we asked him about his leadership style, George told us: 'I base my leadership on respect for those who are really close to the actual work. I do not have any tendency to tell people what to do. Instead, I base my leadership on trust, respect and open dialogue with all my subordinates. There are no hidden agendas on my part.' George clearly expected that being open, honest and considerate and not telling them what to do would make a big difference to how others saw him. 'I'm quite sure that they think that I am open and that I am very inviting,' he said. 'I tell them about my private life and I say what I can and cannot do. I hope they have caught that.'[20]

Other managers we have studied believe they are doing leadership when they engage their subordinates in small talk.[21] Sometimes they think this can have a dramatic impact on their followers' self-confidence, satisfaction and morale. It seems that when a manager does what many would think is common behaviour in the workplace – being respectful, talking about private matters, drinking coffee together – they think they are doing 'leadership' and something remarkable is happening. However, most subordinates don't respond to coffee with their unit head in the same way as to having tea with the Queen.

Despite these assumptions, most people are not on the lookout for leadership. George's subordinates do not care much for his leadership. Like most people, they are actually more interested in their work tasks, having stimulating colleagues, developing their abilities, finding career opportunities, receiving their salary and protecting their working conditions. Most people appreciate an open, honest and effective manager. These are qualities they probably also appreciate in other people they encounter. But much of the time, this does not particularly matter. They just want to get on with the job. They are often not so interested in ambitious leadership that promises to transform them with superior visions, values or meanings.

Leaders as stupidity managers

How does leadership produce stupidity? Perhaps the most obvious way this happens is through demanding absolute compliance from followers. Authoritarian and cultish organisations are built on a strong differentiation between leaders and followers. Those in subordinate positions are pushed to refrain from thinking outside the box. They should assume that their leader has the big picture and knows best.

Strict authoritarianism is not very popular in today's workplaces, at least not in the West. Followers are now rarely required to show absolute compliance. Virtually all organisations expect members to use some degree of initiative. Even the military encourages junior staff to use their own judgement at times. But this does not mean the end of stupidity.

One way that leaders stupidify their followers is through transformational leadership. It assumes that 'leaders transform followers' and that 'followers are changed from being self-centered individuals to being committed members of a group'.[22] Transformational leadership is a kind of moral improvement scheme. Bad, self-centred followers are turned into good, loyal group members. All thanks to the right leadership. Transformational leaders are thought to give their followers individualised consideration, intellectual stimulation and inspiration. This is said to boost their self-confidence, enthusiasm and identification. Instead of being cajoled, followers enthusiastically comply.

The very idea of transformational leadership means that

leaders position themselves as superior figures who have a clear vision and can transform their disappointed followers into much better organizationally committed people.[23] 'Visionary' leaders, we are told, make their followers less self-centred. This of course assumes that followers are happy to be transformed. To insist on critical thinking would be counterproductive. It would hamper the leader's work of transforming their followers. After all, the task of a transformational leader is to encourage followers to switch off their independent thinking and commit themselves to a leader's vision.

SuperLeader saves the day?

Transformational leadership has proved popular. However, recent years have seen the rise of more 'democratic', 'authentic', 'distributed' or 'facilitative' forms of leadership.[24] These portray the leader as a humble figure who tries to have a positive impact on followers. Facilitative leaders try to encourage their followers to grow. They do this by giving their followers meaningful space to develop.

One of the many new labels for this is 'the SuperLeader'. This is a person who 'focuses primarily on the empowering roles of helping, encouraging and supporting followers in the development of personal responsibility, individual initiative, self-confidence, self-goal setting, self-problem solving, opportunity thinking, self-leadership, and psychological ownership over their tasks and duties'.[25] SuperLeaders should learn from mistakes, listen more, talk less, create independence and interdependence, and avoid dependence. Their role is to support and coach rather than create a vision and give direction.

Followers who enter organisations as raw and moderately competent are developed by the SuperLeader. Sometimes this happens. But more often than not it misfires. Otherwise competent followers become people seen as needing improvement. The developer leader calls for followers who want to be developed. This can encourage a certain form of attachment to the leader which is not actually required.

Through playing their facilitation role, leaders often create needy followers who want support, coaching and counselling. By representing themselves as figures who help followers to grow and improve, leaders can reinforce their subordinates' passivity and dependence. Often this can be about leaders building up their own sense of self-esteem rather than doing anything for their followers.[26]

When people are not being mesmerised by the idea of leadership, they can downplay the role of the manager.[27] One senior manager we spoke with told us that 'mostly it is them [the subordinates] that contact me when they need help with some issue ... They need a leader that is sufficiently technically skilled in order to be able to give them support, but generally I do not think they need or want any interference from the boss.' In this case, subordinates used a wide range of others sources for problem-solving, including work-groups, colleagues and network contacts. The leader was only a relatively peripheral part of the picture.

This is quite common. There is usually some manager hanging around, but most people turn to colleagues and friends to deal with technical problems, emotional issues, and requests for help. In many workplaces employees meet their manager only infrequently. Much of the time, their boss is sitting in meetings with other managers. But in the world of leadership fantasies, managers spend most of the time leading their committed followers.

Reality bites

Leadership sounds great. It seems much sexier than management. Leaders do exciting things like persuade and seduce. Managers do boring things like planning, organising and controlling. It's not surprising that a common cry in the corporate landscape is 'We need leaders, not managers'. Many managers assure us, and themselves, that they are 'a leader, not a manager'. So far so good. But the reality is quite different. Most people ask for leadership but actually want management.

Organisations, particularly large ones, are full of administrative tasks. These call for lots of management and little leadership. There are budgets, IT issues, personnel planning, financial reporting and customer demands to take care of. Making sure things are delivered on time is often more important than trying to transform followers into better people. One former hotel manager we spoke with described his job as frantically running around and dealing with various acute issues. He had little, if any, time to do leadership.

The reality for most managers is administration. They spend most of their time sitting in meetings, dealing with emails and filling in forms. They do budgets, financial reporting and office space allocation, comply with human resource policies and much more. As a result, managers generally feel that they do not have enough time to do leadership.[28] After all, transforming people into better human beings is time-consuming. It is hardly done through a few minutes' small talk. It is hard to fit Superleadership around the relentless stream of brief and abrupt episodes that makes up a typical day for a manager.[29]

Let us return to George, whom we have already briefly met. He suspects that despite his liberal use of small talk, his subordinates do not care that much about his leadership. And he is right. When asked about George's leadership, one of his

subordinates describes their relationship like this: 'Hmm …
what do we do really? We go to his meetings and answer his
questions, and beyond that …' The silence speaks volumes.

When asked about what leaders should do in their organisation, one of the engineers who works for George said: 'It should
be someone who makes… parties and such.' Managerial 'entertainment' seems to be in demand in this company. This has
certainly influenced George's view of his role as a leader. When
we asked what he did to lead people, he told us: 'I walk around
the corridor at five to nine and tell people "Breakfast is served".
I think it is appreciated.' In addition to breakfasts, George also
introduced beer-tasting just before Christmas, something else
he thought was 'very appreciated' by his subordinates.

George's entertainment activities aside, his subordinates
were not that interested in his leadership. George admits that
he finds it hard to lead because he does not understand what his
subordinates do. They work on their own and can be 'secretive'
with how they spend their time at work. 'Mainly they sit at their
desktops and write code,' George said. 'They don't interact that
much with each other under normal circumstances … What
they are working with is among the most complicated things
you can do as a software developer. Therefore it is extremely
hard to comprehend and understand.'

The complex and solitary nature of engineering work
combined with a shared unwillingness among George's subordinates to see themselves as 'followers' made his work as a
leader difficult. Doing 'leadership' becomes about arranging
parties, serving breakfast and doing administration.[30] George
dreams about doing leadership, but there is little demand for it.
The engineers who work for him want autonomy, not leadership. Of course, they are not alone.

There are many would-be leaders like George. Organisational

reality often does not offer fertile soil for them. Spending time hosting parties and serving breakfast between bouts of relentless administration is often the best they can hope for.

Manufacturing stupidity

Stupidity is not created by leaders alone. The leadership industry plays a vital role. This is made up of business magazines, publishers, business schools, management development institutes, management gurus, consultants and others. Virtually all of them promise leadership improvement. It is the business world's response to Hollywood – a dream factory for managers and other leader-wannabes. This multi-billion-dollar sector works by launching new recipes for leadership success every single day. By encouraging public enthusiasm for leadership, the industry inspires people from all walks of life to adopt what are often seductive but also very questionable ideas. While the leadership industry claims to be about manufacturing wisdom, it can also do the opposite. Members of the industry subtly – and sometimes not so subtly – discourage people from thinking more broadly or deeply about many of the often utterly ridiculous ideas about leadership. In this respect, the leadership merchants are also stupidity merchants. They get people enthusiastic about idealised and often very unrealistic understandings of themselves.

One way the leadership industry does this is by investing extraordinary significance in leaders. According to some, all global problems, including wars, ecological disasters and economic turmoil, are due to poor leadership.[31] Others are more measured. For instance, Ronnie Heifetz and Donald Laurie point out that 'a leader is responsible for direction, protection, orientation, managing conflict and shaping norms'.[32] This may sound uncontroversial, but this apparently pedestrian statement implies that followers are *not* responsible for these basic aspects of organisational life. It simply makes them into people who implement the leaders' direction, receive the leaders' protection, have their conflicts managed by leaders, and whose sense of what is normal is manipulated by leaders. Non-leaders are reduced to recipients of leaders' impressive work.

The leadership industry also mystifies leaders. This happens when leaders are seen as having superhuman abilities. If you look at some best-sellers on the topic you will find individuals who have amazing vision, extraordinary stamina and unmatched levels of empathy – all in one. Such a faith in the innate goodness and transformative power of leadership means that people shy away from considering the more mundane mechanics of getting the job done. It also means they stop asking whether leadership is actually necessary at all.

The leadership industry projects a sense of moral superiority onto leaders.[33] Put in the crudest form, it is assumed that a real leader is always really good. If he or she is bad, then they are not a leader.[34] Steve Jobs, for instance, was an extremely influential and successful person, but he also acted in psychopathic ways sometimes.[35] Those staffing the leadership industry prefer to ignore such contradictions and preserve more idealised images of well-known leaders. To their minds, good leadership is simply good: it is transformational and authentic.

From good to great, or from mediocre to stupid

Jim Collins's book *Good to Great* is probably the most influential leadership book of the last two decades, selling over 2.5 million copies around the world. It promises to offer the secrets behind lasting excellence and asks why a number of firms have maintained an above-average performance over a long period of time. Collins thinks the big difference was the quality and characteristics of the firm's leaders. These fantastic figures were leaders who appeared to be unremarkable and saw themselves as such. They attributed success to their co-workers. According to Collins this was wrong. The true secret was their style of leadership – what he calls 'level 5 leadership'.[36] These level 5 leaders stuck to their way of doing business, they worked hard and they gave their subordinates a lot of credit.

As with most books that offer to unveil the secrets of business miracles, Collins provides an oversimplified and misleading recipe. Of the eleven companies he examined, many did not do so well in the years after the study and two went bankrupt. This dented the credibility of Collins's claims that the secrets of leadership he had uncovered were 'built to last'. The idea that you might be able to produce and run an excellent company by just applying self-evident management principles should be a source of great suspicion.[37]

Collins's explanation for lasting success has a feel-good effect on managers who hope to be great leaders but are wary of charismatic ideas about leadership. Being professional, hardworking, persistent, modest, sticking to a success formula and giving credit to co-workers seems quite easy. Most managers can imagine themselves doing that. If they suddenly learn that by doing it they become a 'level 5 leader', then naturally they will feel good. After all, it would mean promotion from being good to being great. To find out that what are often viewed as mediocre abilities are not just good but actually great can help to boost the egos of wannabe great leaders.

Self-stupidifying leaders
During unruly and turbulent times, status anxiety runs riot. This means that managers are eager to find status and self-esteem

boosters. One way to do this is by becoming a 'leader' – being a follower is far less appealing. Naturally, some resist it, but many are seduced. It allows subordinates to see themselves not as mundane workers carrying out boring administrative or operational tasks, but as part of a great enterprise. Humdrum activities become about performing a 'mission' or an opportunity for self-development. The result is that ideas about leadership get incorporated into the way both leaders and followers see themselves. As these ideas are so closely connected with narratives of oneself, they come to be jealously guarded by many leaders and some followers.

We often over-attribute both positive and negative results to leaders. They are held responsible for any kind of significant outcomes, good or bad. This responsibility can far exceed what can be reasonably expected from a person.

When we over-attribute powers to leaders, we fall victim to well-known cognitive biases, including some of those addressed in Chapter 2.[38] One is the fundamental attribution error: we are likely to overvalue our own internal characteristics and downplay the influence that situations have on our behaviour. Cultural attribution biases also interfere. People from individualistic cultures like North America are more likely to look for individual causes of behaviour. This means they grow obsessed with the role of leaders in creating success and failure – something which blinds us to the fact that 70 per cent of corporate performance is driven by situational factors rather than CEO characteristics.[39] Finally there are self-serving biases: individuals are more likely to credit their successes to their own individual talents. As a result, leaders are likely to reinforce the importance of their own contribution and undervalue what others bring. By focusing on leadership, both leaders and followers are able to short-cut much of the difficult thinking and ambiguous information required to make more accurate assessments of why firms succeed or fail.

Consider the case of Jim, a sales manager in a global hi-tech company. When we spoke with one of Jim's sales agents called Ralph, he praised Jim's ability as a leader. 'He has turned the ship around,' he told us. 'He has the best results in the [360 degree evaluation] survey and he has the best financial results in the whole EMEA [Europe, Middle East and Africa].' At last a manager who is really effective, we thought, and decided to study this star closely. But quite a different picture appeared when we spoke with Steve, another of Jim's sales agents. 'When we [the sales agents] talk we all agree that these figures we could have done without Jim,' Steve said. 'He is totally offside! The only thing he says is: Full speed ahead!' Others shared Steve's view, but some thought the good results indicated that Jim had some good qualities that were difficult to grasp. If we compare these two accounts of Jim's leadership abilities, we can start to see how the contributions of a leader can be quite ambiguous. For some, the success of the division is down to Jim's great work. For others, Jim's only contribution is to utter empty phrases. It seems that much is in the eye of the beholder.

People enthused by ideas about leadership are often faced with contradictory information. Sometimes leaders do good things, sometimes bad things. Most people are unwilling to see Hitler as a transformational leader, even though he had many of the features of such a leader.[40] Celebrated figures like Steve Jobs or Winston Churchill have many bad traits, but we see them as all good. Such conflicting information does not usually lead people to abandon their belief in the importance of good leadership. Rather, they disregard contrary evidence and focus only on the information that confirms what they think at the outset. They look for the good and overlook the bad. As a result, we are often willing to provide irrational levels of support for leaders who appear to be charismatic. A study by Francis Flynn and Barry Staw found that investors were more willing to put money into companies with charismatic CEOs – even if their performance was the same as firms with non-charismatic CEOs.[41] This reminds us that most people develop consistent yet simplified understandings of leadership. Investors are even willing to put their money on it. This kind of Disneyland reasoning about a beautiful and harmonious world of leadership is reassuring, but not particularly insightful.

The mixed blessings of mindless leaders

Buying into ideas about leadership can sometimes be stupid, but it can also be effective. It can help to bolster fragile self-esteem, enable simplistic modes of attribution and reduce cognitive dissonance. All this can help individuals avoid the ambiguity and anxiety that are endemic in complex organisations. The sense of purpose that comes from being a leader who inspires and motivates others is quite different from being a manager who does administration.

To confidently say 'I am a leader, not a manager' is not just good for self-esteem, it is great for impression management. It makes it easier to be perceived as a person on the way up. To appear – in talk, dress and manner – as a leader, without any signs of doubt, hesitation or self-irony, can create success. To show ambivalence and doubt can be a career-stopper. Reflection often messes things up for people.

Promotion calls for 'leadership skills'. A person eager to progress in their career is wise to be enthusiastic about leadership. In many cases, this can be pure pretence, but that doesn't matter too much. Doubt about leadership is a source of uncertainty and distraction. It can lower self-confidence and diminish a person's commitment to work. Being able to bypass doubt in favour of a strong commitment can help individuals make their way through the organisation.

Buying into notions of leadership can also help the organisation as a whole. Individuals are encouraged to put aside disruptive and difficult criticism of individual leaders or ideas about leadership more generally. This can help to get people enthusiastic about the visions of a leader. By doing this, they can build commitment to a course of action. Although the premises of action may be suspect, the very idea of leadership can help to make things happen.

Actively encouraging leadership-induced stupidity is, however, a mixed blessing. For individuals, an irrational commitment to leadership means they can easily become separated from the realities of management. The gap between ideals and performance can become obvious when an individual leader promises significant personal transformation but creates something far less lustrous. Frustration often follows when individuals who are striving to become leaders prove to be ineffective. The clash between the idolisation of leadership and the imperfections of organisational life will sooner or later come to light.[42] The result is jilted leadership junkies.

To deal with these disappointments, some simply move on to the next fad or fashion offered by the leadership industry. Others become bitter cynics who find it hard to buy into any ideas about leadership at all – even when leadership may actually be needed. Still others become virulent anti-leadership activists who oppose all attempts to wield leadership.

By mindlessly buying into ideas of leadership, organisations can become overcommitted to practices that do not work. This happens when organisations cut short broader reflection and discussion about when leadership is useful, how much leadership is needed and what kind of leadership they may need. For instance, an untrammelled attachment to 'facilitative' ideas of leadership can cause organisations to devote significant resources and time to quasi-therapeutic rituals. This can mean they become unable to respond adequately to pressing emergencies. Real work gives way to psychobabble.[43] As a result, production, customers and markets receive less attention than they deserve.

Finally, an overriding belief in the importance of leadership can mean that followers ignore many other forms of coordination that can take the place of leadership. Bureaucracy, self-managed teams, professional coordination and other control mechanisms are ignored. This can create one-dimensional organisations where no matter what the problem, leadership is seen as the answer.[44]

Conclusion

Leaders are often thought to be superior characters who possess cognitive prowess, creative intelligence and practical wisdom. This idea is popular, but it does not capture the entire picture. In this chapter, we have argued that leadership is often intimately related to stupidity.

The quasi-religious belief in leadership all too often offers a Disneyland vision of organisations. It is unrealistic and naïve. But it is also comforting and hopeful. Far from being a negative thing, selective stupidification can sometimes prove to be functional. Reducing independent thinking and reflection can yield positive outcomes. Common thinking, shared values and a sense of order can all be outcomes of an obsession with leadership. Leadership can spare individuals the anxieties of thinking for themselves.

While functional stupidity may take hold through an undue

emphasis on leadership, there is another side to the story. Sometimes ideas about leadership may not be as powerful as we often assume. Efforts to do leadership often simply means highfalutin talk, which the audience treats with a mixture of mild amusement, disdain and boredom.

Think about the quintessential leadership act – 'communicating a vision'. In many organisations, subordinates can be actively hostile to these visions. Instead of seeing the vision as profound, many think they are 'corporate bullshit'.[45] Others find such visions to be a mild distraction or even completely irrelevant. Still others might entirely miss the vision. After all, organisations are full of messages that easily get lost. In most organisations, leadership is not as potent as most people seem to believe.

Attempts to do leadership do not always have the intended impact on followers. Rarely can (aspiring) leaders cook up their favoured recipes for leadership. For this reason, the real stupidity may lie in the belief that leadership has any large impact on organisational life. Perhaps leadership talk actually stupidifies the people who are most committed to it – the members of the large and expanding leadership industry. Some may be cynical, but most sincerely believe what they are preaching. And taking these ideas so seriously can call for a powerful dose of functional stupidity.

5

Structure-Induced Stupidity

Routine thoughtlessness

A couple of years ago one of us took part in a workshop with about twenty personnel managers who worked for a large municipality. Some preliminary results from a study of Human Resource Management (HRM) work were presented and discussed. One finding from the study result was that members of the HRM profession often felt they were not appreciated and had a low level of status and influence in their organisations. They wanted to do more work with strategy and less with service. However, people from other departments wanted the opposite from HRM professionals: less strategy and more service. One person in the group suddenly felt that she should give the others some feedback. She had once worked in HRM but had recently shifted to a position as a unit manager. This led her to realise the sheer amount of steering documents that existed which all units were supposed to consult and follow. It was a shocking experience: 'Friends,' she told the group, 'you don't know how many documents we have developed and we are supposed to relate to in our work. We must change the way we work.'

The audience did not respond to this provocation. They all

put on their poker faces, signalling that such strange comments were best passed over unnoticed. At the end of the workshop we brought up this topic again and urged the audience to take the feedback seriously. Perhaps they could elect some of their number to explore reducing obstructive HRM bureaucracy. Given the negative reputation of the HRM function, this appeared to be an ideal opportunity to take an initiative. The response? Total silence.[1]

We are frequently told that we live in post-bureaucratic times. It is common to hear that organisations are not run by hierarchies, rules and regulations any more, but by vision, leadership, organisational cultures and networks. But if you take a careful look at any organisation, bureaucracy is as strong as it ever has been.[2] In the HRM function of the municipality we discussed above, the central task seemed to be to create bureaucracy, though by another name. More and more pointless forms now require filling out. The difference from the past is that much of this work has to be done online. Rigid plans, rules and procedures continue to be features of working life. In most industries there is more regulation than ever. There are many whose sole job it is to create plans, rules and procedures, and even more who spend their working life ensuring that these are followed. Other employees find that ever-larger chunks of their days are taken up with following rules and procedures.

These bureaucratic processes have their advantages – they can provide order and impartiality. But they are often a source of disorder. Bureaucratic structures can be practical, but they can also breed impracticality. Rules can sometimes force us to think, but more often than not they foster thoughtlessness.[3]

People at work are regularly pushed to conform with bureaucratic imperatives that free them from thought and decisions. At the very same time they are told that bureaucracy is

bad. Now and then we may get angry with a particularly troublesome rule, but mostly we mindlessly comply. We stop asking
questions and thinking for ourselves. We just go along with the
rules and routines and hope that they make our lives easier.

Most of the time, structures, rules and routines do the
thinking for us. We give them no thought, and mindlessly
carry them out. This can be practical and efficient. Spared
from the effort of assessing what needs to be done, and how
and why, instead we can simply focus on the procedure. When
you just have to tick boxes, then you don't have to think outside
the box.

In this chapter, we look at how rules and routines in organisations create stupidity. We will argue that sometimes a deep
faith in structures is due to the existence of stupid jobs. These
are roles which are designed to be as simple as possible and
allow very little space for individual initiative or reflection. But
another driver of our faith in structure is an explosion of professional idiots. These are experts who find it hard to see beyond
their own professional obsessions associated with specialisation and division of labour. This potent mixture often promotes
an unquestioning faith in structures. Employees assume that
such structures are good, even when there is strong evidence
to the contrary. In some cases this can yield highly functional
outcomes, for the individual as well as the organisation, but
just as often, mindless rule-following can breed chaos. The
result of all this is what we call a society of superficial scrutiny:
a world where almost any organisational activity is the subject
of oversight. As people focus more on complying with the rules,
substantive issues remain unaddressed.

Smart people doing stupid jobs
Breaking up tasks in a detailed and regimented way can make

things more efficient, but it can also make them more stupid. One aspect of this that we discussed in an earlier chapter is 'deskilling'.[4] Breaking up complex tasks into simple activities has been common in industrial production lines for over a century. One of the early champions of the creation of stupid jobs was the industrial engineer Frederick Winslow Taylor. In his famous 'pig iron' experiment he broke down an already simple task (carrying blocks of iron and loading them onto a cart) into even more simple parts. According to Taylor, 'one of the very first requirements for a man who is fit to handle pig iron as a regular occupation is that he shall be so stupid and so phlegmatic that he more nearly resembles in his mental make-up the ox'. Due to the supposed 'stupidity' of the pig-iron handler, 'he must consequently be trained by a man more intelligent than himself into the habit of working in accordance with the laws of this science before he can be successful'.[5] For Taylor, the task of the industrial engineer was to design complex tasks to enable people he assumed to be stupid to do them. (The irony here is that Taylor's supposedly stupid pig-iron handler was not so stupid. Though Taylor referred to him as Schmidt, his real name was Henry Noll. During his spare time he built his own house and was also a volunteer at the local fire department.)[6]

Although scientific management is unfashionable today, large parts of the service sector use techniques that Taylor would find familiar. Think about the call centre where operatives follow a script, the delivery industry where drivers rely on a computerised GPS system for directions, or fast-food restaurants where chefs cook by numbers. To become a registered black cab driver in London, it takes years to gain 'the knowledge'.[7] Now anyone can turn their car into a taxi by registering as a driver with an electronic guidance service like Uber. In each case what had once been smart jobs requiring continual thinking have been made into relatively thought-less tasks.

We might assume that routinisation is only the fate of low-level highly routine service jobs. It is not. Many professionals now follow routine steps when delivering services. Medical doctors have to go through a series of steps when they see patients to ensure that they have done everything correctly. Similarly, the work of a teacher is increasingly dictated by detailed 'education systems' that tell them what to do and when. Some consultants talk about their work being like working in McDonald's – they serve up standardised products by following routine processes.[8] More generally, the sociologist George Ritzer has pointed at the McDonaldisation of society – the spread of the principles of the fast-food industry into all aspects of society.[9]

At the same time as the number of highly routinised jobs is expanding, there are also rising numbers of people with, on paper, high levels of education who expect their jobs to offer plenty of scope to exercise their intellect. As a result, many of these aspiring knowledge workers feel frustrated. Sometimes, this can translate into cynicism or even outright hostility.[10] In other cases, jilted knowledge workers just withdraw from their work and look for intellectual stimulation elsewhere: reading the newspaper online, playing video games or working on other personal projects during work hours.[11]

This creates a problem for many organisations: how do you get smart people (with high levels of education and matching aspirations) to endure 'stupid' work (highly repetitive, and often requiring skills that can be acquired in a few days) with a happy demeanour?

One way organisations try to solve this problem is by using labels that frame mundane jobs in more uplifting ways. Inflating job titles is a popular trick. A secretary becomes an executive assistant; a bookkeeper becomes a financial manager; a publisher's sales representative becomes a senior higher education consultant; an in-house training coordinator becomes a strategic human resource development leader. A mid-level banker becomes a vice-president, promoted some years later to senior vice-president, even if the job remains the same. These grandiose titles help people to feel that their rather trivial jobs are actually quite sophisticated. The titles can help them ignore the boring bits of their job and focus on the exciting parts. Even if they do routine work, they can tell their friends and family they have a smart-sounding job. 'I manipulate spreadsheets' sounds much less impressive than 'I am a senior analyst.'

Professional idiots

The great majority of people in the knowledge economy do routine work, but there are also many experts. In fact, the past three decades have seen an explosion of experts on almost every imaginable issue, from different sub-diseases and parts of the human body to all aspects of human life, from diversity management to sexual therapy. These experts are often given lots of autonomy within boundaries, yet they are marooned in a very narrow universe. They usually have a standardised education, follow a set career path and spend their days tied up with other experts. They often live their entire working lives within a specific sub-tribe: Human Resource Management, Communication, a specific branch of Law, Branding, X-ray Medicine, Mechanical Engineering, whatever.

These tiny professional worlds often narrow people's outlook. These experts can struggle to think outside the well-defined perimeters of their own hard-won knowledge. They may do their particular job well, but they do it without much heed to the broader issues. This is illustrated in a recent laboratory study which showed that when individuals were prompted to think they were experts, they became more closed-minded and dogmatic.[12] This meant they were less likely to consider the views of others. A similar process seems to prevail with real experts: as they pour all their intellectual energy into specialised work, they can become what Germans call *Fachidioten* – roughly, professional idiots. They know a lot about a specific issue, but are clueless beyond their very narrow domain. They also become rather rigid and negative about what does not fit into their worldview.

Increased professionalisation has pushed the ideal of the specialist to an extreme. Each specialism has splintered into clans of sub-specialisations. Consider contemporary medicine. Once doctors specialised in a particular part of the body, such as lungs, or a specific disease, such as cancer. Now they can specialise in a single treatment or a very rare disease. The same goes for the business world. We once had accountants, logistics specialists, human resource specialists and so on. Now there are multiple specialisms in each of these areas. In the field of human resource management there are specialists in how to administer personality tests, how to advertise for new employees, how to pay people, how to keep track of employees' records, how to promote them, how to deal with them if they are angry, how to fire them and how to manage their diversity. It seems that they cover almost any eventuality.

Of course, the days of the universal genius are long gone. In many technical and scientific fields, specialisation is necessary. However, the construction of ever-narrower sub-specialisms is often less about solving complex technical problems and more about allowing a specialist to work in a very narrow area they have a nerdish fascination with. This can have some important benefits for the specialist. It can help them build an identity in a world already crowded with experts. No longer do you have to say: 'I work in accounting.' Instead you announce: 'I am an expert in forensic accounting for mergers and acquisitions transactions.' Rather than: 'I'm a human resource officer', you can say: 'I'm an expert at executive remuneration in the insurance industry.' In our own little world of research we often come across scholars who say they are specialists in applying one aspect of one theory to one industry using one method. In fact, many courses which are designed to coach doctoral students in developing their careers often leave them with the impression that an exceedingly narrow focus is an excellent strategy for building a thriving career. The advice seems to boil down to this: do the same narrow thing over and over again and you will become a world expert in it – no matter how mediocre your ideas or technical abilities are.

By claiming a narrow sub-discipline, you can exude an aura of technical expertise. This can give the would-be specialist a sense of power, status, and self-confidence. It can also have the lucrative side effect of helping them carve out and defend what can often be very lucrative market niches with few competitors.

In many cases, strong specialisation has taken a step too far. People may sub-specialise even if they could, in principle, master a much broader terrain. In social science, for example, there is a growing tendency for researchers to focus narrowly. It increases their productivity, but also leads to predictable and boring research and only marginal improvements in knowledge.[13] In the natural and biological sciences researchers are often encouraged to narrow their focus down to just one or two minor issues.[14] This is potentially damaging because innovation gains from a broader outlook, an ability to see potential connections between different subfields, the capacity to question assumptions and to think differently. An over-emphasis on expertise and sub-specialisation hinders this. When specialism rules, we get the problem of people who only have a hammer in their toolbox, and as a result are inclined to treat everything as if it were a nail.

As a consequence, organisations are full of specialists who work on problems as they know them. However, most problems are not isolated. Having many experts each working away on their own little aspect of a wider problem can create many unforeseen problems. For instance, organisations can find themselves expanding because there are more experts employed. Inevitably these experts will start to develop plans, procedures, rules, routines and activities and demand compliance from everybody else. The result is often to multiply bureaucracy, with an organisation's core work suffering as people are forced to spend time responding to the experts' demands. As well as being costly in itself, the division of labour and the inclinations of all these people not just to be supportive but also to demand responses to all their initiatives and requests can be very resource-intensive.

With specialisation and division of labour we get a lot of boxed-in thinking. Few people have a comprehensive understanding of the situation. They do not make connections. Different groups specialise. Top management seldom has a full overview and doesn't understand what units and people are doing. This is often a breeding ground for functional stupidity.

Faith in the system

A few years ago one of us did a study of a global management consultancy firm we will call Excellence.[15] In this firm we found many young, hopeful consultants, eager to learn and build a fine career, who had been promised great opportunities for career development. 'This is a feedback culture,' a senior manager told us. 'Staff are taken care of, given advice about their performances as well as their strengths and weaknesses.' The new recruits were promised a wealth of opportunities to develop and progress. Much was made of education, seminars, a wide variety of assignments, frequent mentorship, careful assessment and promotion. The new consultants were told that significant time and resources were devoted to this. The firm seemed to be an ambitious young person's dream.

However, when we examined what was actually happening in the firm, a rather different picture emerged. There was a strong discrepancy between the claims of senior people and how things actually worked. Despite all the talk about this being a meritocracy that developed its staff, we noticed difficulties. There were tight time constraints, it was tough to assess what people actually were doing, judgements were frequently clouded by bias, and politics often trumped productivity when it came to promotions.

One particular issue of concern was how people were assessed. One partner told us: 'The problem is that sometimes there is a lot of inflationary grading. You participated in a reasonably successful project, and you think that you have worked with somebody who was really great, and tend to give them good grades. And then when you look at the whole population, if we should just look at the grading, everybody would have been promoted and we obviously can't do that.' Problems with the assessment system were also a concern for junior people. One consultant told us: 'I wrote my own assessment sheet again on a project. I've even written the evaluation, both contribution and summary. Then the project manager edited it somewhat. It is not supposed to work this way, but it does.'

Given these problems with the performance-management systems, the art of getting ahead in the firm seemed to be less about ability and more about politics and networking. One consultant confessed that 'the art of surviving here is to team up with a superior who has already teamed up with his or her superior. Then you work together.'

The fact that a large professional service firm was driven partly by politics, and that fine structures and procedures were seldom followed, came as a surprise to the naïve new recruits. They had been told that high levels of performance was all that counted, yet they learned that the people who got new projects or were promoted were those who concentrated on building good relationships with important people. But what was perhaps even more surprising was that despite this insight into the harsh realities of life in a professional service firm, they still maintained a strong faith in the human resource management system.

Many members of the firm said that the firm's excellent HRM explained its people's good reputation. 'Our reputation is very good concerning our employees,' one manager said. 'If you have five years at Excellence on your CV, then they don't look at your degree. They practically don't care to look at anything at all, they just say: "Okay, here is the job if you want it." They know that the quality of the people we hired is assured, and that we have trained and developed them. This makes our employees very attractive.' A more junior consultant confirmed this view. Other firms 'know that we have rigorously tested them [the employees] before they were offered a job and that we also have developed and educated them,' he said. 'Our people are very attractive.'

Because people had a faith in the system, they identified strongly with the firm, worked exceptionally hard and rated it highly to the wider world. But for all this to work, it was necessary for employees to suspend their doubts. People's strong beliefs in the HR system meant that they often did not believe their own experiences. When they came across a moment when the system was not working as it should, they simply dismissed it. The system was sound, they thought. These snags were just unfortunate exceptions. Shit happens, they would say.

If employees gave more thought to their own experiences, they would easily see that the HR system didn't work as it was supposed to. But such a realisation would bring problems. It would probably undermine faith in the wider HRM system. It also might make it less likely for people to comply with it. To avoid such a sticky situation, most people working for the firm seemed to prefer to remain ignorant and thoughtless, overlooking their own experiences in order to preserve a faith in the system. This allowed the firm to go on claiming that it was recruiting, developing and promoting the best and the brightest.

Another important aspect of the HR system was that it made employees feel like they were part of an elite. One consultant we spoke with told us: 'The Excellence brand stands for professionalism. It means that I'm serious and professional in my work.' He went on to say: 'I like the aura of the Excellence brand. I know that I was recruited to an elite group and that I am still considered to be worthy of an organisation that recruits the best students, has the best clients, and makes a lot of money. We hire one out of a hundred who apply for work here. We have long and trying tests and evaluations and I have passed them all. Excellence is successful.'

Seeing oneself as part of a professional firm that develops the best and the brightest is great for business. People feel good about themselves and the firm they work for. They have self-confidence. This comes across when they speak with clients and to other external parties. It reinforces the firm's good reputation and promotes recruitment, commitment and staff motivation – if I belong to a selected group of the best and the brightest, I am strongly inclined to demonstrate my worth. It also helps the firm to sell services. But keeping up this self-confident front requires people to overlook the many instances where the best and brightest don't get ahead.

The success of Excellence, and many other professional service firms like it, is based on a culture of functional stupidity. People working in these firms are happy to believe in the myth of promoting only the best and brightest, despite significant evidence to the contrary. When people can overlook these contradictions, they are able to preserve an image of themselves as the best and the brightest. So even if the systems at Excellence did not work as intended, the faith in the systems did.

Of course, often it does not fully work like this, and contradictions are too obvious to be denied. An interesting case is the Danish hearing-aid company Oticon. Its CEO, Lars Kolind, was a visionary leader. His vision was to 'develop a truly knowledge-based company, which could make a difference in the form of a breakthrough in user satisfaction with hearing aids. This not only requires a creative combination of technology, audiology and psychology, but also a much closer cooperation between the different professionals involved in the actual selling, fitting and fine-tuning of the hearing aid to the needs of each individual user.'

Kolind tried to abolish formal hierarchies. Official job titles were avoided and a flexible work space established. Employees were encouraged to buy into a set of corporate values: trust, empowerment, open communication and respect for the individual. They put in place challenging goals and supported individual development. Employees were encouraged to 'think the unthinkable'. They were also asked to challenge managers' views and always eliminate any activities that didn't add value to the customers.

Kolind wanted to empower his subordinates. He told them: 'When in doubt – then do it. If it works, it's good, if not, you're forgiven,' and: 'It's easier to be forgiven than to get approval.' He encouraged his employees to think about themselves as part of a 'football team where each individual knows the objectives and the strategy and can kick the ball immediately without having to look up the rules and ask why'.

Kolind's bold vision seemed to pay off. Oticon became a great success story. It was widely reported in the media around the world as 'the Spaghetti organisation'. The case became standard fare in many business schools.

For a time there was a good match between the write-ups that appeared in the media and what was actually going on in the firm. But after a while, the company's practices started to sharply diverge from the glowing image. The Spaghetti organisation soon existed in nothing more than name. One employee described how 'the magic has gone. It has become a more ordinary workplace … Of course, we still have open-space offices and we can still move our shelves-on-wheels around, when we need to – but then that's it.'

Despite these changes, the media continued to tell upbeat stories about the Spaghetti organisation, its originality and progressive nature. People who worked there recognised that what was being reported might be misleading, but they did not correct it. There was some disquiet, but on the whole people liked the upbeat image and continued to play up to it. They had become engrossed in a story about who they were that did not stand up to reality.[16]

As in Excellence, people in the firm became absorbed in the image to the point of supporting a narcissistic faithfulness to a narrative that did not match reality. This was a way to cling to peace and happiness, even though people sometimes chafed at their experience of the gap. To fall in love with the public image, when it is positive and narcissistically gratifying, to stick to it as closely as possible and minimise both recognition and communication about its false nature, can help a lot to smooth over the bumps created by discrepancies between what people like to think and how it really is.

How structure creates turmoil

A strong faith in a system can often produce positive outcomes, both for the people employed and for the organisation as a whole. At Excellence, we met employees who had a strong faith in a system that didn't work, yet this faith created some good outcomes: belief that they were part of a world-class meritocracy helped them to sell the firm to clients. But all too often a strong belief in systems can create negative outcomes. This is what often happens when people get too excited by a formal system and lose touch with the day-to-day realities of work. It happened at Costen Elementary school when a new principal, Mrs Kox, took over.[17]

Costen Elementary is a relatively large school with ninety teachers. It is located in a state in the US which had problems with its schools system. To deal with these problems, the school board decided to standardise the curriculum and instructional techniques. They hoped that if schools followed standards, performance would improve. The state established clear – some would say rigid – benchmarks for student progress. It also threatened to close down poorly performing schools. In this context, Mrs Kox was seen as a rising star. As an assistant principal at an improving school, she attended an education programme run by an elite business school and an education school. Kox loved the programme because 'business people have a different orientation to improvement', she said. 'They have a better sense of urgency.' She was particularly enthusiastic about the idea of accountability.

The board of Costen Elementary thought that Kox was a great candidate for the role of principal. Her enthusiasm for accountability appealed. 'She's very opinionated and has very high standards,' one board member said. She was seen as 'very tough' and had a 'no-nonsense' approach. After she was appointed, the board continued to see Kox as a strong leader. She guided the school into the new era of accountability, had exhaustive knowledge of education policy, was tireless, and held firm to her convictions. Her results were also decent, at least to start with. The school's test results were above the city average – but they fell short of Baxter Elementary, Costen's sister school. Senior management continued to give Kox outstanding reviews and they enthusiastically renewed her contract. She seems to be a success story. Yet if you scratch the surface you find a rather different picture.

For a long time, before the arrival of Kox, Costen responded to the diverse student body by given teachers lots of autonomy. The teachers described the previous principals in glowing terms: 'They hired good people who let them do their jobs,' one teacher said.

When Kox arrived, all of this changed. Accountability and standards became central to how the school operated. The teachers had been 'running the school without a principal for six months', Kox said. 'Everyone took full advantage of running in every direction that they chose to. Well, that's not going to happen with this administration.' Kox liked to work in a hands-on way and give clear directions. She fleshed out her ideas about accountability through strict surveillance of the classroom. She instituted new student-management and grading systems, as well as curriculum and instruction reforms. While the previous administrations had rubber-stamped grades, Kox scrutinised them carefully. She now said that teachers were 'panicking' and that one was 'very worried because she had never seen anyone review her grade book for the last 26 years'.

Teachers felt frustrated by Kox's reforms. They claimed they were being micro-managed and exposed to rigid controls, and felt that their work was being standardised. This created a sense of turmoil. One teacher described how 'I'm constantly defending what I'm doing in my classroom'; another said: 'You'd have to be psycho to stay here more than one or two years.' Unsurprisingly, many teachers resigned. Those who remained started to mobilise against her. These efforts were spearheaded by Mrs Drew, who gathered a large number of complaints into a 119-page document with the title 'Turmoil at "KOX"sten School'. A campaign began to get Kox fired.

Some might see Kox as a dreary slave to accountability, others as an empowered entrepreneur who brought accountability to Costen, a task-oriented despot (the teachers' view), or an intrepid leader (the board's view).[18] We see Kox as a typical example of someone with an unreflecting commitment to structural solutions. She rigidly stuck with the system and had little sensitivity to the local culture. She focused on policies and procedures and ignored the impact her system had on the staff. This created problems: many teachers described the school as being 'in turmoil'. Many staff left. Results began to decline. But despite all this, Kox continued to have strong backup from the school board.

Kox's behaviour may appear to be rigid and lacking in sensitivity, but we live in a society that is more and more focused on accountability and scrutinising organisations. Massive amounts of resources are wasted on checking whether organisations have the correct formal structures in place. In this sense, Kox was a paradigm of the society of superficial scrutiny.

The society of superficial scrutiny

'Formally speaking we have done everything right. We complied with the rules. We are looking at our procedures.' Today, this has become a standard formula for managing organisations.

Complying with formal regulations is sensible, but more often than not the sheer weight of externally imposed rules means that people put more effort into ensuring all the boxes have been ticked than actually getting the job done. In sectors like social services, health care and education there are so many standards and formal regulations to be complied with. Organisations dig deep into precious resources to ensure that regulatory requirements are met. Less and less time is devoted to serving vulnerable groups, caring for patients or educating students. There is little assessment of the substantive work done. This is viewed as too complicated. Instead the focus is on superficial scrutiny.

We live in a society of superficial scrutiny, of constant checks to see whether we comply with some arbitrary standard. This is something that Mike Power recognised over twenty years ago when he coined the concept of the 'audit society'.[19] What has changed is that now many of these checks are only skin-deep – stage a routine of complying, and that suffices. Compliance becomes all about image-creation. Organisations get geared to live up to what is scrutinised.

To show that they are doing the right thing, many organisations simply copy what others are doing. They imitate others not necessarily because it is the best thing for them to do, but rather so as to reduce reputational risk. If you have been copying everyone else and something goes wrong, it is unlikely you will be singled out for blame. Blame becomes diffused, so you can point out that everyone got it wrong. Government inspectors and special-interest groups who closely monitor organisations and punish deviations also play a big part. The media are also happy to chip in when there is an instance of rule-breaking. And of course there are lawyers on hand to see everything done 'by the book'.

That is what has happened in the medical sector in the UK. Doctors find they are increasingly exposed to an ever-expanding range of legislation, regulations and protocols. Many of these measures are what Gerry McGivern and Michael Fischer have called 'spectacular regulation'[20] – these are the policies cooked up to deal with the media fallout from a high-profile scandal. Spectacular regulations are not primarily designed to work. They are designed to shut the media up and placate the public. As doctors find they are subjected to more and more of this spectacular regulation, they feel 'guilty until proven innocent'. Naturally they find this stressful – dealing with pointless regulation takes time, and always feeling like a potential culprit is a big psychological challenge. The main group that gains from this system is an ever-growing blame business of lawyers, regulators, the media and patient advocates who find ever more opportunities to 'hold doctors to account'.

The disadvantages of all this are obvious. It contributes to inertia, hyper-caution and weak results. Organisations develop a planning fetish. Error minimisation becomes the primary job. Education, health care, the police and many other sectors devote ever more of their time to ensuring that their documentation is done correctly. If anything goes wrong, they have chapter and verse: all procedures were correctly followed.

By carefully following all the right rules and routines, people are able to avoid greater responsibility for the substantial practices or outcomes. Even when people in an organisation do things that everyone recognises as daft, they are approved. For instance, it is preferable to have an anti-bullying plan and 'follow routines' rather than deal directly with a bully in the workplace. If a hospital has a problem with cleanliness and hygiene standards, it might be enough to show that you have a 'strategy' to deal with it. Actually obliging people to wash their hands or properly cleaning wards is often an afterthought. Making an effort to follow the rules and routines is good enough. It enables the hospital to avoid blame.

What this gives rise to is increasingly inefficient organisations that are more and more costly to run. While they might be weak at delivering on their core purpose, they are strong at doing everything formally right. They say the right things and look good to the external world, yet they find it hard to do their central tasks. The driving force here is to rule out errors. Courage, creativity and good results grow less important. A safer strategy is to ensure you have ticked all the boxes, followed procedures and have formally 'done the right thing'.

In a society of superficial scrutiny the media, regulators and interest groups all carefully monitor whether organisations are living up to norms. They check that everything is done 'correctly'. However these checks go only so far. The more they monitor plans, routines and documents, the further they stray from the practical work being done. Typically the only thing all this superficial scrutiny is guaranteed to produce is more superficial compliance. In the words of a municipal director: 'After having done all the plans and have the documents in order, you don't have time to work with them.'

A typical example of this is a social welfare director of a municipality. Following the annual inspection by the social services regulatory body, the agency received about twenty-five comments. After the following year's inspection, the director received no remarks from the regulator. When we asked him if they had changed anything substantive, the director replied: 'No, but we've written down twenty-five new routines.'

Legislators push for stronger or more detailed regulations to solve problems. The media and pressure groups call for 'something to be done'. Regulators monitor those who actually do the work and ensure that correct procedures are followed. Managers comply with what regulators want by implementing new plans, policies and practices. Professionals follow these routines. Everybody seems to benefit from this process. They all feel they do things correctly. The only problem is that as people dutifully ensure that boxes are ticked, the organisation may be run badly. Those supposed to benefit from all this box-ticking often end up suffering, but this happens below the radar: superficial scrutiny focuses on structures, routines and procedures. Are they there? Are they followed? Yes, fine. Do they lead to something good or bad or nothing at all? Well, it is hard to say. So who cares?

Conclusion

Formal structures, rules and routines can be a source of significant stupidity in organisations. They are necessary, but many organisations overdo them. Structures are often mistaken for guarantees of quality, productivity and reliability. Far-reaching division of labour encourages tunnel vision and box-ticking. Most people have a limited overview and do not make much effort to carefully look behind surface structures.

At the apex of organisations, senior executives are supposed to integrate all these specialists, but top managers often focus on rules, regulations and routines as well as on the most easily manipulated performance indicators. They live in their own world, spending their time meeting other managers. They rely on PowerPoint presentations and carefully massaged numerical indicators to sum up what is happening down below. Many senior people have very little real knowledge of what goes on in their organisations. This is fortunate, because they often don't want too much knowledge. Knowing too much can be frustrating and stressful. Wilful ignorance is a good practice.[21]

Further down the organisational hierarchy, most people are encouraged to just focus on their work and not think about the broader picture. They end up doing narrow, specialised work and avoid looking into its outcome. Increased specialisation creates problems for organisational functioning, but this is not an issue for those safely located in their functional stupid worlds. Normally problems are not clearly understood or communicated. Widespread thoughtlessness can feel comfortable for experts and senior executives alike. But it can also create a lot of problems that remain undetected and misunderstood.

A strict division of labour is reinforced through the mushrooming of experts in ever narrower areas of speciality. These experts often become good at rigour and rationality within their own narrow world. However, they frequently lack a wider view of problems. They become smart and stupid at the same time. They can solve some problems, but they often create others.

The mixture of narrowly focused experts, myopic senior managers and routinised workers creates organisations where rule-following trumps good results. People develop a faith in processes and procedures – even when they don't necessarily deliver the goods. In the short term this produces many good things: it helps individuals build a career and organisations to operate smoothly. It looks good on the surface. But it can also be a source of many problems in the longer term. Instead of focusing on doing the core tasks, an organisation becomes more focused on superficial compliance with rules and regulations.

6

Imitation-Induced Stupidity

Following the crowd

In the middle of the twentieth century most US corporations saw themselves as an unrelated portfolio of different activities. The largest corporations typically owned a wide range of different businesses which had little to do with each other. At the time, business leaders assumed that these loosely related business conglomerates were the best way to operate a firm. It gave firms the advantage of being able to manage risks across different sectors and countries, it helped them share resources, and it brought ample opportunity to grow.

By the late twentieth century this had all changed. The idea of the conglomerate operating in multiple business areas had gone out of fashion. Firms began to radically restructure themselves by selling their unrelated businesses. They focused on what they thought were their 'core competencies'.

What caused such a radical shift?

The typical reason provided is that a focus on core competencies was simply better. Companies that concentrated on activities where they had a genuine edge were more likely to survive and thrive. Capital tended to flow towards those firms that had a genuine advantage in a particular sector. Hence resources would not be tied up in substandard operations.

However, a more careful look reveals a quite different picture.[1] Often companies decided to focus on core competencies because other organisations were doing the same. The concept was popular, and like any bandwagon, people wanted to jump on it. There were also many influential people from management gurus to academics and consultancy firms calling for firms to refocus their operations in this way.

One particularly influential group who championed the idea of core competencies were securities analysts. These are the people working for large financial institutions who recommend whether investors should buy, sell or hold shares in a particular company. They estimate how much a company is worth. Often these estimates can have a big influence over how much companies' shares will actually be traded for.

Analysts are often seen as people who make objective assessments of the value of a company, but their judgements often depend on prevailing fashions. During the tech boom, for instance, analysts rallied to overvalue the shares of technology companies. This also applies in the case of core competencies. When the idea came into fashion, analysts started to systematically overvalue the shares of companies that claimed to be refocusing their business to that end. This gave companies big incentives to follow the herd and engage in corporate restructuring around core competencies. If they did this, they would probably get positive recommendations from analysts, the companies' shares would go up, and the CEO's bonus along with them.

This all sounds fine in the short term, but in the longer term it would often create problems. Many of the predictions about the benefits of refocusing companies did not come true. Restructuring a company around core competencies sometimes produced superior returns, but often the financial results would be disappointing. As a result, the analysts' predictions were often wide of the mark. You might think this was a big problem for them, but mostly it was not. If an analyst followed the crowd and made similar predictions to everyone else, then they would not seem so stupid. However, if they went against the crowd and showed independent thinking, then they would stand out – and much of the time this was not desirable. They might be viewed as making chancy predictions and find their career prospects dwindling. It should come as no surprise that recent research has found that the most successful investment analysts are usually people who make recommendations with only moderate levels of novelty.[2] Real independent thinking is usually dangerous for an analyst's career prospects.

Systematically rewarding companies that focus on core competencies (despite the fact they had low returns) is just one example of a form of functional stupidity widely practised by many organisations: imitation. All too often companies do things not because they produce the best results, but because everyone else is doing it. By following the crowd, they avoid thinking too much and sidestep difficulties that might come from having an idiosyncratic position. This kind of thoughtless herd-following is often richly rewarded, but it also creates risks of pursuing the crowd off a cliff.

When image is everything

Executives who control modern organisations – in particular large and public ones – are eager to show they are up to date. They do this by adopting the latest practices, whether it be corporate social responsibility, social media, authentic leadership development, branding, balance scorecards, talent management or whatever else is hot at the time. This means that new initiatives abound, sometimes effective and sometimes not. Most of the time it is impossible to know. One study of American corporations found that firms that implemented popular management fashions did not have on average better financial performance than other firms.[3] The only significant difference the researchers found was that after implementing the management fad in question, the CEO's pay tended to go up. This gives us cause to be suspicious about management fashions. All too often doing the same as others means doing something that technically or economically just does not make sense. While these new practices might create a mix of problems, advantages and ambiguities, they come with a significant advantage: they make the organisation look good.

Copying what others are doing can create problems. It can further entrench received ideas of how things should be. It can undermine the efficiency of an organisation's operation. It can also mean that organisations adopt practices which are unsuitable because they are seen as 'normal', 'appropriate', or the 'right thing to do'. Of course, it may be smart to adopt some practices. In embracing the fashion, an organisation appears to be respectable. This can attract resources: it can become perceived as an attractive business partner or gain access to key opinion-makers.[4]

But what about substantive issues like performance? Is it not good to identify 'best practice' and then implement it? Sometimes this is true, but there are problems. 'Best practice' is often the airbrushed version of a business practice that is peddled by pop management authors, the business press and consultants, but is not durable enough to be moved between organisations. The many recipes for corporate greatness which have seduced numerous executives have proved to have a limited shelf-life. Japanese management was very popular among Western executives during the 1980s, but as Western executives were searching for inspiration in Japan, and piles of books celebrating Japanese-style management appeared, the Japanese economy started to falter. When the Spaghetti organization of Oticon was celebrated in mass media, the firm had already started to abandon it. What fits one successful company (or industry, or even a nation) does not suit another. Best practice is often a matter of local specificity and is hard to cultivate. What may work is dependent on context, networks, organisational culture and local competences. Imitation is often very difficult. You may install formal structures and practices that try to replicate the admired source firm, but outside the context they came from they can operate quite differently.

It is sometimes smart to manipulate surface-level images, but more often than not, to do this involves significant functional stupidity. If positive results are lacking, it may go unnoticed or only be recognised after a long delay. When this happens, bad corporate memory, shifting careers and intense indifference to learning can make superficial imitation quite acceptable.

Jumping on the bandwagon

Copycatting is an important skill in corporate life, but one that needs disguising. It is much easier to follow others than think for yourself. The desire to keep up with fashions and the fear of lagging behind others plays a major role in corporate life. Deviation from the crowd is fraught with problems. Fortunately, bandwagons keep you safe.

We often assume that senior executives are independent, strong-willed, rational people who on the whole make wise decisions. Jan Wallander thinks otherwise. Wallander was for many years one of Sweden's most highly respected business leaders. He sat on the boards of many companies and was the key figure behind the development of Handelsbanken into one of the most admired financial institutions in Europe. Wallander thinks that senior executives are largely driven by a desire to be in tune with their time. Uneasy to diverge from the crowd, they readily follow new management trends and fashions. This means they may shuttle between ideas, often with little to show for it. 'Business leaders are just as fashion-conscious as teenage girls choosing jeans,' Wallander wrote. 'They are like a herd of sheep munching at the grass. If they hear that the grass is greener on the other side of the hill, they rush away, and then all the others follow.'[5]

Wallander has proved to be right. Managers often make decisions in the manner of sheep in a flock. They just troop along with what others in their industry are doing. This is exactly what James Westphal and his colleagues found when they looked at why hospitals in Texas started using Total Quality Management techniques.[6] The idea of TQM was developed largely in the manufacturing sector. At first it was not completely clear that the techniques used for building a car could also be used for treating a patient, but in the mid-1980s a few hospitals in Texas began to run experiments. They found that the techniques needed to be tailored to their own organisations, and spent some time on making modifications.

After about 400 hospitals had adopted some kind of TQM system, duly customised to their needs, other hospitals started to follow suit, but instead of going into detail, and tailoring in line with local needs, they just followed the flock and copied what others were doing. Quite soon two thousand hospitals had implemented some kind of TQM system. If past studies are anything to judge by, it was likely that these latecomers would not get the same efficiency gains from applying these systems.

So why apply them? The answer seemed to be, that everyone else was. If a hospital was directly linked with another that had adopted TQM, then it would be more likely to do it. By tagging along, hospitals ended up with a new management technique, but perhaps more importantly, they contrived to be seen as legitimate by their peers, and by others who mattered.

These dynamics in Texan hospitals are almost exactly like the teenagers shopping for jeans that Wallander describes. Daring first movers try out a new style and customise it. Then the mass starts to copy the first movers – often with little thought and no customising. Peer pressure rules – if people you are close to have the new jeans, then you should too. Often the new style of jeans doesn't fit everyone – on some they look positively awkward. But no matter – looking good is not the point. The teenagers are buying the new jeans to fit in and gain approval by their peers. It was the same with the Texan hospitals: implementing a TQM system might not make much difference, but it did align them with their peers.

One of the main reasons senior executives are so fashion-conscious is that corporate life is plagued by uncertainty. Often managers do not know for sure whether a new practice works. Cost–benefit analysis is often little more than guesswork. The only thing we know about the future is that we don't know it. When uncertainty is high, it often is safer to go where the rest do. Then you avoid too much blame. There are always business gurus, consultants and professionals willing to tell you what everyone else is doing or what they plan to do. Executives, like the rest of us, are often eager to hear positive news. The promise of quick fixes is appealing. Falling behind the times can ruin careers.

Over thirty years ago, two sociologists recognised that many organisations were trapped in an iron cage of their own making. While looking at many sectors, Paul DiMaggio and Walter Powell noticed that most organisations were much alike.[7] They had similar organisational structures, similar strategies, HR systems, and brands. If you asked people within each company, they would say they were unique, but look at each company in a sector, and they were to all intents and purposes the same. Powell and DiMaggio asked themselves, why is there so much similarity? They came up with three reasons: regulation, shared thinking and common norms.[8]

The first reason for so much similarity is regulation. Firms were often subject to the same rules and laws. In responding to these regulations, companies tend to generate the same kind of rules and internal policies. For instance, in many countries around the world companies are legally required to ensure that they are not damaging the natural environment too much. Accordingly, companies have developed policies, instituted procedures and employed staff whose task it is to see that the firm is in compliance. With globalisation, many rules and laws have gone international. This means that companies worldwide face increasingly similar laws. One result is that they have started to look increasingly similar – on a superficial level. For instance, large banks across the world have had to respond to the Basel regulations on liquidity. In response, they have taken a more and more uniform approach to managing the amount of capital they have on their balance sheets.

The second reason why companies can be so similar is shared thinking. As we have seen, executives are often very uncertain, groping to know what makes a company successful. To deal with this uncertainty, they often simply look at what other successful firms are doing and try to do the same. For instance, many companies conclude that they need to be more innovative. To increase their rates of innovation, they look at firms well known for being innovative, such as Google, then dispatch their executives to Silicon Valley to visit tech companies' corporate campuses in the hope that they will learn something. They often ignore the fact that Google is an entirely different sector to them, and the lessons in view probably of limited value. They also overlook that even if they do learn something, actually implementing it within their organisation is likely to be difficult, if not impossible.

The final driver of copycat behaviour that Powell and DiMaggio identified is normative pressure. This involves pressure to follow along with social norms prevalent in an industry. To appear well adjusted, a firm needs to echo all the rest. They should adopt the same structures, processes, policies and language as other firms in the field. You prove environmental awareness by introducing paper recycling in the office. You show that you are concerned about your employees' wellbeing by providing a company gym. You show you are 'strategic' and 'ambitious' by presenting a corporate vision that states you will rival the best in the world in your industry by some date way in the distant future. To show concern with gender equality, you appoint two female board members. To show concern with racism you set up a diversity office staffed by one of the few obviously non-white people in the company. You show you deplore child labour by doing an ethical audit on your supply chain. Sometimes a high moral tone even leads to a company forbidding employees from using hotel chains that show erotic films. Small firms may be let off the hook, but large, well-known organisations in the glare of the media spotlight find themselves under pressure to comply.

What one company does can often be highly idiosyncratic. Outsiders often find it hard to understand exactly what is going on inside a firm, and this will make it difficult to copy. So when

companies try to imitate one another, it is often very superficial. Genuine, 'in-depth' imitation is another matter. For
instance, many companies have some form of CSR activity.
However, there is a huge degree of variation in what goes on
under this label – even within the same industry. Some firms
have environmentally friendly buildings, others get their staff
to read to impoverished children. Fortunately, superficial labels
are sometimes enough to make people happy.

This superficial learning can lead companies to make
dangerous assumptions. One reason for this is that when
companies want to learn something, they often look only at
the best-known companies. These are usually the winners in
a particular industry, and we tend to like success stories. But
the problem with focusing only on winners is that you learn
from a very biased sample.[9] You ignore the great majority of
companies which have either gone out of business or are still
limping along. Looking at these companies could presumably
tell you something insightful – even if it is what you should
not be doing. By only looking at winners, you rule out many
of the painful lessons you could learn from people who have
tried and failed. But there is another trap lurking. By focusing
only on winners, you are picking a sample of firms which are
likely to have followed risky strategies. These are the ones that
got lucky and made it. They could just as well have failed. What
this means is that all the firms in the world who are trying to
copy Uber's business model are making a big mistake. They are
focusing on only one example that happened to make it in a sea
of many hundreds that failed. If a firm really wants to learn, it
should look at failures too.

As well as being misguided, attempts at imitation can be
rather ham-fisted. Consider the adoption of total quality management by the Swedish armed forces. In one regiment, an

officer instructed to describe a new operational control system to her colleagues talked about 'main processes', 'support processes' and 'leadership processes'. This whole system, she said, would result in 'process development'. Sensing a sceptical response, she went on to explain why the Swedish military should implement the control system: 'There is presumably a good reason, because the business sector has implemented ISO 9000 certification in a great many companies and they require their subcontractors to be certified. And this is presumably something you benefit from, since this is what they do in the private sector.'[10] Strong reasons indeed: as the private sector may benefit from this, then we should do the same. This is functional stupidity in concentrated form.

Looking organised

During the mid-1970s, the Stanford sociologist John Meyer was studying schools. He noticed that schools in the United States were rather strange.[11] On the one hand they claimed to have particular organisational structures. Each of the schools he looked at claimed to follow a standard model. But when he looked a little more carefully, he noticed that the structures a school laid claim to were quite different from how they actually worked. Why was there such a big difference between how schools claimed to run themselves and how they actually ran? Would it not be much better if formal structures and practice were in tune?

To answer this question, he and one of his doctoral students, Brian Rowan, looked at whether there was a big split between what they called 'legitimizing structures' and the underlying organisation of work.[12] The legitimising structures were the public face of the organisation. They were how the schools claimed to be organised. The work organisation was the nuts and bolts of how the schools actually got the job done. They also realised that the public face of the organisation was mainly a ceremony: it was about putting on a show. But like any ceremony, this was largely unrelated to everyday life. The way things got done was something else altogether.

But what Meyer and Rowan found most striking was that large parts of organisations like schools are largely protected from immediate practical demands. Instead of focusing on the actual work process, schools spend most of their time on ceremonial activities. They develop plans, set up meetings, write reports, develop policy statements, prepare presentations and all the other things a 'proper' school is supposed to do. All this ceremonial activity often had little or no impact on the immediate work process. In fact most of the time it was a distraction. But this did not mean it was a complete waste of time. Making sure that the ceremony was up to scratch was actually a key part of ensuring that a school kept going. If a school performed the ceremony well, and satisfied people's expectations, then it would be rewarded. Important stakeholders would be more likely to give it resources, or at least to leave it alone. But if the school did not go through the ceremony, then it was likely to be punished.

Soon Meyer and Rowan realised that this insight did not apply just to schools. They also played out in many other modern organisations with objectives that were hard to pin down. This is a common characteristic of human service organisations such as hospitals, prisons and care homes, as well as of schools and higher education institutions. Here, it is ceremony that counts. The entire organisation can grow obsessed with getting the ceremony right, even when it undermines its wider purpose.

One common ceremony in human service organisations

is accumulating quantitative indicators. Hospitals track the number of hospital beds occupied, schools monitor the grades students achieve, universities measure the number of papers staff publish and how happy students are with their courses, police measure the number of alcohol tests carried out, and airport authorities count the number of passengers who are 'delighted' to have their bags searched. But all too often this measurement backfires. Ensuring that all hospital beds are occupied can mean delaying patients' release. Ensuring that students get high test scores can mean they are taught how to pass exams, but little else. Carrying out lots of breath tests can mean that motorists are breathalysed at inappropriate and inconvenient times. Making sure that passengers are delighted may mean you do not scan all their luggage. As a result, fulfilling the overall purpose of the organisation can easily take second place to producing nice-looking statistics.

The question of what the actual goals of an organisation are can be hard to answer, particularly in the public sector. As a result substantive goals matter less and impressions matter more. One result of this is rousing vision statements that say great things about what an organisation sets out to achieve, but usually these are just an interchangeable collection of management buzz words cooked up on some senior management retreat and then finessed by a communications consultant. There is often little, if any, real relationship between these empty words and the actual goals of an organisation.

Charles Perrow, a sociologist at Yale, realised this was the case.[13] He asked himself what public-sector organisations, in particular in human services, are actually steered by. One thing he thought was important was what he called the 'external function' of these organisations. This was all the unrecognised services they provided to the external community. For instance, schools keep young people occupied and off the street; universities help to keep young people out of the unemployment statistics; social service organisations employ people, including many coming out of an overinflated higher education system. Perrow also thought there were some important internal motives within these organisations. They included maximising resources, making working conditions as comfortable as possible, preserving peace and harmony, avoiding open conflicts and scandals, and conveying a good impression to outside audiences. These functions and objectives often take the upper hand, partly because there are no clear indicators of how successful organisations are in substantive terms. It is, for example, often unknown what a university accomplishes in terms of improving the intellectual functioning of their students. All we know is that a certain percentage graduate. As we saw earlier, many of the graduates do not get any brighter from their education.

The unofficial drivers of an organisation do not necessarily contradict official objectives. Sometimes they can even help to achieve them. But if managers took these objectives very seriously, they would quickly face an arduous task. Changing the allocation of resources irrespective of established precedents, redefining areas of responsibility irrespective of existing claims to roles, changing people's goals without considering their interests – these are things that will not be met with open arms. Doing what appears to be rational rather than following set conventions will often lead to amazement and dismay. Too much thinking for yourself is likely to prompt hostility. Following formal rituals, avoiding conflicts and not risking negative publicity is often the safer option. A strong faith in formal structures and procedures creates problems through complicating matters, but having a belief in these formal structures makes life easier for managers and others involved.

Corporate window-dressing

Window-dressing is a vital part of running any organisation, whether in the public or in the private sector. This involves attempts to make the public face of an organisation look good. Policies and practices are adopted to impress external groups like activists, customers, politicians, the media and public authorities. It matters very little whether some new policy actually makes the organisation run more smoothly. What is vital is that it makes things look that way – even if they are not.

We often hear that the hard commercial facts of the private sector mean that image cuts no ice if you can't create products and services that customers want. While this is sometimes the case, many private-sector organisations are no less image-obsessed than their cousins in the public sector.

The concern for image-preening has fuelled a spectacular expansion of the corporate beauty industry. Decorative surfaces in the form of architecture, premises, letterhead design, brochures, posters, PowerPoint presentations, company uniforms and attractive employees are on the rise. For instance, we were told about one well known French company that recently remodelled its offices in central Paris. The office was huge and stood in the city's most prestigious district, but it housed hardly any employees. Most of the staff were located at offices on the outskirts of town where land was cheaper. When the firm was asked why it had this expensive facility with no employees, their response was: it creates a good impression.

Whether the public or customers benefit or lose from this corporate beauty contest is hard to tell. It may be pleasing to watch, but it also means that resources and attention are taken away from core processes. This can mean that as the organisation looks more beautiful from afar, it looks much less appealing close up. Consider the example of banking in the United Kingdom. Many of the large banks have devoted greater shares of their resources to window-dressing activities. They have redesigned branches, run expensive advertising campaigns, instituted CSR initiatives and much more. Yet at the same time customer satisfaction ratings continue to be very low. It seems that as banks have built impressive images, their customers have become increasingly grumpy.

Promising rainbows

Diversity management is something most organisations are eager to champion, particularly if they have a prominent public face. Organisations originate diversity policies, create mentorship (or reverse mentorship) programmes, build affinity networks, implement unconscious bias training and much more. All this work can be a positive step towards changing discriminatory workplace practices, but often this does not happen. Sometimes diversity management is more symbolism than substance. It is about publicly signalling that a company takes diversity really seriously and is doing something about it. By showing that they have put systems and procedures in place, organisations can 'prove' that they are good employers. Little may have changed in terms of who does what in a corporation, or how 'minority' employees are treated, but doing diversity management ticks the box.

The demand for diversity-management policies has created a multi-billion-dollar industry in the United States.[14] Companies active in the sector need to continually assure their clients about the value of their services and products. One client, a personnel manager in a Canadian oil company who was responsible for diversity training, justified his choice of consultant because 'they were not into the same old ideas – you know the hippie images of the seventies. They are real professionals, and are willing to change their programs to give us something new each time.'[15] Their assumption seemed to be that 'something new' means 'something better' – or at least that it will look better. Consultants also stressed the importance of coming up with something new. One of them said: 'That old sensitivity training stuff has no selling power any more. You've got to give it [diversity] more management appeal – link it to efficiency or performance, somehow connect it to saving money. That's the feeling of the times.'[16]

Coming up with something distinct is important: it needs to be presented as clearly different from 'the old stuff', and needs to be well packaged. Diversity experts also monitor other companies and imitate their latest initiatives. They try to link their activities with other fashionable themes such as teamwork. The sales message is that diversity pays. Diversity is usually sold by using appealing images like 'rainbow cultures' and 'mosaic workplaces'.

The profitable, harmonious and beautiful world of diversity promised by consultants and craved by clients is not so easily achieved. One problem is that the local relevance of diversity programmes is often limited. For instance, a study of diversity management in the Canadian oil industry found there was a mismatch between what companies provided and what course participants wanted. Many of the leading companies in North America were often based in North Carolina and Georgia and influenced by themes relevant for African Americans and middle-class women with jobs. However, for people working in the Canadian oil industry companies, diversity issues were often linked with quite different matters such as 'francophones' – French-speaking Canadians from Quebec. This created a perception that the content of diversity programmes on offer was barely relevant.

While diversity was often presented using images of harmony, participants were aware that this did not always fit the facts. After participation in one such programme, a manager said: 'It really is a feel-good exercise. You know, we can all feel good that we are this happy multi-colored family – that's going to bring in all this money for the firm. The truth is quite another matter. If people are really different, they don't get along that easily, they want to do things differently, and they get upset about how they are told to do work.'[17]

Oil companies often have a bad reputation for being conservative and backward, yet they want to give the impression that they are forward-looking and up-to-date. Large and well-known consultancy firms offering the latest programmes were engaged to do the job for them, but this had a mainly cosmetic effect. Fashionable, standardised programmes did not win over staff at the local level. They merely made participants sceptical. In the end it meant that diversity-management programmes were more about chasing rainbows than delivering practical change.

Sceptical responses from some participants could complicate things. If expressed widely and honestly it might undermine the ambitions and hopes of such initiatives. Luckily the risk of this happening is low. Participants are often hesitant to spell out their scepticism. They may worry that these kind of remarks could mark them out as someone who is 'off message', 'out of date', or who 'doesn't get it'. Top management are often more concerned to convey that they are doing something than worried about what the outcome actually is. Often participant compliance and executive ignorance rescues meaningless corporate activities from extinction.

Conclusion

Many aspects of organisational life are not about making things function more efficiently. Instead they are about creating the right external image and complying with broadly shared expectations of how an organisation should be. This is because managers and others in organisations are often conformists – they aim to do what everyone else is doing and avoid standing out from the pack. They imitate others and follow fashions as fervently as any teenager. Structures and formal practices that look good are adapted. This interest in looking good is often most pronounced in public-sector organisations, but companies are also increasingly scrutinised on the basis of whether they live up to a formula of what a good firm should exhibit: corporate strategy, outsourcing, CSR, branding campaigns, HRM policies and strategies, diversity management and much more.

An increasingly important part of work is just about polishing the image of the firm. Often this comes with problems. A disconnect between the rosy images a company tries to project and sharper practices can lead to frustration, low commitment and cynicism. This can often be bad business. So many organisations try to convince themselves – and others – that what looks good actually is good. If this is not the case now, then perhaps it will come in the future. This eagerness to have faith in, and be proud of, window-dressing structures and to deny that one is a fashion-following conformist is significant. It helps to boost identity and self-esteem. Avoiding sceptical thinking about all this is vital for morale. It also helps to encourage people to commit to exhibiting the right surface and maintain the belief that this matters. In a surface-loving society, this is not as hard as it seems.

The current fascination with branding helps a lot. In the next chapter we explore this goldmine of functional stupidity.

7

Branding-Induced Stupidity

A damn fine omelette?

Some years ago, the Swedish military decided it needed to change. Compulsory service had been dropped a few years earlier. No longer was the force made up of lots of foot soldiers who provided the brawn for defending the country. Instead it was staffed by a smaller number of professional military personnel who were supposed to provide the brains to run peacekeeping missions. However, some thought there was a problem. The image of the military lagged behind the times. What was needed was a rebranding campaign.

The idea of rebranding the armed forces would have seemed ridiculous only a few decades ago. After all this was a non-profit outfit and there was hardly any need to differentiate it from other organisations. There was – and is – only one military force in Sweden. Nevertheless, the Defence Forces wanted to show that they were up to date, so they persevered. A smart new communication director was hired. He set out to 'rebrand' the Defence Force, hoping to rejuvenate it, and put it in tune with the times. This meant changing the logo. The generals liked the notion of being up to date, so the communication director got a green light.

What the new brand actually looked like was uncertain. It had been classified. However there was reassurance that the new logo would be similar to signs on Sweden's military aircraft: 'three yellow crowns on a blue background with a yellow ring around it'. In a 'spring-clean' this new logo was to be applied to 'everything from billboards, websites, letterheads down to the ashtrays. All the old guns and badges will be removed.' The communication director realised that this would be a major move. 'You have to break eggs to make an omelette,' he said. 'It is clear that some will think it's tough along the way, but it will be a damn fine omelette.'

The rebranding project was announced to the mass media, who inevitably kicked up a fuss. The cause of their interest was not the brilliance of the branding. Rather it was triggered by poor timing and a clash of priorities. Replacing all the old signage with new ones would cost a lot. At the very same time the military had become aware of budget problems and had cancelled a big planned manoeuvre. This looked bad: spending money on a new logo when there wasn't enough for basic operations was seen by many as stupid. An added complication was that the great majority of the military personnel were attached to the old logo. They protested at its removal and supplanting by something they saw as inferior. Other stakeholders were also upset. They felt that Swedish heritage was being denigrated. An employee of the Swedish national archives spoke to a national newspaper, pointing out that 'in one sweep this wipes out the use of the heraldic weapons, many of which have centuries-old traditions. It would be a very unfortunate development for the heraldic heritage.'

Faced with all this negative publicity, the Defence Force decided to abolish the project and keep the old logo. The director of defence forces admitted: 'We have made mistakes.'[1] It seems that a combination of strong resistance and bad timing meant that this damned fine omelette was never cooked.

Another notable case was that of British Airways when it sought to rebrand itself as a global rather than a British company. This seemed a good idea, top management thought. After about half of all the aircraft had been repainted to reflect this new global look, the harsh reaction from customers forced the company to issue different orders: repaint the planes to look as they did before they went global.[2]

Nevertheless, branding remains a hot topic. BA's top management and the generals in Sweden are not the only people that have found themselves swept away by this enthusiasm. In some parts of the economy an interest in branding makes sense, rather as the cattle-owners branded their cows to distinguish them from their neighbours' and discourage thieves. But often the urge to apply the hot iron to everything does not lead to success.

These two cases speak volumes about the stupidities that can be set in motion by the brand-obsessed times we live in. The Defence Force is an organisation that has no call to differentiate itself, but still the top people felt compelled to undertake an expensive and disruptive branding initiative. When the idea was floated within the military top brass, people seemed to go along with it. Most other bodies seemed to need periodic shifts of branding; why shouldn't the defence forces do the same? At first sight this looked like a good idea – it showed that the military was up to date and part of the contemporary world. However, the repolished image clashed with deeper underlying realities. The new logo undermined centuries of traditions within the military, creating a wave of resentment in the process. But perhaps more worryingly, the rebranding initiative showed that senior figures in the military seemed more ready to devote their resources to image warfare than to core business. Eventually these problems became too much to bear, and they returned to their old logo. Something similar can be said about British Airways.

Such a fatal fascination with rebranding is by no means unique to the Swedish military and BA. It has captured almost all sectors of society. Routine branding and rebranding initiatives can be found in companies, public services and non-profit organisations. These kinds of initiatives easily attract the enthusiasm of marketing and top managers. It is easy to be seduced by the idea that a new logo, a coat of paint and an ad campaign will transform and rejuvenate an organisation. It appeals to hubris and wishful thinking. In reality, it is not so easy to recreate a company with a touch of branding magic. Don Watson reminds us just how silly it can sometimes be: 'branding frequently means changing an impossibly mundane name into a marvellous new one: National Bank of Australia to National Australia Bank and Australian Opera to Opera Australia, for example'.[3] At one level these initiatives seem entirely stupid, achieving little or nothing. But looked at more carefully, branding initiatives do achieve things: they show that an organisation is actively doing something, and they keep marketing officials and senior executives busy.

The dancing brand-name

When Karl Marx wrote about capitalism in the late nineteenth century, he claimed that society had become gripped by a dangerous affliction he called 'commodity fetishism'.[4] When people saw something like a table, all they saw was a commodity. They often overlooked many important features of the table – who made it, how it was made, what wood it was made of, where that wood was grown and so on. They did not think about how useful it might be. Instead, what they saw was the price tag.

Times have changed. The average furniture shopper today certainly looks at the price. They are usually happy to overlook complicated questions about the source of the materials it is made from and who actually made it. But they are seized by a new kind of fetishism – brand fetishism.[5] Often the first question that many people ask about an item – whether couscous or a car – is what brand is it? If a piece of furniture carries the brand of a famous designer, then buyers assume at once that it must be excellent. With a well-known brand attached, they are often willing to waive more searching questions like how was it made, how good are the materials, and even is it a decent price.

This is not true just for people who buy products in private life – it happens in business life as well. Displaying a well-known brand on the front of a consultancy report means that the advice is often taken more seriously. A common piece of back-room wisdom in the corporate world is: 'No one ever got fired for hiring McKinsey.' It is not the contents of the report that count: the brand outranks them.

Our attachment to brands can make people incapable of looking at products, services, or the organisations that produce them in a sober way. Too often we fixate on the brand and ignore the rest. The reason we have grown so myopically focused on brands, according to one expert, is that:

In an extremely complex, noisy, almost insanely competitive world when there is much that is so familiar to choose from, where choice based solely on rational factors is now almost impossible in most fields, brands make choice easier. Brands are the device we use to differentiate between otherwise almost indistinguishable competitors. Without clear branding, in some fields we literally could not tell one product or service from another.[6]

In some parts of the economy an interest in branding makes sense. Every market is flooded with similar mass-produced products. Whether it is a new pair of trousers or a total quality management system you want, you will find hundreds of varieties available. Naturally, we find it difficult to distinguish between so many products and services. The choice can make our heads spin and rouse anxiety. To deal with these unpleasant feelings, we often just focus on the brand. Differences are played up and we attach distinct meanings to indistinct products. Massive similarities are hidden by massive marketing efforts.

Branding efforts are by no means new. In 1956 a leading proponent of corporate image creation explained that 'What you are trying to do is create an illogical situation. You want the customer to fall in love with your product and have a profound brand loyalty when actually content may be very similar to hundreds of competing brands.' To create this illogical loyalty, he said, the first task 'is one of creating some differentiation in the mind – some individualization for the product which has a long list of competitors very close to it in content'.[7]

This form of illogic has now spread. It is no longer manufacturers of fast-moving consumer goods who try to make indistinct products seem different. People in all kinds of organisations are preoccupied with brand. When this happens they come to be seduced into loving specific products, services or even entire organisations, despite their lack of remarkable qualities. Name recognition and reduction of uncertainty is one thing. Finding meaning and paying a hefty premium for a product due to branding is another. The latter is what most business and communication people want, but often this is hard to achieve outside high-status and symbolically loaded contexts.

Absolut bullshit?

Today, most people see brands as an undisputed part of life, but take a look back at their history and you see how strange they are. Brands were initially used as a tool for marking cattle. Today they are used by people to mark themselves. Most of the time this is metaphorical but in some cases it is literal. There are people who proudly have their favourite brands – say Harley Davidson or Nike – tattooed onto their bodies.[8] Some companies have even encouraged their employees to advertise their logo on their bodies. One Manhattan real-estate firm offered an immediate 15 per cent raise if employees tattooed the firm's logo onto their body. Forty people took up the offer.[9]

Branding often involves small variations on the same basic product. VW's and Porsche's sports utility vehicles are basically the same SUV. The difference is the brand and the design. However these relatively insignificant differences are amplified. This strategy is known as 'gold-plating'. 'To sell a basically standardised thing, the seller will magnify the value of minor differences quickly and easily engineered, so that the surface is what counts,' writes Richard Sennett. 'The brand must seem to the consumer more than the thing itself.'[10] This is often a question of a 10 per cent difference in content and 100 per cent difference in price.

Paying a massive premium for what is almost the same product does not appear to be particularly smart. Of course one can – and many do – buy things for status reasons. A person can simply expect that there is a pay-off from consumption of highly symbolic goods. But often building a sense of status or impressing others is not the only motive. Branding often works when people start to look for 'meaning' and even 'love' in relatively indistinct products. This search is helped along by functional stupidity: people stop asking serious questions about an underlying product or service and focus only on the superficial brands.

Today, consumer goods often have a completely arbitrary relationship to the meanings attached to them. Absolut vodka is a revealing example. According to the manufacturer, the 'core values of the brand are Absolut clarity, simplicity and perfection'. The company tells us you can experience these qualities simply by looking at the bottle. The clarity and simplicity are emphasised by the absence of a label, while the perfection is clearly linked to 'rinsing the bottle with something absolutely pure' before filling it with vodka.[11] Absolut's market strategy is about minimising the importance of the product by stressing 'a blank bottle-shaped space that could be filled with whatever content a particular audience most wanted from its brands: intellectual in *Harper's*, futuristic in *Wired*, alternative in *Spin*, loud and proud in *Out* and "Absolut Centerfold" in *Playboy*.'[12]

The clarity, simplicity and perfection that the Absolut brand is claimed to embody often pass the consumer by. In most cases, clarity and perfection are not the outcome of drinking vodka. Believing in 'these core values' – as a producer as well as a consumer – probably requires you to turn your intelligence down, but a dose of intelligence minimisation can be rewarding: you can feel that you fit in, you may feel better about yourself, and you might even feel clear, simple and perfect.

Sacred toothpaste

Brands are supposed to accomplish all sorts of remark-able things. We are told they can evoke deep emotions like love, envy, joy and even sadness. They can give people's most mundane activities meaning – cleaning the toilet or withdraw-ing money from your bank can become a deeply significant experience. They boost people's sense of self. They create a sense of value around the intrinsic qualities of a product or service. Don't they?

Many of the overblown claims about the impact of brands come from a limited number of companies and products that are status symbols with a long history, global reach or cult status. Unfortunately for brand enthusiasts – but perhaps luckily for the rest of us – most brands are not status symbols, they don't have a long history and they lack special cultural cachet. The reality of brands is often much more mundane. Some products trigger a semi-religious emotion in consumers. But in many cases, the enthusiasm for brands is very modest indeed.

One context where we saw the sacred beliefs in branding meet the mundane realities of business life was a pharmaceuti-cal firm that sold, among other things, toothpaste. The people we spoke to introduced themselves as brand managers. They were lyrical about brands and branding, and grew particu-larly animated when talking about well-known and successful brands: 'Adidas. Their "Impossible is Nothing" campaign. I don't think anything's come close to being as good as that, to be honest,' one brand manager told us. 'The language that they use is so specific to a person like me. It's quite inspirational. It's quite motivational.' Apple, Nike and Coca-Cola sparked similar enthusiasm, as when another brand manager informed us: 'When you have a Coca-Cola, you're experiencing – you could say maybe – happiness.' The shared wisdom in this group was that brands were a deeply existential issue. 'We live and die by them,' one of the brand managers told us.

The picture the brand managers painted of their work seemed impressive. We were told they worked with life, creativity, emotions, expressiveness and value creation. Who could ask for more? There was only one problem: the customers did not really care about the existential aspects of toothpaste. Customers mainly cared about prices. The company focused almost exclusively on short-term sales: 50 per cent of products were sold as part of some kind of deal. This left very little room for uplifting branding. The focus of brand managers was actually on much more mundane things. One of the brand managers admitted that her work was about making the products visible and ensuring they were properly placed on shop shelves. It was about 'the pack, what the pack looks like. How it looks on shelf. How it stands out.'

One source of frustration for these brand managers was that consumers did not find their work so important. 'They don't really understand it,' one person told us. 'They'll just pick up anything on shelf that's on promotion.' Another brand manager admitted that 'People aren't really interested in toothpaste.' They realised that consumers were really largely motivated by price. 'Loyalty to the product is really, really low,' we were told.

The customers, the product and their work fell short of their own fervent beliefs in branding. This could mean that the naïvety and thoughtlessness about 'brand value' would be solely dysfunctional. However, they dealt with this depressing reality in two ways that allowed them to rescue their branding ideas, and create some sense of hope and happiness. First, they held on to the ultimate significance of the brand. Sooner or later they hoped that the dream of ideal branding will come true. One brand manager told us that 'For our consumers, our shoppers and, really importantly, for our customers, there's an intangible thing they can't do without.' This mystical intangible thing is presumably the brand. Another told us that 'A lot of it is sold on deal and that's one of our ongoing challenges but, without our brands and our branding, we wouldn't sell what we do.' The message seems to be that even though price is seem-ingly all that matters, brands are important too – even if the customers don't know it. There is a mystical, hidden brand force out there somewhere.

The other way brand managers justified their beliefs in the face of mass indifference was by claiming that branding is useful for selling your ideas inside the company. They thought that brands could be used to market products to senior manag-ers (for resources) and to sales forces (who flogged the stuff to shops). Creative campaigns, amusing events and other displays of success were seen as an important way of catching other people's attention in the company. 'You'll see people sending emails out [saying], We've won this award. Look how fantas-tic we are,' one brand manager told us. 'You've got to market internally. You've got to market yourself and your brand as well.'[13]

The glamour and joy of brands can help to make the working lives of marketing people more remarkable and uplift-ing. Rather than focusing on selling a very respectable, healthy and necessary product they can pretend that they are doing something much more grandiose. This ambition seems hard to live up to – particularly when you are selling a mundane product like toothpaste. But the brand managers we spoke with had become adept at overlooking these problems and reassur-ing themselves about the vital nature of branding. By doing this, they were able to maintain the idea that they were doing something much greater than flogging toothpaste to price-driven, indifferent and disloyal customers.

A sceptic may think that marketing toothpaste is unlikely to be particularly meaningful. One may of course say that selling sugary water like Coca-Cola would be an even less likely candidate for all the fuss. But let us leave this issue aside. What happens when the product being marketed is something that is more important? Like for example a leading university, where good students spend years (and huge sums of money) and leading academics spend their careers (often working sixty hours per week or more)?

Say it like you mean it

Midshire is a leading university in the United Kingdom.[14] It has an excellent reputation, at least among people outside the academic community, and usually comes out in the top ten in national ranking exercises. Surely this temple of intelligence should be a source of excellent organisational practices? Perhaps not.

Recently, the university attempted to improve its brand. It redesigned its logo – a process that cost £80,000 and prompted much displeasure among students (4,000 of whom signed a petition protesting about it). The university also implemented an internal branding initiative it called the 'Midshire tone of voice'. One day, academic staff at the university received a message in their inbox about this new initiative. Attached was a document explaining how 'Midshire is a place that fundamentally rejects the notion of obstacles – a place where the starting point is always "anything is possible". This can be best communicated using the language of what could be and a phrase "what if".'

Having laid down this upbeat theme, the document continued:

> What if there were a place of infinite possibilities, where your only boundaries were the limits of your energy, imagination and potential? Comfortable with breaking new ground and taking risks, the people around you would be the very best and their focus would be to make you the very best too … What if you were to work somewhere every day so different, you might never want to leave? Where lines of command were short and you were empowered to act on ideas, provided they were first class. And if you were to move on, your distinct approach would successively influence the people and organisations around you. So what if all these things existed in one place? We think they do: the University of Midshire. What if?

Having established this visionary message, the document continued, providing staff with clues about how to develop a 'Midshire tone of voice'. These included looking to the future, keeping positive, starting dialogue, being proactive, and saying it like you mean it. It even gave examples of how the would-be user of the tone of voice might talk with people – including tips for starting a sentence. Naturally, the phrase 'what if' featured prominently.

For some, this was an excellent example of internal branding that could help the university to stand out. Many others agreed – it helped the university stand out – but almost for entirely negative reasons. A common response when reading this was summed up by one academic who forwarded the 'voice' document to us: 'Should I laugh or cry?'

All the clichés are there: look to the future, keep it positive, sound uplifting, do the impossible, be proactive and so on. But it all sounds very unrealistic, simplistic and – yes, quite stupid. Many people find this kind of empty rhetoric lightweight and superficial. The 'very best' in the academic world are likely to be allergic to such clichés.

The 'Midshire tone of voice' says that 'we', the top management of the university, know what is best. We know how you ought to express yourself. Your tone of voice is not for you to decide. We don't trust the judgement of the 'very best' who are supposed to populate Midshire University. And as for the final principle of 'say it like you mean it', it may be wise not to 'say what you mean', at least when those behind the tone-of-voice principles are monitoring you. But it is unlikely that you will actually mean what the Midshire tone of voice suggests (or commands). Some people may go along with the belief that they are 'the very best' and work in a place with 'infinite possibilities'. But doing so requires a serious lack of reflection.

Given that the impact of the tone of voice on academic staff is likely to be limited, we might ask what motivated the people behind this initiative. It must have required the work of many people. It was presumably signed off by Midshire top management. So how can the 'best and the brightest' do this? How can we explain the tone-deafness of the 'Midshire tone of voice'?

Many senior managers and staff spend time cloistered in their own little professional worlds. Their days are taken up with meetings, giving talks, working with policies, plans and PowerPoint presentations. They can easily grow detached from the reality of what happens in the rest of their organisation. Fine-sounding formulations, impressive images and wishful thinking often take over. When senior managers start to live in their own world, they are liberated from the everyday challenges and frustrations that make up so much of organisational life.

In an age where branding dominates, there is a growing expectation that the corporate world should be packaged and presented in impressive ways. We live in a world of grandiosity. Any chance to beef up stories of who we are, what we do and what we will do in the future is enthusiastically embraced. Primitive fantasies like 'infinite possibilities' become attractive. There is all too often a naïve hope that with a vision, some inspiration, the right values, and the courage to embark on a 'journey', surely great things lie in store. We can become excellent, world-class, the very best. Say it as loud and as often as possible, and it might just come true. At the very least, you might start to believe it.

Functional stupidity is a must if you want to understand this kind of empty rhetoric about the future. What exactly does talk of 'infinite possibility' mean? Won't it make people feel embarrassed? Will it not seem ridiculous? We suspect that most of the target group will answer 'Yes'. But the good people at the top of Midshire seem to have a great talent for putting these questions aside. They don't seem so worried about the meaningfulness or integrity of the Midshire tone of voice. Instead, they seem to be seduced by positive thinking and the fantasy of standing out as an institution where everyone talks in a similar tone of voice.

Manufacturing consumers

Most people in the developed economies live in a post-affluent society. The central economic problem has shifted from one of scarcity to one of abundance. It is not that we don't have enough. It is that we have too much. This means the big issue is not about producing more. We already have significant overproduction of goods and services. Rather the challenge becomes creating demand for all these products and services that are produced. Marketing becomes an important way to do this. Enormous resources and talents are invested in trying to convince people that they need all the products and services which are created every day. This is the core of what we briefly addressed in Chapter 3 as the economy of persuasion.[15] Its logic is by no means restricted to the capitalist market. It starts to infiltrate all sectors of society: from education to politics, from mass media to high culture, from health care to the military. In the economy of persuasion, what counts is what looks good in order to seduce and sell.

In the past, the main idea of advertising was to demonstrate – and often exaggerate – the advantages of a product. The contemporary advertising industry is not content with such a modest goal. 'Now it manufactures a product of its own: the consumer, perpetually unsatisfied, restless, anxious, and bored,' Christopher Lasch wrote nearly forty years ago.

> Advertising serves not so much to advertise products as to promote consumption as a way of life. It 'educated' the masses into an unappeasable appetite not only for goods but for new experiences and personal fulfilment. It upholds consumption as the answer to the age-old discontents of loneliness, sickness, weariness, lack of sexual satisfaction; at the same time it creates new forms of discontent peculiar to the modern age.[16]

These words seem even more relevant today.

Consumption is all too often about creating dissatisfaction: with products, with services, and most importantly with your general standard of living. If you are completely satisfied with your car, your clothes, your mobile phone or your skin, you have no reason to consume further. But if you feel something isn't quite right, that is another story. The advertising industries try their hardest to create a discrepancy between what you have and what you might have. They promise an improved personal appearance, higher status, greater self-esteem, and a more enjoyable life. When faced with these images you often end up feeling worse about your current situation, but also more willing to consume.

People who work in marketing are usually aware of some of the negative impacts of the images they create. They are often the most enthusiastic readers of the growing genre of anti-consumerist literature. Naomi Klein's *No Logo* is frequently seen on the shelves of branding agencies around the world. So how exactly do marketers deal with these negative views of what they do? It might be amusing to be ironic every now and then. In some cases, marketers have actually incorporated anti-marketing messages into their own campaigns. However, such irony is likely to wear thin. To avoid this existential peril, many people working with brands can simply avoid thinking too much. They try their best to control their doubts and stop uncomfortable questions bubbling up. One common trick here is to outsource these questions to 'the market' or 'the customer'.

When what the customer wants is always right, it is easy to refrain from asking tough questions. In a study of business ethics, a British manager said that he was in favour of environ-mental issues. When asked about how that influenced him at work, he said: 'It is not for me to bring personal prejudice or my own opinions into the marketplace. What's important from my point of view is to reflect my customer's requirements. So whatever I happen to think is irrelevant. I must give the cus-tomers what they require.'[17] For this manager, the customers' requirements stand above prejudices or opinions. Or to put it in another way: You should not let your own prejudices and opinions interfere. Rather, you should be willing and ready to obey the prejudices and opinions of the customer. Of course, a high degree of respect for the customer's views is necessary, but one may still try to influence or persuade them. But in a customer-oriented economy, people tend to focus on giving the market what it wants. Thinking is outsourced: the customer knows best. Just follow him or her.

With the marketisation of ever wider spheres of life, there is a tendency to treat people as customers in all aspects of their lives. No longer are they seen as clients, patients, passengers, students or citizens. They are customers. Even prisoners are considered to be customers in some prisons.[18] This leaves you wondering whether one day enemy fighters will considered to be 'customers' who need to be 'served' by the military.

When people focus on customers, they may put significant resources into reflecting on what they need and how to fulfil these needs. But any more serious thinking is avoided. Instead, people see the marketplace as the centre of the universe and the customer as someone who is always right. Broader questions are removed from the agenda. This whole process is oiled by a strong dose of functional stupidity.

Conclusion

Sixty years ago John Kenneth Galbraith argued that we lived in an affluent society.[19] Today, we are on average about three times richer than when Galbraith coined the term. There is serious overproduction in many parts of the economy. Household items are used only a few times before being thrown away. Thousands of books are published every day – the vast majority find only a few readers. Medical procedures which are of little real benefit to patients are routinely prescribed. Millions of scientific articles are produced every year, and less than half of them are ever read by anyone apart from the editors, reviewers and authors.[20]

To help us dispose of this massive surplus we produce every single day, we have created an economy of persuasion. The sheer size of this operation might lead people to ask 'What the hell are we doing?', but most are aware that asking these questions too persistently is potentially harmful – for their own psychological wellbeing as well as for their professional prospects.

Convincing people about things they do not need or want has become crucial for many businesses, public organisations and employees. In some contexts this is not a big deal: calculative and even cynical attitudes dominate. Some people do the job, and do not expect anything beyond a pay cheque. But most people want something more than that. They want a sense of meaning in their work, and to feel as if they are doing something worthwhile. The cruel fact is that many jobs are experienced by their occupants as meaningless.[21] Creating a sense of worthiness in this kind of work is a challenge.

Branding offers one solution. It helps to transform what are often dull jobs into something that sounds exciting and interesting. Instead of creating packaging for toothpaste, people can say they work with a brand. What are clean teeth compared with a deeper meaning and love for the toothpaste? Instead of selling overpriced vodka, people can say they help to create purity, clarity and perfection. Instead of teaching bored students and writing pointless research articles, you can say you are a world-class scholar with infinite possibilities.

All this is far from easy. Branding activities are often met with indifference or cynicism. Employees often ask critical questions. To ensure that branding works, organisations need to gag the killjoys. Moaning and groaning are often marginalised and good news is celebrated. Denying reality can be helpful in all this. It calls for cultures of positivity. We will look at this topic in the following chapter.

8

Culture-Induced Stupidity

Tell us something enjoyable!

How do you avoid talking about negative things? This was a very practical problem that a group of people working for a newspaper were trying to deal with. Some time ago one of us did a study of a daily tabloid newspaper.[1] We witnessed how it operated, how decisions were made, and how people working there thought.

One of the most important events at the newspaper each month was the review meeting. It was one of the few times when all the major people in the organisation came together, a basic organisational ritual. Members of the tribe gathered and expressed commitment to a shared set of values. But instead of a totem pole they focused on headlines. The stated aim of these meetings was to review what they had done right and what they had done wrong in the previous month, and perhaps to learn from this. The meeting was one of the few places where senior people at the paper could ask big questions about what they were doing and how it might change.

The meetings had a typical routine. When senior people from each department at the newspaper shuffled into the room, they were faced with a wall covered with the front page of all the 'best-sellers'. Another wall was covered with 'disaster' issues.

There were about twice the number of front pages on the best-seller wall as there were on the disaster wall, as the first covered all work days and the second only weekends and the worst-selling day per week. After the obligatory small talk was out of the way, the group started to discuss declining sales figures. They all found this a bit depressing. One of the editors chipped in: 'Tell us something enjoyable!' They quickly changed the topic to some success stories, such as issues which had sold particularly well, but as they worked their way through the best-selling issues, a sense of confusion arose. The people in the room had little or no idea why one issue had outsold another. Sometimes a relatively dull issue had sold well while an issue with an eye-catching news scoop had done poorly. The pattern of sales seemed to be almost random. The same was true for disaster issues.

Naturally, people in the room tried their best to understand why it was that some issues sold well while others did not. They offered all sorts of theories: 'It's Monday, so sales are down'; 'It's a holiday, so sales are up'; 'People are changing their buying behaviour, so sales are down'; 'The weather was bad, people are watching TV, so sales are down'; 'The weather was good, people are on the beaches, so sales are down'. The result was a system of 'almost Ptolemaean complexity'. But at the root of it all was a very simple but seemingly unshakeable assumption: great front-pages sell newspapers.

On the surface, this meeting was all about going through the successes and failures of the month and providing a set of random explanations. But if you look a little closer, you can see functional stupidity at work. The people in the meeting knew that dark clouds hung over the newspaper industry, but they were not really interested in hearing the bad news. They spent far more time reviewing their successes than their failures. When forced to consider bad news, they came up with all sorts of folk theories about why this might have happened. Any attempts to take a more scientific or systematic look at the situation were laughed off. Instead, they reverted again and again to their favourite explanation – based on their deeply shared common belief – that it is headlines that sell newspapers. This was despite the fact that they had evidence right before their eyes that it was not necessarily so.

Maintaining a deeply held belief in the face of huge amounts of evidence to the contrary is a classic marker of functional stupidity. At the newspaper, a shared culture of newsmaking was built around the belief that headlines strongly affect sales, even though this probably was not the case. In many ways this belief was very functional – wrong but still of value. People liked the meeting, it was entertaining to see the headlines that were 'good' and (though less so) 'bad'. There was a good atmosphere: people cracked jokes and exercised their sarcasm. The meeting worked as a good organisational ritual. It gave people a chance to meet and express their common understandings and beliefs about newspaper work.

For the people who met here, making news was about entertainment, giving an unsophisticated audience what they wanted: celebrity gossip and short articles. The people present recreated their cultural universe and guided the work within the newspaper. It gave them a common sense of identity, marshalled their activities and kept them focused. It helped people feel sure when every twenty-four hours they had to make fast decisions about how to fill forty-eight pages of the newspaper: what to include, what to highlight, what to put on the front page, the back page, how to design the headline. All of this helped to ease the way through the reaffirmation of a shared culture. But it was not on the agenda; it was a tacit function. As a result, they spent a lot of valuable time addressing something that is most likely to be a non-issue: the direct effect of head-lines on sales. Focusing on this and basing their work on false assumptions meant that the newsmakers overlooked many of the profound changes that were going on in the industry, some of which would eventually become an existential threat.

Organisational culture calls for people to take certain assumptions and beliefs for granted and refrain from think-ing about them. If the people working at the newspaper were to have begun to think seriously about the (non-)relationship between their assessment of the quality of the headlines and the actual sales, the entire organisational ritual would have been ruined. Being mindless about this helped to recreate and rein-force the organisational culture.

Marching to the same tune without thinking about it

Most organisations are held together by a stubborn attachment to an overall set of beliefs, a common language and practice. This is what is known as organisational culture. According to the anthropologist Clifford Geertz, culture provides the meaning human beings use to interpret their experiences and guide their actions.[2] As soon as human groups come together for a prolonged period of time they create a shared culture. It gives them a common way of understanding the world and deciding what needs to be done.

Like any other kind of human group, organisations develop cultures. This is a system of common symbols and meanings. It provides 'the shared rules governing cognitive and affec-tive aspects of membership in an organization, and the means whereby they are shaped and expressed'.[3] Culture tells people what exists, how one should relate it, how things should be and what is important to strive for.

Some cultures value collectivism while others value individualism; some focus on quality, others on high productivity. Some firms proclaim a sales orientation, others a long-term customer orientation. Some organisations have highly committed employees while others have highly exploited human resources. In one organisation, rules may be viewed as strict, almost holy principles to be obeyed at all costs. In another, they could be seen as loose guidelines that can be bypassed. Age may be viewed as a source of wisdom in one firm, a sign of inertia in another. Some cultures celebrate hierarchy and differentiation, others egalitarianism and community. Pepsi and CCC (to be addressed below) offer nice contrasts.

Culture comes from a wide range of sources in an organisation – top management is only one of them. Often people at the top are less in control of the culture than they would like to think. The reality is that most people throughout the organisation play a role in creating the culture. In his study of a hi-tech company, Gideon Kunda noticed that power to shape culture was 'clearly possessed by those invested with formal authority and high status', but the firm's 'open and shifting environment, reputation, status and real rewards are in the hands of numerous, often unknown, others'. Everyone being able to create and shape culture might sound attractive. Kunda was not so sure. In these kinds of meritocratic cultures 'agents of control are everywhere', he wrote. 'One is surrounded and constantly observed by members (including oneself) who, in order to further their own interests, act as spokespersons and enforcers of the organizational ideology.'[4]

When there is a 'strong' culture, there is also likely to be a strong tendency for people to think in homogeneous ways. Culture does the thinking for them. It can give them a sense of integration and direction, but it can also trap them in set ways of understanding the world.

Often individuals internalise a strong culture. Their sense of who they are becomes almost indistinguishable from what the company is. As one partner in an accounting firm put it: 'At one level we are completely independent, but we all march to the same tune without even thinking about it.'[5]

Compass or prison?

Organisational culture is a compass that gives people direction, but it is also a prison that limits their freedom.[6] Culture guides and integrates, but also blinds and stifles thinking.

A cultural compass makes it easier to find your way at work. It directs you in what to think, feel, say and do. Often it works automatically. You don't have to think that much about basic issues, and it allows you to move around an organisation without too many problems. When you follow the compass, you get along with other people in the organisation. The cultural compass at Pepsi pointed staff towards competition and chasing market share. Delivering results was the only thing that really mattered. Complications that might come from family commitments, loyalty and friendship were to be ignored.

Culture can also imprison people. This is what happens when shared beliefs become a shared blindness. When all people in an organisation think in the same way, they also find it hard to imagine anything outside their narrow cultural universe. Culture is partly unconscious, an assortment of ideas, beliefs and meanings that we take for granted and rarely think about in any sustained way. Certain values in an organisation are seen as self-evident; we think they are undoubtedly superior. When we stop reflecting on the values of the organisation, an organisation can start to operate like a psychic prison. This is what happened at the newspaper. Despite lots of evidence to the contrary, the newsmakers remained locked into the

assumption that it was headlines that sold papers and that discussions around this would improve the situation.

Strong organisational cultures are often fuelled by powerful unconscious forces.[7] For instance, people can start to treat
leaders as father figures who they imagine can punish or protect
them. Emotions infuse many organisational cultures. Sometimes cultures can be paranoid: in these kinds of organisations,
people feel that the environment is hostile. They are oversensi-
tive to critique. Other organisations can have an obsessive need
for order. Many bureaucracies are characterised by obsessive
and often irrational rule-following. In these kinds of cultures,
openness, freedom or creativity is viewed as a sign of disorder.
Fantasies about lack of control and chaos make people nervous.
As a result, organisational members are eager to punish even
the mildest rule-breaking.

Organisational culture is often used to control subordinates. A strong culture means that employees think similar
things. This liberates people in the firm from being disturbed
by alternative ideas. It also has some benefits for employees: it
can help them feel comfortable and secure. In some cases, the
culture can function so smoothly that they hardly notice it at
all. Undisputed assumptions rule.

Cultures of optimism

All organisational cultures are to some extent unique. However
there are themes that many of the organisations we have looked
at share. One of these is optimism. This is the idea that you
should always look on the bright side and do your best to be
upbeat. You do this by encouraging an unbroken stream of
upbeat messages. Crucially, negative stories and news should
be avoided.

One organisation that was seized with a culture of optimism

was the Finnish mobile phone-maker Nokia. In their in-depth study of the company, Timo Vuori and Quy Huy found that the organisation was dominated by a widespread preference for optimism.[8] Middle managers were extremely hesitant to share bad news. 'If you were too negative, it would be your head on the block,' one middle manager explained. People working in the company tended to jib at asking critical questions – both of their boss as well as each other. One middle manager described how: 'Nobody wanted to rock the boat … I didn't want to be labelled as a mean person who was constantly criticising the hard work of others.' Another pointed out that: 'Critique was seen as negative; the mindset was that if you criticise what's being done, then you're not genuinely committed to it.' Middle managers tended to focus on creating good-news stories. One person described how middle managers 'wanted to give them [senior managers] good news … not a reality check'. Another described how 'the message about each product area had to be kept positive so [the units] would be allowed to continue [to operate]'.

Top management were seduced by this relentless stream of good news. When they found they were not receiving the upbeat news that they wanted, then they simply replaced someone who was a bearer of bad tidings with someone else who was more optimistic. 'New blood' with a 'can-do' attitude tended to be favoured. One middle manager described how top management 'trusted these people when they said it's going to work out. They had blind faith. The management team … knew a lot of people – but they picked some young, fast-talking guy who said: "I have this little trick, I'll fix this thing."' The top management team were largely unable to make accurate judgements about these optimistic promises because they had little or no background in the technical aspects of the job. Instead, what they were more interested in was the business plans that were presented. One senior manager described how: 'People [in Nokia] learned to speak the [new technical] language quickly; they became quasi-experts. They gave the impression that they understood [this new area], but [I realised later] it was only skin-deep.' This meant the company became committed to increasingly unrealistic timescales and projects. When things went wrong, they were often overlooked or covered up with a sheen of good news or pseudo-expertise. All this was useful for people in the short term: it meant that top managers could tell their investors they were doing something about the strategic challenges they faced. It also meant that middle managers could hang on to their job, avoid finding themselves in uncomfortable situations and keep their division open. But the relentless optimism gave rise to serious problems in the longer term. It meant that timescales kept on slipping, and some of Nokia's new products which were supposed to be responses to Apple's iPhone were either of inadequate quality or late to the market. This meant Nokia's position as industry leader was eroded and it was eventually taken over by Microsoft.

Another place where we found a culture of optimism was CCC, a renowned and rapidly growing IT consultancy with about 500 staff.[9] When one of us studied the firm, we noticed that employees were encouraged to look on the bright side of the organisation. 'Don't criticise if you don't have a constructive suggestion' was an important norm. Moaning and groaning were cardinal sins. This stopped any 'negative' thoughts being shared. When no one in the organisation shared problems or contradictions that they came across, individuals started to feel that any negative experiences they had were either mistaken or just an exception. A culture of positivity made it feel odd when you faced a problem. It was even more odd to talk about it.

People who did indeed register problems were likely to start to think that there might be something wrong with them, as they were the only ones who seemed to be bothered.

There are apparently many good things about being optimistic. At CCC it meant that employees were motivated. Because uncomfortable issues went unmentioned, there was an absence of conflicts. This meant that people in the firm were more likely to get along. They felt that the workplace culture was generally positive. But the relentless optimism at CCC had some downside. It created a reluctance to face up to problems. The emphasis on being positive meant that setbacks, bad news and difficulties that did not have clear solutions attached to them went unreported. This left little space for doubts and critical thinking. At CCC, it meant that when problems arose during a serious downturn in the economy, the organisation was slow to respond. It didn't want to dwell on the negative, so it preferred to overlook anything that smacked of bad news.

Cultures of change

One thing executives are frequently very optimistic about is change. They assume that it is always for the best – no matter what the change actually is. This change fixation is supported by a bloated change-management industry whose various experts and advisers make their living by propagating the need for drastic changes and promises of great accomplishments. Every new management fashion offers an opportunity for ever more change. When organisations become fashion victims, they start too many projects – many of which are dropped too soon or performed with too little enthusiasm.[10] The results are often cynicism and time-wasting. People start to secretly harbour negative expectations from the outset. This tends to make change more difficult next time. If it happens too often, organisations can get stuck in what Eric Abrahamson has called the 'repetitive change syndrome'.[11]

A hi-tech company that one of us studied had a serious case of repetitive change syndrome.[12] The firm was undertaking a cultural change project. It started with optimistic ideas about promoting a customer orientation, developing visible leadership and facilitating teamwork. All units in the firm ran workshops to discuss these issues. After the workshop, they reported what they had done. Then nothing happened. Top management believed all the units were feeling inspired and had continued to work on these themes. Middle managers expected that top management were driving the initiative and waited for new instructions. Everyone assumed that someone else was the change agent.

People in the company didn't know about this collective myopia. We only uncovered it because we spoke with people across the company. As we were outsiders, employees would often admit to things they would not tell to colleagues or superiors. Armed with this new-found knowledge, we spoke with two senior managers in the company who were involved with the project. It quickly became clear that they did not want to hear bad news. They started out by saying that they were eager to hear about our findings. Then they added that they understood the change programme had been broadly seen as a success. We told them this was far from being true: the response to their change project was overwhelmingly passive and/or negative. People thought it was based on good ideas but they were frustrated that nothing happened. We relayed some typical responses to the initiative: 'just talk and paper', 'bread and circuses for the people', 'just another sign of top management hypocrisy'.

The senior managers listened. When it became time for

them to respond, they suddenly changed their talk. They said that they had realised that the change project hadn't worked, but they were not really responsible. They had only got involved fairly late. The CEO and CTO owned the project. They blamed others for the misfortunes. It quickly turned out that these managers were not interested in more detailed feedback. They didn't want to learn why the initiative had not worked. They just wanted the programme to be forgotten about as quickly as possible. Some time later, one of us described this case to a group of managers during an executive development programme. Most seemed to recognize the process and outcome. One of the managers on the course responded: 'It ends like this every bloody time.' Careful feedback, learning, doing it better the next time? No. Bad news and honest feedback are usually avoided. Organisational amnesia usually wins the day. All that is sought for is positive news about change. Any other form of feedback is bad for your reputation, bad for your self-esteem and bad for your career. So when there is a chance, unwelcome feedback is swept under the carpet. Deliberate ignorance and mindlessness protect people from feeling obliged to think through issues and contribute to more rational organisational behaviour. The ideal of learning and rationality is preached. Functional stupidity is practised.

Cultures of now

As well as being optimistic, many organisations have a strong emphasis on the present. The present (and the near future) counts more than the past. Managers think in the short term because they are evaluated by their superiors and colleagues on their short-term results. Some managers say that 'Our horizon is today's lunch' and like to make quips like 'I know what you did for me yesterday, but what have you done for me lately?'[13]

This short-term mentality equates to an endemic lack of responsibility. Managers are keen to claim responsibility for things that have already worked out. This means 'big corporations implicitly encourage scapegoating by their complete lack of any tracking system to trace responsibility. Whoever is currently and directly in charge of an area is responsible – that is, potentially blamable – for whatever goes wrong there, even if he has inherited others' mistakes.'[14]

Sometimes things go wrong and a negative outcome or a growing awareness of a problem emerges, often triggering 'blame time'. Rarely are there in-depth investigations of who is truly responsible for a bad result. Rather political expediency and limited accountability are what counts. Actors will bypass responsibility for bad outcomes, just as they rush to assume it for positive results.

Talk and appearance – their behaviour in 'high-visibility' situations such as presentations to senior managers – may matter more for employees' promotion than solid work and competence – what they have actually accomplished. In cultures that value action and decisiveness, senior people often rely on their perceptions. Lengthy investigation, deep analysis, careful reflection and rational decision-making are usually avoided.

Most organisations feed this culture of now. They place a huge premium on the present and the near future while forgetting the past and entirely ignoring the medium or distant future (except in sporadic jargon-filled mission statements). An exponent of the dominant recipe for senior managers is Dan Eliasson, head of the national police force in Sweden. The publication of a book on the treatment of nine police employees involved several very serious allegations of severe bullying, ostracism and even baseless criminal complaints against police

officers who were considered to have been critical of ineffi-
ciency and poor working conditions. In an interview Eliasson
responded: 'My mission is to create a strong, open and empa-
thetic organisation here and now. I won't spend time dwelling
on historical injustices.'[15] These were the words of a man well
suited to the culture of here and now. Like many who ply their
careers in an age of functional stupidity, he knew which way
to look.

Cultures of uniqueness

Another common theme in many contemporary firms is the
idea that they are unique. We found this theme at work in
CCC, an IT consultancy we briefly discussed above. Managers
and other employees repeatedly told us that the work climate
was great. People had excellent relationships with one another.
There was a close sense of community across the firm. The
organisational structure was flat. Staff thought this firm was
unique, and the best in its field. Their clients were very satisfied,
they were growing fast, they had high profit margins and very
low turnover. 'Fun and profit' were the overall values. The CEO
emphasised the firm's ability to create a positive work climate:
'If there's anything we're good at it's this, we are damned good
at this.' This was viewed as affecting commitment and work
cooperation. People stayed in the firm and were willing to put
in extra work hours. The culture was based on a 'we-feeling'
and loyalty. There was a strong group pressure to help out.
Many employees felt that they could work hard at CCC. They
really made an extra effort, they said.

CCC was established at a time when the market for IT
consultancy and bespoke software development was expanding quickly. The firm talked up its unique 'business concept',
which involved combining IT expertise with knowledge of

management and strategy. Consultants were encouraged to establish contacts with senior managers in client companies. Their aim was to make IT into a top management issue rather than a concern of the IT department. 'This is our strength, this is what we're good at,' one consultant told us.

Most people in the firm believed that CCC's success was largely a result of their fantastic business concept. One consultant said: 'Linking the development of a new system to the customer's business concept and area of operations is our basic philosophy.' Another said: 'I don't believe we are any better [than other companies] from a purely technical point of view. We are better at some things. And that is precisely the fundamental business concept: management and IT development. But we are no better at IT development, perhaps worse in some cases. But on the management side – our way of handling customers – that's where we're better. Our target group is corporate managements, not IT departments.'

A few employees had a rather different picture of the firm's business concept. They pointed out that very few people had much expertise in management or strategy. The vast majority of employees were programmers and systems analysts. This suggested that the business concept might be rather hollow. Talking about developing as well as implementing strategic IT solutions sounds much better than what people were actually doing – programming.

Some things helped to preserve people's pride in this business model. A few projects in line with the ideal of doing strategic IT were highlighted. People also stressed development: they claimed that while they might be doing operational work now, in the future they would be doing strategic work. Some interpreted the 'strategic' aspect of the company's work as having contact with senior people. By focusing on the future and using unconventional interpretations, the 'strategic' aspect of the business concept was preserved.

A few years later, we spoke with a handful of senior managers who had worked at CCC at the time, but had since left the company. One of them told us that the business concept was 'a myth, a sales trick'. 'We did not have that type of competence among the consultants. We did not have that type of management consultants,' he told us.

> It was a skilfully fantasised and carefully nurtured myth – I claim somewhat maliciously. But I think it is true, also. I still don't think there is anything wrong with doing so, because it worked at the time. That is not a bad character. If the consultants feel that we are good at combining management and IT – fine. They were happy about it, it worked in their projects and earned money through programming, that's what it was all about.

The shared belief in the 'unique' business concept worked as a social glue and identity booster. It guided employees' sense of how they saw themselves and the company. It bound them together and helped them feel good about themselves. It allowed them to tell themselves: 'We don't just do programming, we do strategic work' and 'We are one of a kind.' This seemed to work, even though it didn't stand up to the reality test.

However, this obsession with the uniqueness of their business model came with problems. Managers who came from other firms sometimes felt that their colleagues were 'a mutual admiration club'. They assumed that CCC was the best, and did not think there was much to be learned from other firms. In some parts of the company, managers took the firm's ideas too seriously. For instance, some subsidiaries took its business concept of fusing IT and strategic advice to heart. They recruited experienced, qualified and expensive people who could offer both IT and strategic expertise. However these individuals turned out to be overqualified for the simpler and less costly tasks that customers typically asked for.

Cultures of flatness and community

Alongside a celebration of the uniqueness of the firm, employees at CCC talked a lot about how flat the organisation was. There was little hierarchy, we were told. Subordinates had a lot to say about appointments of new managers. They could veto candidates they did not approve of. Managers were expected to socialise with staff, be excellent at communicating with people, great raconteurs, be supportive and be a visible presence at parties and other social events. On top of all this, they should be liked by their subordinates. This was all part of the 'fun-and-profit' culture that was espoused.

Hierarchy is hard to avoid, particularly when a firm grows. However, individuals are often inclined to overlook this. At CCC, some people noticed there was a widening distance between themselves and the senior executives as the number of employees grew to 500, but many others claimed they were working in a flat company. When we asked one staff member what was different about CCC, he pointed out the lack of hierarchy: there were only two levels in the company – subsidiary managers and consultants. But when we asked whether he could select or even influence his assignments, he said this was not usually the case. His most recent assignment had come when someone showed up and told him which project he would be working on. We asked whether the person who had given him this assignment had managerial responsibilities. 'Yes, he works directly below the subsidiary manager,' he responded. Apparently the flat structure was not so flat after all.

Propagating a rather selective view of the company as flat and social differentials as low reinforced a sense of community and of gladness to work for CCC. Many employees said that they were willing to go the extra mile for the firm. Some staff members we spoke with pointed out that wages were average, while the firm charged clients premium prices. Most thought that was not a big deal, because 'you get so much else out of working in the firm', one consultant told us. This included a positive work climate, a sense of intimacy at work and the feeling of being part of a great company. One client said: 'CCC is not a firm, it's a religion.'

The non-hierarchical view at CCC cultivated a naïve belief that the firm had few power differentials. People followed hierarchy while believing it did not exist. Employees were willing to be seduced. This great company and the excellent managers who run it probably know what they're doing, employees seemed to think. Behind this lurked a wish to avoid cognitive dissonance: they wanted to see an organisation that was in line with their beliefs. A strong feeling of community in the firm reduced the inclination to ask awkward questions. They didn't want to disturb what were relatively harmonious workplace relationships.

Encouraging staff to turn a blind eye to hierarchy had advantages for them: it promoted a good climate, fostered loyalty and pride, supported a sense of community. Employees all found this motivating. The image of the firm was also very positive. It made the company seem as if it was at the cutting edge. Clients were often impressed.

But this aversion to hierarchy was never exclusively good. It came with considerable risks. Seductive messages started to lead the firm astray. This became even more difficult when the firm faced a deep recession that damaged business. CCC was slow and reluctant in responding. With a strong norm of always being positive and a deep belief in the uniqueness and superiority of the firm's business concept, they found it hard to discuss problems openly and frankly. Also community ideals made it hard for managers to take difficult decisions about letting people go. Instead, they swept difficulties under the carpet. As problems piled up, smaller difficulties started to become crises that were impossible to ignore. The shake-up and transition was difficult to cope with.

Conclusion

Cultures make organisations work. A shared culture helps to make collective action happen: it coordinates people, offers a shared sense of purpose and creates a common identity. People see their work reality in similar ways. Conflicts and confusions are reduced. But cultures have drawbacks too. They can create tunnel vision and conformity. Divergent thinking is inhibited. In this sense, a strong culture is a mixed blessing. It works simultaneously as compass and psychic prison. Cultures always include a degree of functional stupidity. It helps coordination and integration, which makes it a key resource for effective organising.

Many of the organisations we have looked at in this chapter, and indeed throughout the book, embody this tension. The stress on being optimistic, being change-oriented, focusing on the present, being unique and being non-hierarchical is common in many organisational cultures. On the one hand, these values come with some strong benefits. Optimism means that people assimilate good news; an obsession with change means that organisations are dynamic; a focus on the present makes people action-oriented; a celebration of uniqueness makes them proud of their company; values of non-hierarchy means they feel they belong to a community. All this can bond people together and help them to be collaborative, engaged in their work and feel good about themselves.

However, each of these common cultural themes creates a dangerous oversight. Optimism means that talking about bad news is taboo. An obsession with change means people drift from one change initiative to another with no real benefits. A strong focus on the present means that they overlook lessons from the past and discount the medium to long-term future. A belief in its uniqueness can make an organisation self-obsessed. An abhorrence of hierarchy means important power differentials are ignored.

Each of these oversights can underpin some serious long-term failures. When you can't mention bad news you often can't adapt to important changes. When firms drift aimlessly between change initiatives they waste resources and generate cynicism. When people look at the past they are unable to learn. Those who grow self-obsessed grow blind to others. Ignoring power makes it harder to get things done.

Sometimes culture can be dominated by functional elements, but at other times stupidity can take over. Usually, cultures are a bit of both. Quite how much is hard to assess more precisely, but they can easily slip from being functional to being stupid. This tends to happen sooner or later.

Part Three

Managing Stupidity

9

Stupidity Management and How to Counter It

Why we need to be stupid

We are often told that organisations need to be knowledge-intensive – they should encourage smart people to do smart things in order to compete in a smart economy. But much of the time, being too smart can be dangerous. It can lead to conflicts, uncertainties, doubts and reduced motivation. People may then not be particularly productive. This is why most effective organisations are also well versed in stupidity. These organisations are not just full of enlightenment, reflection and knowledge. In many cases they actively discourage these possibly subversive qualities.

Earlier in the book, we cited management gurus who claimed that the most effective way for firms to remain competitive is to 'hire smart people and let them talk to one another' (p. 24.[1] Although this sounds great, it could be very risky. Smart people talking openly can come up with dangerous ideas. These ideas might not just be about how to create more advanced financial models to make very rich people richer, or brilliant ways to market more cola. Instead, these smart people might start asking questions. They might look at the awkward truth behind many organisational practices. They might see empty shams in arrangements and ideas that senior management prize. Encouraging smartness may lead people to reflect on bigger issues like the overall purpose of their work. It could also lead people to query organisational arrangements. They might start asking for justification for common practices and unreasonable inequalities. All these questions are likely to make many people feel a little uncomfortable.

Given these potential difficulties, it should not be so surprising that stupidity management is an important activity for managers – although it is never presented in explicit ways.

Stupidity management involves interventions that reduce or narrow thinking at work. The stupidity manager tries to make sure that people don't transgress the mindsets prescribed by the organisation and industry. These common assumptions are to be taken for granted. People should concentrate on the means, not the ends.

There are many tools at people's disposal to boost stupidity. These include culture, branding initiatives, referring to industry best practice, organisational structures and systems and leadership. Organisations often want fervent acceptance of things that could be challenged: visions, strategies, fashionable ideas, change initiatives, structures and human resource management procedures, to name a few. Challenging all these things could lead to pluralism, conflict, confusion, endless debate and ultimately, indecision. To deal with these threats, stupidity management is sometimes necessary.

The vice chancellor of the university that one of us works at recently gave a speech. 'We must make sure that the organisation becomes more effective,' he said. 'Decisions need to be implemented. No longer can decisions be viewed as arguments in a debate.' Here is a senior figure put out by the surplus of independent thinking and discussion. He is worried that people insist on thinking and expressing their own views rather than assuming that top management is sure to know best.

Stupidity management poses a dilemma. Greater functional stupidity can have benefits. It can facilitate decision-making, create a good workplace climate, safeguard people's sense of self, and offer a sense of direction. But too much functional stupidity may have drawbacks. It can obstruct clever decision-making and problem-solving, build a conformist workplace, undermine identities, and desensitise people to problems.

The two sides of stupidity management go together. This means that any budding stupidity manager faces a trade-off. Do they want more stupidity and functionality, or do they want more smartness and less functionality? Whereas in some situations it may be beneficial to make a quick decision that people don't question, in others the manager might want to encourage decision-making to be as thoughtful as possible. But they should also be willing to accept the time, resources and effort this will require. After all, free thinking and open discussion creates conflicts and disorder, as well as change that people may not be willing to follow.[2]

Decision-making is easier if you reduce complexity by asking people not to think too much. It takes less time, energy and cognitive resources. It also avoids the risk of getting bogged down in analysis paralysis. But when you limit people's thinking, you lose a lot of information, you don't fully interrogate your ideas, and you may end up making bad decisions. We often prefer to save time and energy rather than consider all the issues. As a result, decisions regularly involve a significant degree of functional stupidity. This is bound to happen when organisations imitate others, when top managers confuse PowerPoint presentations with solid information, and when organisations create new structures without thinking about how they will work in practice.

Workplace relations can sometimes be improved if openness and the potential conflicts this can bring are curtailed. When firms have a shared culture, it can mean that people think and behave in the same way, they talk in the same kind of language, and celebrate a shared identity. This creates consensus, positivity and strong communal bonds and facilitates a shared sense of purpose. But it also comes with increased conformity and limitations on thinking.

Identities are secured and strengthened when people start to define themselves in closed, secure and stable ways. This happens when people confidently state things like: 'I am a leader', 'I am a great communicator', 'I'm a change agent', or: 'I'm part of an elite firm which only employs the best and the brightest.' In an increasingly fragmented world, the identities we try to build for ourselves are often not as reliable as they seem. The leader may find she has no followers. The alpha communicator might find himself being misunderstood, or even worse, ignored. The change agent might find she is just another follower of fashion. The best and brightest may be seen by outsiders as brainwashed organisational automatons. When this happens, a hard-won sense of self can rapidly evaporate.

People deal with the contradictions and dilemmas that crop up at work through stupidity management. It helps them buy into fluffy ideals that are valued by external audiences. It enables them to develop a faith in systems they can see do not work as they should. It can persuade people to perceive corporate imitation as innovation, or help them develop a zeal for meaningless tasks. Ultimately a good helping of stupidity management can aid people to accept much of the empty talk and baseless ideas that are hallmarks of contemporary corporate life.

To explore how stupidity helps people to deal with contradictions, let's take a closer look at a typical scene from corporate life: an off-site meeting. One person who attended the meeting described how: 'A consultant led a session on "how we feel toward each other." It's just an opportunity to see how you handle yourself in that kind of session. The only one who believed all that California bathtub crap was the consultant. I'd believe it too for fifteen hundred bucks a day.'[3] Clearly this employee did not find the session particularly enjoyable. However, those who set up and ran the session would probably not rejoice to hear it described as 'California bathtub crap'.

But let's do a quick thought experiment. Imagine you are managing this unenthusiastic seminar participant. He comes to you after the off-site and starts grousing about the 'California bathtub crap'. You too may have some misgivings, but the top brass told you to roll out a relationship-building session to your staff, and you're trying to make the best of it.

What options do you have to deal with this in-house critic? You say: 'You're probably not negative about everything in the whole session. You must have got something out of it' ... 'Think about the positive aspects' ... 'That was just your experience. Maybe you should be more open' ... 'Other people liked the event. Maybe your view is just an outlier' ... 'You're entitled to your feeling, but sharing your negativity with them may spoil it for the others' ... 'You're just being simply too negative, and coming across as a grouch. That is bad for you.' You might point out: 'The company doesn't appreciate people who don't make positive contributions and can only moan.' Or: 'It's up to the participants to use the session productively. Any negative aspect is your own failure to get it and co-create a powerful learning experience.' All this can be followed up with hints that your dissatisfied subordinate may not be leadership material.

Some of these tactics may work. If they do, then our grumbler might turn to some stupidity self-management: 'Perhaps there were some insights in the session after all' ... 'Do I need to be a little more open-minded and less critical?' ... 'Maybe my evaluation is not so grounded in reality' ... 'I should support others so they can get something out of it' ... 'I don't want to appear to be negative, so I'll try to be more positive' ... 'I need to help create a good workplace climate and stop myself from so much groaning and moaning.' Or simply: 'I need to watch my step here.'

Of course, stupidity self-management may happen – even without that help from the manager. But often stupidity and stupidity self-management work in tandem. When this happens, they can save the 'California bathtub crap' as well as its champions. They can also ensure that sceptics don't have such bad experiences and feel shame for not speaking up about the crap.

Behind these specific actions are likely to be matters like leadership, structures and formal processes, following fashion, organisational cultures, appraisal practices, career systems and other forms of more systematic stupidity management.

We don't know what the outcome of this little instance was. It is likely that the person only shared their feelings with the researcher. But the story is familiar. Similar scenes abound in corporate life, but are often contained. The lubricant of functional stupidity, aided by the engineering work of stupidity management and the careful maintenance work of stupidity self-management, helps to make the organisational machinery tick. At least on the surface.

Stupidity management: some tricks of the trade
There are many ways managers try to encourage functional stupidity. However, there are four common forms that we think

are worth highlighting: authority, seduction, naturalisation and opportunism.

The first trick of stupidity management is using *authority*. This is when a manager makes use of her formal position in the hierarchy and their ability to distribute punishments and rewards. Often, actually using rewards or punishments is not as effective as subtle reminders that they could be used. Respect for authority discourages more junior staff from thinking too much. People are often reminded that 'the boss knows best' or that 'leadership will show followers the way'. People are made to think that as subordinates they should follow policies and orders. They should focus their minds on their task, not asking what should be done or what assumptions are being made. This can train people into a sort of thoughtlessness. They slowly get used to not thinking outside of their hierarchical level, formal routines, accepted ideas and established systems. Instead they put their effort into making systems work more efficiently. They don't ask whether it is the right system in the first place. Milgram's famous studies of authority and obedience showed clearly how many people blindly followed authority and refrained from thinking by themself.[4]

The second trick that managers can use is *seduction*. When they do this, they try to persuade people by enlisting attractive ideas or arrangements. A flurry of buzzwords, an impressive PowerPoint presentation and a well-dressed consultant can easily divert from a lack of substance. Being spellbound can make your audience feel great. Attractive stories about corporate greatness – now or to come – are often mindlessly accepted and retold with great enthusiasm. The future is usually a great thing for any stupidity manager – it is not sullied by the mistakes of the past or the problems of the present. People can be seduced by being encouraged to think things are great. Being upbeat, assuming that change is always good and lauding the organisation's excellence are all vital parts of this.

A third trick of the stupidity manager's trade is to make even the strangest practice appear to be natural. This we call *naturalisation*. The assumptions that are made in an organisation, its view of reality and its dominant goals need to be seen as self-evident. This involves the stupidity manager going out of their way to convince colleagues that 'There are no alternatives'. They might do this by reminding them that 'This is how we've always done it', or even better: 'This is how everybody else is doing it.' For instance, they may point out that you need to have strategies, budgets, annual appraisals, CSR initiatives (or whatever else) because everyone else in your industry has these things. By doing this, they may project even the most tenuous arrangement as normal. If everybody else is doing something, then it seems self-evident you should do the same. It is just a natural thing to do.

A final trick is the appeal to *opportunism*. You do this by speaking to people's self-interest. When incentives are stacked up in the right way, people can be schooled to avoid asking too many difficult questions. This may mean buying into trends that they know to be questionable because good things will follow. An employee might be swayed into thinking: 'OK, this may be an empty management fashion, but the CEO is interested and the project will support our unit's position in the firm. It may also really work.' A touch of stupidity management may help the opportunist to disguise naked self-interest and show commitment to empty ideas. With enough incentives, it is easier to explain away and rationalise even the gravest doubts. Functional stupidity can be a useful way to reduce or even avoid unpleasant feelings that come with opportunism.

Functional stupidity can be accomplished through authority, seduction, naturalisation and opportunism. Often there is a mix of these elements. When any or all of these stupidity strategies work well, they can help us to minimise anxiety, avoid feelings of emptiness, sidestep doubt and neutralise moral dilemmas.

In some organisations, one in particular of these stupidity-management techniques dominates. In hierarchical organisations like the military, displays of authority are used to encourage people not to think too much. By invoking rank in an army unit, you can often duck even the trickiest questions. In a firm dominated by a 'transformational leader', seduction may come foremost. By appealing to grand visions and exciting images of the future, these organisations can help people to avoid thinking and go straight to believing. In bodies wrapped in tradition or convention, such as many public-sector organisations, naturalisation is common. Following what has always been done, or doing what others are doing, can become a proxy for careful thinking. Finally in professional service firms, appeals to opportunism can be common. For instance, a consultant can easily be encouraged to overlook problems with a prospective client if they offer a lucrative contract.

More often, these typical tricks of the stupidity management are used in tandem. If we return briefly to Pepsi, we find all four being used together. The strict hierarchy encouraged the Pepsi executives not to think independently or express deviant ideas. They feared that independent thinking would stymie their careers. The Marine Corps of the Business World were seduced into believing that they belonged to the best, brightest and toughest. This meant they avoided asking the kind of negative questions that a more neutral and sober observer might. By portraying a steep hierarchy and fierce competition as natural, Pepsi made executives allergic to raising issues that might shake their position in the corporate pecking order. Finally, there was a strong self-interest of executives buying into the dominant cultural universe. Of course, they could cynically play along and privately confess that this was corporate bullshit nobody seriously believed in, but it is likely that the rewards and status that come with such a position would slowly remind them that manure can grow roses.

Stupidity management at CCC

One company we have already looked at which is quite effective in fairly soft and productive stupidity management is CCC.[4] This IT consultancy firm worked mainly with seduction. Through a strong process of socialisation, new recruits were encouraged to develop a deep-seated love for the company. Through the use of rich symbolism, people were guided into seeing their work as extremely meaningful. Through being given the right to veto the appointment of managers, subordinates were encouraged to think of themselves as working in an egalitarian workplace. Through having a warm and open style of leadership, employees viewed the company like an extended friendship group. When all this was put together, it created a strong feeling of identification with the firm. It started with a one-week 'project management philosophy' course, which everybody from new subsidiary managers to secretaries had to take part in.

The tone at CCC was set by the founders. They recruited people from their network, paraded values like community, informality, social activities and openness, and stressed the firm's uniqueness. The founders were admired. They nurtured their image and taught other managers how to do leadership. This together with selective recruitment created a homogeneous organisation and meant there was little in the way of encouragement to think differently.

It had the effect of disarming suspicion and reducing critical thinking. Trust and a willingness to be seduced were encouraged. Employees seemed to think that this fine company and its fine managers knew what they are doing. A strong feeling of community reduces the inclination to stand out. Conformity breeds a desire not to disrupt harmony by thinking like an outsider. People were constantly reminded that they should see themselves as being loyal group-members.

People were encouraged to be to be positive and optimistic. Fun and profit were the slogans. They were reminded 'not to be critical if you didn't have constructive suggestions'. Moaning and groaning were to be avoided. This was not seen as repressive. Instead, it was a way of committing to a happy community and a fine workplace climate. However it also entailed an implicit risk of sanctions. This meant that seduction and anxiety coincided. By preventing people from airing criticism, they started to avoid recognising problems such as inconsistencies between corporate messages and practices. And given the right mood and mindset, you could always disregard or explain away what did not fit your idealised view of the organisation.

Managers were an important part of organisation life and also played a role in activities like parties, corporate cooking classes, and a company choir. This meant the company took up quite a lot of the time of its employees, many of whom were young – the average age was just over thirty. It also meant that managers were well informed about the thoughts and feelings of their employees. It prepared them well to deal with any negative emotions or criticism which might arise.

Encouraging functional stupidity at CCC also had some positive effects for the organisation as a whole. It helped to create a positive climate, a sense of loyalty, pride, identification with the firm, a feeling of community, the experience of work being meaningful, and increased motivation. It also helped to polish the external image of the firm. Consequently, clients were often impressed.

But functional stupidity cuts both ways. It also comes with considerable risks. Blinkers and norms of positivity foster low levels of critical scrutiny and reflection. The ability to learn is reduced. Incoming managers from other firms sometimes felt their new colleagues were a mutual admiration club, with little to learn from outside. But perhaps the most worrying part is that people at CCC had great problems dealing with a deep recession and a rapidly shrinking market. They were allergic to bad news. To pick up signals and communicate awareness of crises was out of tune with the speciality of looking on the bright side of corporate life.

In such a situation, it was time to call off stupidity management. Sadly, this was not easy to accomplish. The effects of skilful stupidity management are often deep and lasting.

Anti-stupidity management

Often the problem that organisations face is not too little functional stupidity, but too much. Society and working life is full of grandiosity – high-flying vision, branding baloney, leadership nonsense, fantasies of the knowledge society and fashionable pseudo-solutions.[5] In this book we have looked at many organisations that have been seduced by grandiosity. They have encouraged their employees to stop thinking outside narrow areas, and this has brought serious consequences. Everyone from CEOs to low-level employees is regularly put at risk of overdosing on stupidity management. We believe that reducing this kind of corporate no-think is one of the most urgent, yet most challenging, issues that organisations face today.

To start to destupidify our otherwise (technically and operatively) smart firms, we need to drop the myth of relentless positivity. In recent years people have been grabbed by the notion of positive thinking. The message is that by looking on the bright side and building up an optimistic demeanour, then you will succeed. The roots of this idea run deep in North American culture and have filled many pages of self-help books. But in recent years, it has taken on the mantle of science. Psychologists like Martin Seligman have promoted the idea that by being optimistic you can succeed in every aspect of your life, including your work. The problem, of course, is that just being optimistic can mean that you overlook some of the very real negative problems that can plague organisations. Relentless optimism may keep us happy for the moment, but it can also mean that we become deluded.

Perhaps instead of encouraging only optimism, organisations should try to build up a virtue that the poet John Keats defined nearly 200 years ago – negative capability. Writing to his brother, Keats described negative capability as the ability to be in 'uncertainties, mysteries, doubts, without any irritable reaching after fact and reason'. For Keats this meant being able to experience, and recognise experiences, and remain open to the world. For him, this found its best expression in poetry. Over the following two centuries people have seized upon this phrase to describe something that is often lacking in our knowledge- and positivity-obsessed culture: the ability to face up to uncertainty, paradoxes and ambiguities.[6] Instead of trying to superficially resolve or ignore them, we should be able to work with them. Negativity capability involves 'the ability to tolerate anxiety and fear, to stay in the place of uncertainty', and so to allow for 'the emergence of new thoughts or perceptions'.[7] According to the political theorist Roberto Unger, negative capability is one of the central motors of economic development. It is the ability to escape from the 'false necessity' of belief that the institutions we work within are natural and enduring. For Unger, our negative capabilities are our ability to autonomously challenge and recreate these institutions in a quest to bring about new forms of wealth creation.[8]

For us, negative capabilities are the ability to think critically – the ability not to be constrained by the false necessities which are set up by rules, routines, cultures, brands, and many more of the mechanisms of organisational life. It means the ability and willingness to ask questions and to be reflective. This means querying the assumptions that we make, asking for and being prepared to give justifications, and considering the outcomes and broader meaning of what we do. Doing this requires mature thinking – something that is sorely lacking in most of our organisations as well as society at large.

Fostering and exercising negative capabilities may be tough. Demands for order, discipline, consensus and optimism often make it hard to ask questions. As we have argued throughout the book, critical thinking takes time and effort. It creates uncertainty and often it upsets people. Ongoing inquiry and reflection might be a virtue in the university seminar room, but it can easily turn into a dangerous vice in the boardroom.

Having said this, we think that negative capabilities are an absolutely essential part of any thriving organisation. It is this capability that can stop organisations becoming ossified into outdated or fashionable mindsets. It is also this capability which can help firms avoid the kind of corporate bullshit that increasingly clogs up so many organisations. It is these negativity capabilities that can help an organisation to learn and hold on to vital lessons from the past. But perhaps most importantly, it is these negative capabilities that can enable an organisation to create new and more thoughtful lines of action.

Exercising negative capabilities

Much has been said about the techniques of critical thinking. Often it is held up as a special skill possessed only by a few great thinkers, path-breaking innovators or political revolutionaries. This may be true when it comes to very sophisticated problems, or when we break with firmly established ideas, but critical thinking is not just something for professional critics. It is a practice that most people can – and sometimes do – engage in.[9] We engage in critical thinking when we ask some fairly simply questions – both of ourself and of others: What is going on here? What do others think is going on here? What the hell do we think is going on here? Let's look at these questions in a little more depth.

Observe

The first thing any good critical thinker does is to observe. This means asking the deceptively simply question: 'What is going on here?' To answer this, critical thinkers need to carefully look and listen, and then try to capture what is going on in the situation. Observations need to be open. It is easy to fall into pre-established categories like leadership, information and decision-making. A good observer looks beyond the categories and sees what people are actually doing.

Good observers note what is not so obvious. Beneath the surface or beyond common sense there may be different things going on. A discussion about strategies may be more about people at work trying to boost their identity as 'strategists'. People listening to a persuasive management guru talking about excellence may be more into enchantment than learning. A manager talking to subordinates may be less about visionary leadership and more about reinforcing their position as immature followers.

If you are trying to solve a business problem, understanding all the facts first and being able to accurately and clearly describe the issues is an excellent start. It is what we, as university teachers, try to get the experienced managers we teach to do. Often they find it hard because they don't want to describe the problem in a broad and open-minded way. They just want to apply a pre-packaged solution. The difficulty here is that it is pretty hard to solve a problem that you don't accurately understand and cannot clearly describe first.

This points to one great pitfall that any good critical thinker has to avoid: premature problem-definition and *solutionism*. As we saw in chapter 3, there is a tendency for skilled people to jump to a solution before they can accurately describe the problem in detail. Avoiding solutionism means stopping oneself – and indeed others – from reaching too fast for the tools. Like a good pathologist or a skilled mechanic, you should spend some time thinking about the problem first.

Interpret

Once you have a good understanding of the issues – and can carefully describe them – the next step is to find out how other people understand it. This involves trying to figure out the way people talk about the issue, what they think and how they see it. The aim at this stage is to answer the question that every good anthropologist asks: 'What do the natives think is happening here?' Your aim is to gather people's views – however wrong-headed or upsetting they might appear – and try to start seeing it their way. This should lead to a number of different perspectives on the very same issue. By asking a range of people, you will quickly find that the same issue can appear to be radically different depending on who you talk with. For the marketing department, it may be about poor branding; for the engineers, poor design; for the financial folks, inaccurate costing. For some people it may not be a problem at all – just an unavoidable issue that we have to live with. Good managers can understand the issue from each of the main groups' perspectives. Really good managers can talk to them in their language. Excellent managers can translate between the different groups' languages – helping marketers to understand engineering-speak (and vice versa).

At this point a second trap raises its head. This is *myopia*. All too often it is easy to feel comforted in your own perspective. Most of us have been trained in a particular professional language and have been rewarded for using it for years. As a result, we quickly become professional idiots who are trapped within this language. 'I have the solution. Now, what is the problem?' is how many operate as true *Fachidioten* (professional idiots). As a result, we see only a narrow aspect of a problem. We turn a deaf ear to all the other voices and ways of understanding an issue. When this happens, we become one-dimensional men and women who are trying to deal with multidimensional issues. Good interpretations resist and transcend fixed ideas.

Question

Having understood how different people describe the same problem, you need to take the next and final step. That is asking questions about these different perspectives. A critical thinker does not naïvely accept what they see on the surface. Nor do they blindly accept the views of others. They need to question their views. They do this by asking the question: 'What the hell is going on here?' This means doing the kind of things that stupidity management typically puts a stop to. It means asking: 'What are the assumptions we are making here?', 'What are the reasons why we are doing this?' and 'What are the wider outcomes or broader meaning of this?' By beginning to ask these disruptive questions, many of the unseen or unthought issues and problems may begin to come to light.

When looking at an issue critically, it is possible to ask a range of questions. You can ask cognitive questions such as: Is this correct? Does this idea or practice stand critical scrutiny? You can pay attention to emotional issues. You might ask yourself: Does this feel OK? Is there some anxiety or fear that I need to take seriously? Or does it feel too good? You might also attend to moral questions like: Is this ethically defensible? What are the wrongs involved here? Finally, you can ask yourself motivation questions: Why is someone doing this? What is driving them? How do they benefit? What do you get out of it? And why are you interested in the first place?

Often the ideas that come up at this stage can be disturbing, both for the person addressing the issue and more often for the organisations. Once you have first-hand impressions from observations, and have scanned the available perspectives, the central questions that you need to start asking are: What assumptions are we making, what are the reasons behind what we are seeing, and what are the wider implications or meanings of this? Answering each of these questions is likely to flush out many of the real issues that have been lurking in the background.

The final trap that can raise its head at this stage is *naïvety*. This happens when you take people – or indeed your own observations and 'solutions' – at face value. All too often there are deep meanings or broader problems which are lurking behind what you see on the surface. By avoiding scepticism and not asking difficult questions, you are likely to simply end up dealing with symptoms and not getting to the deeper causes.

Dispelling stupidity

Critical insights can be provoked in many different ways. We believe some of the following nine processes are a useful trigger for people to engage in critical thinking and serious reflection.

Reflective routines. You could build routines that encourage reflection into projects or your working schedule. In your work group or department, you could try asking critical or reflective questions once a week or once a month. For instance, instead of just asking what you have done this week or month, you could get a sense of what others think you have done. Even simpler questions, like 'Why?', 'Where is the evidence?' or 'What does this mean?' could be useful for flushing out much of the bullshit. In addition to this, you could run 'what the hell' sessions where people are asked to bring along one example of strongly questionable corporate practices they have come across recently. You might create time and space for reflection and thinking. Many public-sector organisations have lectures and seminars with outside experts. Sometimes these are outside the organisation's core business. They are expected to give some broader food for thought. Some more commercial organisations hold lunch seminars. One US boutique investment bank, for example, regularly had an outside speaker with expertise on a topic which was completely unrelated to the firm. This was appreciated by the staff: it provided them with some space and time to think. But it also allowed them to continue their broad education. Sometimes such inputs can just remind people that other ways of thinking are possible.

Devil's advocates. Sometimes it is tough to ask critical questions yourself. Often our internal censor cuts them out. If this is the case, then you can appoint a professional critic – otherwise known as a devil's advocate (DA). There are many PAs, why not also DAs? This is a person whose job is to challenge what is going on, to question, to pose counter-arguments and so on. The idea is that by asking these critical questions, we are forced to think further and articulate justifications. The process might be annoying and sometimes painful, but it typically results in better decisions and less blind optimism. Individuals could find a devil's advocate in the form of a friend or adviser who is willing to ask them the right critical questions, and by doing so force them to think again. A team could choose someone inside it as a devil's advocate – their job would be asking tough questions, poking holes in arguments and strategically undermining consensus. The role of devil's advocate could be supported by allocation of some time and resources (say a half-day per week for doing the observing, interpreting and questioning as sketched in the section above). People could rotate through the role, taking turns. Others could express views to the DA, who then could summarise and then pass them on. Their role is to 'ask anti-stupid questions'.

Post-mortems. We are supposed to learn from our failures, but we rarely do. One of the big reasons for this is that when things go wrong, we look for ways of hiding it. When this happens, organisations and individuals often make the same mistake many times over. As one manager said when one of us presented a study of an organisational change project leading to nothing, apart from wasted time and lower trust in corporate management: 'This happens every bloody time.' If we were actually interested in reducing the risk of mistakes being made again and again, then we would take a long cold look at what went right, and see that what went wrong is a good place to start.

Pre-mortems. Often we learn lessons only when it is too late. A common refrain heard when projects go wrong is 'We could see that coming'. The frequent answer to this is: 'Why didn't you say something?' One way to ensure that people speak up before it is too late is to hold a pre-mortem at the start of a project.[10] This involves a fairly simple routine of saying to the team: 'Imagine you are two years down the line and this project has been a disaster. What do you think went wrong?' Typically, if you have a group of experienced people they will identify a list of issues that typically trip up a project like the one you're setting out on. After you have worked out the top five or ten potential issues, you can use these to start coming up with ways of avoiding the problem in the first place. This kind of exercise tends to do two things. First, it generates preemptive solutions. But perhaps more importantly, it helps to deflate the kind of self-serving biases that so frequently haunt projects.

Newcomers. Often people who are new to an organisation come up with a fresh perspective. They see things that old hands do not. They ask the kinds of questions that are deemed to be taboo by others. All these qualities make newcomers ideal critics. To harness this potential you could ask them questions like: What do you find strange or questionable? What surprised you here? What has struck you as different from other work-places? Do you experience something as exotic or stupid? Have you asked yourself what do they really do here? Answers to any of these questions are likely to be very revealing to the people who have been around for some time.

Outsiders. Sometimes organisations can gain from learning from an outsider. One way to do this is to understand what an outsider sees in your organisation. This might involve inviting people in from other organisations to observe what is happening and report back. Sometimes, this genuine outsider perspective can be revealing. Another way to get an outside perspective is to become an outsider yourself. This means going into another organisation that you are not familiar with to see how it works. For instance you could shadow someone in a different type of organisation for a few days. By doing this, you might begin to see your own organisation and routines with fresh eyes. This is sometimes done in management development programmes. Participants switch organisations, or shadow each other for a work day, and then they get some perspectives.

Engage your critics. Many organisations already have critics, but they do their best not to listen to them. If you are genuinely interested in understanding the systemic stupidities within your firm, then engaging your critics could be useful. This might mean speaking with pressure groups, academics or social movements that have been critical about practices within your industry. It also might mean trying to learn from critics who are inside the organisation, or perhaps from those who have left. Often these critical communities can be a source of pain, but they can also be a source of potential insight. Even if they turn out to be wrong, you might learn something.

Competitions and games. Games can be a useful way of rooting out stupidities. One well-known example is bullshit bingo: people are encouraged to look out for clichés and other meaningless statements and make notes when they hear or see them. The first to spot ten items of bullshit wins a prize. You could also hold a stupidity-spotting competition. People would identify the most stupid organisational arrangements. Anonymous proposals might be made and anonymous voting take place. By giving a degree of humour to these often difficult things, it may be possible to make people less anxious about expressing honest opinions.

Anti-slogans. All too often we take management-speak too seriously. Perhaps we should learn something from 'culture jammers' and start to develop a kind of anti-management-speak.

Concepts like functional stupidity, stupidity management, window-dressing and bullshit bingo could all be part of it. There are a few fine dictionaries of management jargon. How about writing a local dictionary of anti-management jargon? These concepts and anti-slogans can become part of the popular culture of the corporate body, and hopefully serve to remind people not to be too stupid.

Anti-stupidity task force. Much in organisational life is about adding positive projects, structures, systems, procedures and activities. But sometimes the discontinuing or cancellation of activities and arrangements matters much more. Often this is done slowly and informally, but a better and more effective arrangement may be to systematically go through issues and make conscious choices, after careful discussions, about what is to be dropped. In most organisations there is plenty to choose from. These kinds of cancellation projects may face stiff resistance from people with a career interest in a specific issue, or who fear looking bad to the outside world. But the benefits may far outweigh the costs of the operation.

We think it is vital that organisations provide some systematic backup to destupidification. Many of the proposals involve groups of managers, departments and others, but there are of course informal groups within organisations capable of waging insurgency against managerial claptrap. We can imagine clandestine groups springing up in many organisations to challenge the kind of corporate bullshit that we are routinely faced with. In fact it would not be outlandish to call for a wider anti-bullshit movement where people vow to fight against the word viruses of management-speak that have invaded so much of our language. This merry band of anti-bullshit crusaders could easily mount surprise attacks on the worst examples of corporate claptrap. They might learn from the tactics of 'culture jammers' who have created their own perverse examples of advertising to show the stupidities of branding. Instead of a Joe Camel with cancer, the management jargon busters could create management anti-fashions like fat thinking (instead of lean thinking), Level Zero leadership (in place of Level 5), debranding (instead of rebranding), deficiency drives (instead of efficiency drives) and much more. Each of these movements might rid us of some of the pointless management guff that is increasingly clogging the arteries of our organisations and stopping them from actually carrying out their core tasks.

As well as being a collective movement, we think that much anti-stupidity management can be done on the individual level as well. Being reflective is central. This means cultivating your ability to ask about assumptions, give and demand justifications and think about the broader meaning of your work. Doing all these things requires the kind of emotional and intellectual maturity which is sadly all too often discouraged by contemporary organisations (and society at large), but there are ways to support and develop this maturity. Creating time to read, think, cultivate relations, network and develop negative capacities outside workplaces is vital. Anti-functional stupidity is, however, ultimately not a one-band show. It needs to be supported by groups, both informally and formally. It can be systematised and institutionalised. Rather than these endless – and often stupid – measurements of happiness at work, resources could well go into assessments of stupidities there.

Doing anti-stupidity management with finesse and feeling

Doing anti-stupidity management is not easy or uncontroversial. Often it can be dangerous and even career-limiting. People are often unsure about their observations or thinking and they are nervous about expressing any critical or alternative views. And even if they are, in principle, right, it may not be a good thing to point at absurdities – it may create problems. And yet criticism is vital.

When trying to upend stupidities, there are issues to bear in mind. The first is that it can be hard to spot functional stupidities. Often what deserves this label resists assessment. Organisations and work are full of ambiguities and complexities. Stupidities are often in the eye of the beholder, and some have bad eyesight. It is not necessarily that you believe it when you see it. You may see it because you believe it. Sometimes the identification of something stupid is an outcome of self-interest, limited knowledge or bad judgement. In the worst case we just project our prejudices onto the usual suspects (consultants, academics, engineers, top management) and see the stupidities of the others but not our own. Often we remain blind to great stupidities that are right under our eyes. What all this means is that we may need to be humble in our judgements about what is and is not stupid. This requires us to go for reflection rather than just projection.

We also need to be hesitant in assuming that stupidities are always bad. As we have tried to show throughout this book, there are many positive things about stupidity in organisations. Sometimes it can be very useful. Consequently, stupidity should not always be challenged.

We should be wary of hasty anti-stupidity activism. Often there are interests and feelings which are bound up with the stupidities we loathe. Trying to bring them down through anti-stupidity management can easily evoke political and emotional difficulties we may not have expected.

Sometimes we have little choice. Many stupidities are imposed on us and we just have to live with them. When this is the case, one can try to minimise the harm they do through taking them less seriously. But sometimes there is little point in cultivating anti-stupidity against laws or strong pressure from clients and top management. We need to pick our battles.

Finally, dealing with stupidities can often be a costly and difficult business. Dealing with one's own stupidities can lead to existential problems. Often the work of rooting out stupidities in organisational life can take so long and prove so completely thankless that sometimes it is best just to look the other way.

A difficult balance must be struck between the active cultivation, acceptance, mild questioning and direct challenging of functional stupidities. Pragmatism and sensitivity are required. Cognitive and emotional overload as well as political problems need to be considered. Functional stupidity is, after all, a mixed blessing.

But as we have said, anti-functional stupidity is desperately needed – and there are also rewards for this. A more meaningful work experience and making contributions to those who are supposed to be served by organisations – patients, clients, customers, students, the environment, taxpayers, shareholders – can be richly rewarding. And often people are grateful for initiatives and contributions.

Anti-stupidity work needs to be done with finesse and feeling. One needs to be reasonably sure, thoughtful and well formulated. Often it is good to work gradually: talk to others, check observations and interpretations, and raise the questions with people you trust before acting. This is good for making sure you have a point, can express it well, but also have some moral and political support.[11] Acting may involve raising questions and starting discussions. It may also be about taking initiatives, or more organised attempts to decrease stultification. It may lead to some work along the nine lines we suggested above.

At the most general level, anti-stupidity management

requires work in three interrelated realms. First, at the individual level, we should reflect, engage in critical thinking and consider killing off our own stupidities; we need to do anti-stupidity management. Second, it also requires work on the cultural and collective norms. Expressing feelings and thoughts about functional stupidity in social settings should be encouraged and legitimised. Finally, it requires the use of structural arrangements to undermine functional stupidity. This might involve devoting time and resources, making infrastructural arrangements and having formal appointments of individuals and groups to work with anti-functional stupidity.

With some efforts along these lines, a better balance between functionality and stupidity can be accomplished. But one should not pretend that this is easy.

Anti-stupidity management in a hospital clinic

We have painted a gloomy picture of contemporary organisations, but it isn't the entire picture. There are many positive things going on in many workplaces. Many organisations deliver the goods and services required. Given the glut of positive pep talks, we don't need to join this already huge chorus. However, the unreflective practitioner is, our studies indicate, much more common than their more reflective counterpart. The time, ability and interest to reflect is often very limited. We have explored this in these pages. However, let us balance the story with a more positive example.

Stella is the head of a clinic in a Swedish university hospital. She is a highly reflective, critically minded person who is always prepared to question truths and practices. Showing a high level of integrity, she always reacts against unproductive systems, structures, procedures and priorities. She is seen as very competent and loved by her co-workers. But she is not necessarily so loved by senior managers. Let's look at just one example of her actions: her insistence on not spending the clinic's entire budget. In her hospital – as in most organisations – it is usually seen as a sensible thing to spend one's entire budget – even if you don't need to. You can allow yourself some extra advantages through spending the surplus, and why make an extra effort to be economical with resources if you don't have to? Spending the budget may ensure that your allocation continues next year and reduce the risk of budget cuts. Stella, in contrast, is eager to use resources well and stresses that it is good to have a surplus. She explains this to the personnel in an email after mentioning that the clinic did financially extremely well, with high productivity at low cost, but not at the expense of quality.

Why is finance important?
You have all heard the expression 'monopoly money', 'it disappears in the black hole', and there are all kinds of nasty expressions in relation to finance in the public sector. It seems that it is bad to talk about being financially effective, but I say once more: All the money that can be saved through more effective ways of working will contribute to more health care where it is needed. Spending money without any gains for the patients means withdrawing care and treatment from someone else. We have shown that it is possible to make sustainable savings that don't mean we are all 'just running faster'. Our organisation contributes to less stress and to increased control over our own work situation. It is also nice to avoid saving on things that are beneficial for the patients. We don't have to suspend activities that we think are necessary and meaningful. We are not subjected to the 'moral stress' that can occur when you are forced to make savings that affect patients.

You are all part of this clinic's success, and its continuing development. Thanks – once more – for the past year and for being so tremendously fantastic!

This is a good example of thinking independently and taking responsibility. To move outside functional stupidity and narrow mindsets, and pursuit of the mantra that 'everyone is doing this', guides so much of organisational work. Health care is pressed for resources, but a major issue in many cases is not a shortage of resources per se, but people's inability to think through and be responsible for how resources are being used. Anti-stupidity management could be a large part of the solution to many resource problems in many organisations.

In conclusion

In this book we have explored the concept of functional stupidity. For us *functional stupidity is inability and/or unwillingness to use cognitive and reflective capacities in anything other than narrow and circumspect ways*. It involves a lack of *reflexivity*, a disinclination to require or provide *justification*, and avoidance of *substantive reasoning*. Functional stupidity means thinking within the box: overadaptation to set ways of thinking and acting. In many cases functional stupidity can produce positive outcomes. Managers, professionals and many others cultivate stupidity management. We also frequently self-stupidify. We do this when we avoid questioning our assumptions, sidestep giving and demanding justifications, and refuse to consider the outcomes or broader meaning of our actions. We follow authority, are prepared to be seduced, we see things as natural and unavoidable and we rationalise our opportunism. Intelligent people are not immune to functional stupidity. Actually, reasonably intelligent people with successful careers have usually developed high levels of functional stupidity. Careerists are often good at self-stupification. Skilled leaders are often effective stupidity managers. It can help to smooth the action of their working life and economy.

Functional stupidity has big advantages: it helps individuals to manage their own doubts, be happy, feel comfortable with ambiguity, get along with their colleagues and superiors, present themselves as positive and upbeat, be more productive. And ultimately make a fairly steady climb up the corporate hierarchy. Liberal doses of functional stupidity can also help organisations to eliminate difficult questions, engineer a sense of harmony and ultimately make people more efficient. It reduces the frictions and conflicts that so often pop up in firms that are staffed by otherwise intelligent people. In the many image-intensive and seduction-dependent organisations, people inclined functional stupidity find a good habitat.

But functional stupidity is a double-edged sword. For individual employees, not using their intelligence can create a mounting sense of malaise and disappointment. Discrepancy between proclaimed values and actual work can prove to be troublesome. In extreme cases, it can mean that people grow cynical and alienated. Eventually they become completely disengaged from their workplaces. For organisations as a whole, functional stupidity can mean that people start overlooking problems. When this becomes routine, it can build up to large-scale disasters. But also many more modest, suboptimal structures and practices may develop. The result can be an organisation full of smart people that is riddled with stupidity.

Notes

Introduction

1. Felix Salmon, 'The recipe that killed Wall Street'. *Wired*, 23 Feb. 2009.
2. Richard Florida, *The Rise of the Creative Class: And How It's Transforming Work, Leisure, Community and Everyday Life* (New York: Basic Books, 2001).
3. Phil Taylor and Peter Bain, '"An assembly line in the head": work and employee relations in the call centre', *Industrial Relations Journal* 30, 2 (1999): pp. 101–17.
4. Timothy D. Wilson et al., 'Just think: the challenges of the disengaged mind', *Science* 345.6192 (2014): pp. 75–7.
5. Robert Jackall, *Moral Mazes* (Oxford: Oxford University Press, 1988).
6. John Sculley, *Odyssey: Pepsi to Apple* (New York: Harper & Row, 1987), p. 2.
7. Ibid., pp. 4–5.
8. Cited in: Harry Braverman, *Labour and Monopoly Capital* (New York: Monthly Review Press, 1974), p. 142.

1 The Knowledge Myth

1. Peter Drucker, 'The economic race: A forecast for 1980', *The New York Times*, 21 Jan. 1962, p. 66.
2. Peter Drucker, *The Age of Discontinuity* (New York: Harper & Row, 1967), p. 277.

3. Ibid., p. 278.
4. Ibid., p. 285.
5. Alain Touraine, *The Post-Industrial Society* (New York: Random House, 1971), p. 61.
6. Ibid., p. 62.
7. Ibid.
8. Daniel Bell, 'Welcome to the post-industrial society', *Physics Today*, Feb. 1976.
9. Morten Hansen, Nitin Nohria and Thomas Tierney, 'What's your strategy for managing knowledge?', *Harvard Business Review* 77, 2 (1999): p. 106.
10. Solveig Wikström and Richard Normann, *Knowledge and Value: A New Perspective on Corporate Transformation* (London: Routledge, 1994): pp. 1–2.
11. Robert M. Grant, 'Toward a knowledge-based theory of the firm', *Strategic Management Journal* 17.S2 (1996): pp. 109–122.
12. Bruce Kogut and Udo Zander, 'Knowledge of the firm, combinative capabilities, and the replication of technology', *Organization Science* 3, 3 (1992): p. 384.
13. Thomas Davenport and Larry Prusak, *Working Knowledge* (Cambridge, MA: Harvard Business School Press, 1998), p. 88.
14. Paul Adler, 'Critical in the name of whom and what?', *Organization* 9, 3 (2002): pp. 387–95.
15. Robert Reich, *The Work of Nations* (New York: Alfred Knopf, 1989).
16. Michael Hardt and Antonio Negri, *Multitude* (Cambridge, MA: Harvard University Press, 1999), p. 108.
17. Richard Adams, 'Number of students going on to higher education almost reaches 50%', *Guardian*, 24 Apr. 2014.
18. Richard Arum and Josipa Roksa, *Academically Adrift: Limited Learning on College Campuses* (Chicago: University of Chicago Press, 2011).
19. Bent Meier Sorensen, 'Facebook fight: Why we banned laptops, iPads and smartphones in lectures', *The Conversation*, 11 Nov. 2014.

20. Radhika Shanghani, 'Beyoncé studies anyone?', *Daily Telegraph*, 30 Jan. 2014.

21. Michael Foley, *The Age of Absurdity* (London: Simon & Schuster, 2010), p. 119.

22. Paul Jump, 'Academics in the minority at more than two-thirds of UK universities', *Times Higher Education Supplement*, 3 Sept. 2015.

23. Mats Alvesson and Jörgen Sandberg, 'Have management studies lost their way? Ideas for more imaginative and innovative research', *Journal of Management Studies* 50, 1 (2013): pp. 128–52.

24. Jacob Foster, Andrey Rzhetsky and James A. Evans, 'Tradition and innovation in scientists' research strategies', *American Sociological Review* 80, 5 (2015): pp. 875–908.

25. James A. Evans, 'Electronic publication and the narrowing of science and scholarship', *Science* 321, 5887 (2008): pp. 395–9.

26. http://www.pewinternet.org/

27. Cheryl Conner, 'Employees do really waste time at work', *Forbes*, 17 July 2012.

28. Ben Bryantt, 'Workers waste an hour a day on Facebook, shopping, browsing holidays, study finds', *Daily Telegraph*, 22 July 2013.

29. Tyler Cowen, *The Great Stagnation* (London: Penguin, 2011).

30. Mats Alvesson, *Knowledge Work and Knowledge-Intensive Firms* (Oxford: Oxford University Press, 2004).

31. Stanley Deetz, *Transforming Communication, Transforming Business: Building Responsive and Responsible Workplaces* (Cresskill, NJ: Hampton Press, 1995).

32. B. Ernst and A. Kieser, 'Do practitioners know what they are getting from consultants?' (Working Paper: Faculty of Business Administration, University of Mannheim, 2003).

33. Mats Alvesson and Stefan Sveningsson, 'Identity work in consultancy projects: ambiguity and distribution of credit and

blame', in C. Candlin and J. Crichton, eds., *Discourses of Deficit* (London: Palgrave, 2011).

34. Donald Bergh and Patrick Gibbons, 'The stock market reaction to the hiring of management consultants', *Journal of Management Studies* 48, 3 (2010): pp. 544–67.

35. Jeffrey Pfeffer, 'You're still the same: Why theories of power hold over time and across contexts', *Academy of Management Perspectives* 27, 4 (2013): pp. 269–80.

36. Stephen Sweet and Peter Meiksins, *Changing Contours of Work: Jobs and Opportunities in the New Economy* (Sage Publications, 2008).

37. Peter Fleming, Bill Harle, and Graham Sewell, 'A little knowledge is a dangerous thing: Getting below the surface of the growth of "knowledge work" in Australia', *Work, Employment & Society* 18, 4 (2004): pp. 725–47.

38. Alexander Cockburn, 'The myth of the "knowledge economy"', *CounterPunch*, 23 Mar. 2012.

39. Mats Alvesson, *The Triumph of Emptiness. Consumption, Higher Education and Work Organization* (Oxford: Oxford University Press 2013); Mats Alvesson and Paul Thompson; 'Post-bureaucracy?', in S. Ackroyd et al., ed., *Oxford Handbook of Work and Organization Studies* (Oxford: Oxford University Press, 2005).

40. Alexander Cockburn, 'The Myth of the Knowledge Economy', *Counterpunch*, March, 2010.

41. Paul Beaudry, David A. Green and Benjamin M. Sand, *The Great Reversal in the Demand for Skill and Cognitive Tasks*, working paper No. 18901, National Bureau of Economic Research, 2013.

42. Carl Frey and Michael Osborne, 'The future of employment: How susceptible are jobs to computerisation?', Engineering Sciences Department, Oxford University, working paper.

43. Erik Brynjolfsson and Andrew McAfee, *The Second Machine Age: Work, Progress and Prosperity in a Time of Brilliant Technologies* (New York: W.W. Norton & Company, 2014).

44. John Maynard Keynes, 'Economic possibilities for our grandchildren', in *Essays in Persuasion* (New York: W. W. Norton & Co., 1963), pp. 358–73.

45. Peter Fleming, *The Myth of Work* (London: Pluto Books, 2014).

46. David Graeber, 'On the phenomenon of bullshit jobs', *Strike! Magazine*, 17 August 2013.

47. '37% of British workers think their jobs are meaningless', YouGov, 12 Aug. 2015.

48. Avital Ronell, *Stupidity* (Chicago: University of Illinois Press, 2002).

49. Carol Dweck, *Mindset: Changing the way you think to fulfil your potential* (New York: Random House, 2006).

50. Bernard Stiegler, *States of Shock: Knowledge and Stupidity in the 21st Century* (Cambridge: Polity, 2015).

51. Martha S. Feldman and James G. March, 'Information in organizations as signal and symbol', *Administrative Science Quarterly* 26, 2 (1981): pp. 171–86.

52. Ibid.: p. 178.

53. Michael Foley, *The Age of Absurdity* (London: Simon & Schuster, 2010).

54. Jodi Kantor and David Streitfeld, 'Inside Amazon: wrestling big ideas in a bruising workplace', *The New York Times*, 15 Aug. 2015.

55. 'To fly, to fall, to fly again'. *The Economist*, 25 June 2015.

2 Not So Smart

1. Stephan Schaefer, 'Managerial Ignorance: A Study of How Managers Organise for Creativity', PhD Thesis, Lund University, 2014.

2. Cited in Schaefer, p. 225.

3. Lauren Rivera, *Pedigree: How Elite Students Get Elite Jobs* (Princeton, NJ: Princeton University Press, 2015).

4. Daniel Goleman, *Emotional Intelligence* (London: Bantam, 2006).

5. Stéphane Côté, 'Emotional intelligence in organizations', *Annual Review of Organizational Psychology and Organizational Behavior* 1 (2014): pp. 459–88.

6. Christopher Lasch, *The Culture of Narcissism* (New York: W.W. Norton, 1978).

7. Gary Klein, *Sources of Power: How People Make Decisions* (Cambridge, MA: MIT Press, 1999).

8. Richard K. Wagner and Robert J. Sternberg, 'Practical intelligence in real-world pursuits: the role of tacit knowledge', *Journal of Personality and Social Psychology* 49, 2 (1985): p. 436; Richard Wagner and Robert Sternberg, 'Street smarts', in *Measures of Leadership,* Kenneth J. Clark and Miriam B. Clark, eds. (West Orange, NJ: Leadership Library of America, 1990), pp. 493–504.

9. Daniel J. Isenberg, 'Thinking and managing: a verbal protocol analysis of managerial problem solving', *Academy of Management Journal*, 29, 4 (1986): pp. 775–88.

10. Daniel Kahneman and Amos Tversky, 'On the psychology of prediction', *Psychological Review* 80 (1973): pp. 237–51.

11. Amos Tversky and Daniel Kahneman, 'Judgment under uncertainty: heuristics and biases', *Science* 185, 4157 (1974): pp. 1124–31.

12. Henrik Kristensen and Tommy Gärling, 'The effects of anchor points and reference points on negotiation process and outcome', *Organizational Behavior and Human Decision Processes* 71, 1 (1997): pp. 85–94.

13. Franklin Templeton Investments, 'Investors should beware the role of "availability bias"', Business Insider, 6 Oct. 2012, 1 Dec. 2013.

14. Byunghwan Lee, John O'Brien and Konduru Sivaramakrishnan, 'An analysis of financial analysts' optimism in long-term

growth forecasts', *Journal of Behavioral Finance* 9, 3 (2008): pp. 171–84.

15.   Ola Svenson, 'Are we all less risky and more skillful than our fellow drivers?', *Acta Psychologica* 47, 2 (1981): pp. 143–8.

16.   K. Patricia Cross, 'Not can, but *will* college teaching be improved?', *New Directions for Higher Education*, 1977, 17 (Spring 1977): pp. 1–15.

17.   'It's academic', *Stanford GSB Reporter*, 24 Apr. 2000, pp. 14–15.

18.   Jim Holt, 'Two brains running', *New York Times*. 27 Nov. 2011, p. 16.

19.   Ulrike Malmendier and Geoffrey Tate, 'Who makes acquisitions? CEO overconfidence and the market's reaction', *Journal of Financial Economics* 89, 1 (2008): pp. 20–43.

20.   Philipp Koellinger, Maria Minniti and Christian Schade, '"I think I can, I think I can": overconfidence and entrepreneurial behavior', *Journal of Economic Psychology* 28, 4 (2007): pp. 502–27.

21.   James Andreoni, 'Warm-glow versus cold-prickle: the effects of positive and negative framing on cooperation in experiments', *Quarterly Journal of Economics* 110, 1 (1995): pp. 1–21.

22.   Joep Cornelissen, Saku Mantere and Eero Vaara, 'The contraction of meaning: the combined effect of communication, emotions, and materiality on sensemaking in the Stockwell shooting', *Journal of Management Studies* 51, 5 (2014): pp. 699–736.

23.   Paul K. Presson and Victor A. Benassi, 'Illusion of control: a meta-analytic review', *Journal of Social Behavior and Personality* 11,3 (1996): pp. 493–510.

24.   Barry M. Staw, 'The escalation of commitment to a course of action', *Academy of Management Review* 6, 4 (1981): pp. 577–87.

25.   Harry Braverman, *Labor and Monopoly Capital: The Degradation of Work in the Twentieth Century* (New York: Monthly Review Press, 1974).

26.   Garrett Jones, 'The O-ring sector and the foolproof sector: an explanation for skill externalities', *Journal of Economic Behavior and Organization* 85 (2012): pp. 1–10.

27. Mats Alvesson, *Knowledge Work and Knowledge-Intensive Firms* (Oxford: Oxford University Press, 2004).

28. George Ritzer, *The McDonaldization of Society* (Los Angeles: Pine Forge Press, 2004).

29. Peter Fleming, *Resisting Work* (Philadelphia: Temple University Press, 2014).

30. Denise Agosto, 'Bounded rationality and satisficing in young people's web-based decision making', *Journal of the American Society for Information Science and Technology* 53, 1 (2002): pp. 16–27.

31. Ellen J. Langer and Robert P. Abelson, 'The semantics of asking a favor: how to succeed in getting help without really dying', *Journal of Personality and Social Psychology* 24, 1 (1972): p. 26.

32. Ellen J. Langer and Robert P. Abelson, 'A patient by any other name … : clinician group difference in labeling bias', *Journal of Consulting and Clinical Psychology*,42, 1 (1974): pp. 4–9.

33. Blake E. Ashforth and Gadi Ravid, 'Poor service from the service bureaucracy: the role of mindlessness', *Academy of Management Proceedings* 1 (1986): pp. 166–9.

34. Blake E. Ashforth and Yitzhak Fried, 'The mindlessness of organizational behaviors', *Human Relations* 41, 4 (1988): pp. 305–29.

35. Mats Alvesson and Stefan Sveningsson, 'Managers doing leadership: the extra-ordinarization of the mundane', *Human Relations* 56, 12 (2003): pp. 1435–59.

36. Joël van der Weele, 'Inconvenient truths: determinants of strategic ignorance in moral dilemmas', University of Amsterdam working paper, 2014.

37. Robert H. Frank, Thomas Gilovich and Dennis T. Regan, 'Does Studying Economics Inhibit Cooperation?' *Journal of Economic Perspectives*, 7,2 (1993): pp. 159–171.

38. Russell Golman, David Hagmann and George Loewenstein, 'Informational avoidance', Department of Decision Science, Carnegie Mellon University, working paper, 2015.

39. Patrick McGee and Robert Wright, 'VW management back in spotlight', *Financial Times*, 4 March 2016.

40. Mark Zbaracki, 'The rhetoric and reality of total quality management', *Administrative Science Quarterly* 43, 3 (1998): pp. 602–36.

41. Justin Kruger and David Dunning, 'Unskilled and unaware of it: how difficulties in recognizing one's own incompetence lead to inflated self-assessments', *Journal of Personality and Social Psychology* 77, 6 (1999): p. 1121.

42. Andrew Abbott, 'Varieties of ignorance', *The American Sociologist* 41, 2 (2010): pp. 174–89.

43. Linsey McGoey, 'The logic of strategic ignorance', *British Journal of Sociology* 63, 3 (5 Sept. 2012): pp. 533–76; William Davies and Linsey McGoey, 'Rationalities of ignorance: on financial crisis and the ambivalence of neo-liberal epistemology', *Economy and Society* 41, 1 (2012): pp. 64–83.

44. Robert Jackall, *Moral Mazes* (Oxford: Oxford University Press, 1988).

3 Functional Stupidity

1. David Dyer, 'A voice of experience: an interview with TRW's Frederick C. Crawford', *Harvard Business Review* (1991): p. 117.

2. Ibid.

3. Malcolm Gladwell, 'The engineer's lament', *New Yorker*, 4 May 2015.

4. Robert Jackall, *Moral Mazes* (Oxford: Oxford University Press, 1988).

5. Ibid.

6. Stefan Agewall, 'Clever idiot?', *The Lancet* 361.9369 (2003): p. 1659.

7. David Crouch, 'Swedish private jet scandal claims seventh scalp', *Guardian*, 11 Feb. 2015.

8. Robert Jackall, *Moral Mazes* (Oxford: Oxford University Press, 1988).

9. Ibid., pp. 109–10.

10.   Ibid., p. 6.

11.   Mats Alvesson, *Management of Knowledge-Intensive Companies* (Berlin: de Gruyter, 1995).

12.   Markus Perkmann and André Spicer, 'How emerging organizations take form: the role of imprinting and values in organizational bricolage'. *Organization Science* 25, 6 (2014): pp. 1785–1806.

13.   Mats Alvesson, *The Triumph of Emptiness. Consumption, Higher Education and Work Organization* (Oxford: Oxford University Press, 2013).

14.   Gerry Antioch, 'Persuasion is now 30 per cent of US GDP', *Economics Round-up* 1 (2013).

15.   Louise Ashley and Laura Empson, 'Differentiation and discrimination: understanding social class and social exclusion in leading law firms', *Human Relations* 66, 2 (2013): pp. 219–44.

16.   Chris Warhurst and Dennis Nickson, 'Employee experience of aesthetic labour in retail and hospitality', *Work, Employment & Society* 21, 1 (2007): pp. 103–20.

17.   J. K. Galbraith, *The Affluent Society* (Harmondsworth: Penguin, 1958).

18.   Dana Gunders, *Wasted: How America Is Losing Up to 40 Percent of Its Food from Farm to Fork to Landfill*, NRDC Issue Paper, Aug. 2012.

19.   Rebecca Smithers, 'Almost half of world's food thrown away, report finds', *Guardian*, 10 Jan. 2013.

20.   Mabelle Morgan, 'Throw-away fashion', *Daily Mail,* 9 June 2015.

21.   Global mobile telephone sales to end users from 2009 to 2014, http://www.statista.com/statistics/270243/global-mobile-phone-sales-by-vendor-since-2009/

22.   Peter Fleming, *Authenticity and the Cultural Politics of Work* (Oxford: Oxford University Press, 2009).

23.   Hugh Willmott, 'Strength is ignorance; slavery is freedom: managing culture in modern organizations,' *Journal of Management Studies* 30, 4 (1993): pp. 515–52.

24. Clarence Hooker, 'Ford's sociology department and the Americanization campaign and the manufacture of popular culture among assembly line workers c. 1910–1917', *Journal of American Culture* 20, 1 (1997): p. 47.

25. Alexandra Michel, 'Transcending socialization: a nine-year ethnography of the body's role in organizational control and knowledge workers' transformation', *Administrative Science Quarterly* 56, 3 (2011): pp. 325–68.

26. Naomi Klein, *No Logo* (New York: Picador, 2010).

27. Maureen Morris and Abby Klaassen, 'How Dan Widen learned how to fail', *Advertising Age*, 25 July 2013.

28. Robert Jackall, *Moral Mazes* (Oxford: Oxford University Press, 1988).

29. Dan Karreman and Mats Alvesson, 'Resisting resistance. on counter-resistance, control and compliance in a consultancy firm', *Human Relations* 62, 8 (2009): pp. 1115–44.

30. Nils Brunsson, 'The irrationality of action and action rationality: decisions, ideologies and organizational actions', *Journal of Management Studies* 19,1 (1982): pp. 29–44.

31. Tony Watson, *In Search of Management* (London: Routledge, 1994), p. 117.

32. Margaret Archer, ed., *Conversations about Reflexivity* (London: Routledge, 2009).

33. Nils Brunsson, *The Irrational Organization: Irrationality As a Basis for Organizational Action and Change* (London: John Wiley & Sons, 1985).

34. Anthony King and Ivor Crewe, *The Blunders of Our Government* (London: Oneworld, 2013).

35. Jana Costas and Peter Fleming, 'Beyond dis-identification: a discursive approach to self-alienation in contemporary organizations', *Human Relations* 62, 3 (2009): pp. 353–78.

36. Fred C. Alford, *Whistleblowers: Broken Lives and Organizational Power* (New York; Cornell University Press, 2001).

37.   William H. Starbuck and Frances J. Milliken, 'Challenger:
      fine-tuning the odds until something breaks', *Journal of
      Management Studies* 25, 4 (1988): pp. 319–40.
38.   Yiannis Gabriel, David E. Gray and Harshita Goregaokar,
      'Temporary derailment or the end of the line? Managers
      coping with unemployment at 50', *Organization Studies* 31, 12
      (2010): pp. 1687–1712.
39.   John Sculley, *Odyssey: Pepsi to Apple* (New York: Harper &
      Row, 1987).
40.   Michael Pratt, 'The good, the bad, and the ambivalent:
      managing identification among Amway distributors',
      Administrative Science Quarterly 45, 3 (2000): pp. 456–93.
41.   André Spicer, 'The political process of inscribing a new
      technology', *Human Relations* 58, 7 (2005): pp. 867–90.
42.   Andrea Whittle and Frank Mueller, 'Bankers in the dock:
      moral storytelling in action', *Human Relations* 65, 1 (2012):
      pp. 111–39.

4 Leadership-Induced Stupidity

1.   Stefan Sveningsson and Mats Alvesson, *Managerial Life*
     (Cambridge: Cambridge University Press, 2016).
2.   Jeffrey Pfeffer, *Leadership BS* (New York: Harper Business,
     2016).
3.   Sverre Spoelstra, 'Business miracles', *Culture and Organization*
     16.1 (2010): pp. 87–101.
4.   Jeffery Pfeffer, *Leadership BS* (New York: Harper Business,
     2016).
5.   Pierre Gurdjian, Thomas Halbeisen and Kevin Lane, 'Why
     leadership-development programs fail', *McKinsey Quarterly*,
     Jan, 2014.
6.   Robert Kaiser and Gordy Curphy, 'Leadership development:
     the failure of an industry and the opportunity for consulting
     psychologists', *Consulting Psychology Journal: Practice and
     Research* 65,4 (2013): pp. 294–302.

7.   Bernard McKenna, David Rooney and Kimberley B. Boal,
      'Wisdom principles as a meta-theoretical basis for evaluating
      leadership,' *Leadership Quarterly* 20, 2 (2009): pp. 177–90.

8.   Keith Grint, 'Learning to lead: can Aristotle help us find the
      road to wisdom?', *Leadership* 3, 2 (2007): p. 231.

9.   Bill George, *Authentic Leadership* (New York: John Wiley &
      Sons, 2004).

10.   Marshall Sashkin, 'Transformational leadership approaches:
      A review and synthesis', in John Antonakis, Anna Cianciolo
      and Robert Sternberg, ed., *The Nature of Leadership* (Thousand
      Oaks, CA: Sage Publications, 2004), pp. 171–96.

11.   Dennis Tourish and Ashly Pinnington, 'Transformational
      leadership, corporate cultism and the spirituality paradigm:
      An unholy trinity in the workplace?', *Human Relations* 55, 2
      (2002): pp. 147–72.

12.   Winston Churchill made a large number of unwise decisions.
      Sometimes these led to catastrophes like Gallipoli in 1915 and
      Greece in 1941. He was also known as a poor assessor of people.
      He typically preferred to appoint people similar to himself.
      He had a flair for the dramatic and risky action and was often
      overoptimistic. Field Marshal Alan Brooke, the head of the
      British army during the Second World War, felt that he had
      to work close to Churchill and not accept other assignments
      simply to prevent Churchill from making too many blunders.
      This is not to deny Churchill's outstanding virtues: among
      them political insight, decisiveness, rhetorical skills and
      courage. See, for example, Anthony Beevor, *The Second World
      War* (London: Weidenfeld & Nicolson, 2012).

13.   Mats Alvesson and André Spicer, *Metaphors We Lead By*
      (London: Routledge, 2011); Stefan Sveningsson and Mats
      Alvesson, *Managerial Life* (Cambridge: Cambridge University
      Press, 2016).

14.   Mats Alvesson and Anna Jonsson, 'The bumpy road to
      exercising leadership', *Leadership* (forthcoming).

15. Martin Blom and Mats Alvesson, 'Leadership on demand.
     Followers as initiators and inhibitors of managerial leadership',
     Scandinavian Journal of Management 30 (2014): pp. 344–57.
16. Norman Dixon, *On the Psychology of Military Incompetence*
     (London: Pimlico, 1994).
17. Mats Alvesson and André Spicer, *Metaphors We Lead By*
     (London: Routledge, 2011).
18. Helen Delaney and Sverre Spoelstra, 'Transformation
     leadership: secularized theology?' in *Leadership: Contemporary
     Perspectives,* Bridget Carroll, Jackie Ford and Scott Taylor, eds.
     (London: Sage, 2015).
19. Dennis Tourish, *The Dark Side of Transformational Leadership:
     A Critical Perspective* (London: Routledge, 2013).
20. Martin Blom and Mats Alvesson, 'Leadership on demand.
     Followers as initiators and inhibitors of managerial leadership',
     Scandinavian Journal of Management 30 (2014): pp. 344–57.,
     p. 351.
21. Mats Alvesson and Stefan Sveningsson, 'Managers doing
     leadership: The extraordinarisation of the mundane', Human
     Relations 56 (2003) pp. 1435–59.
22. Marshall Sashkin, 'Transformational leadership approaches: A
     review and synthesis', in John Antonakis, Anna Cianciolo and
     Robert Sternberg, eds., *The Nature of Leadership* (Thousand
     Oakes, CA: Sage Publications, 2004) p. 175.
23. Dennis Tourish, *The Dark Side of Transformational Leadership:
     A Critical Perspective* (London: Routledge, 2013).
24. Mats Alvesson and André Spicer, *Metaphors We Lead By*
     (London: Routledge, 2011).
25. Jeffery D. Houghton, Christopher P. Neck and Charles C.
     Manz, 'Self-Leadership and SuperLeadership: the Heart and
     Art of Creating Shared Leadership in Teams', in Craig L.
     Pearce and Jay A. Conger, eds., *Shared Leadership: Reframing
     the Hows and Whys of Leadership* (Thousand Oakes, CA: Sage
     Publications, 2004), p. 133.

26. Tony Huzzard and Sverre Spoelstra, 'The leader as gardener', in Mats Alvesson and André Spicer, eds., *Metaphors We Lead By* (London: Routledge, 2011).

27. Martin Blom and Mats Alvesson, 'Leadership on demand. Followers as initiators and inhibitors of managerial leadership', *Scandinavian Journal of Management* 30 (2014): pp. 344–57.

28. Mats Alvesson and Stefan Sveningsson, 'The good visions, the bad micro-management and the ugly ambiguity: contradictions of (non-)leadership in a knowledge-intensive company', *Organization Studies* 24, 6 (2003): pp. 961–88.

29. Henry Mintzberg, 'The manager's job: folklore and fact', *Harvard Business Review* (1990): pp. 163–76.

30. Martin Blom and Mats Alvesson, 'Leadership on demand. Followers as initiators and inhibitors of managerial leadership', *Scandinavian Journal of Management* 30 (2014): 344–57., pp. 251–2.

31. Robert K. Greenleaf and Larry C. Spears, *Servant Leadership: A Journey into the Nature of Legitimate Power and Greatness* (Mahwah, NJ: Paulist Press, 2002).

32. Robert Heifetz and Donald L. Laurie, 'The work of leadership', *Harvard Business Review* 75 (1997): p. 127.

33. Mats Alvesson, 'The leader as saint', in M. Alvesson and A. Spicer, eds., *Metaphors We Lead By: Understanding Leadership in the Real World* (London: Routledge, 2011).

34. Bernard Bass and Paul Steidlmeier, 'Ethics, character and authentic transformational leadership behavior', *Leadership Quarterly* 10, 2 (1999): pp. 181–217.

35. Walter Issacson, *Steve Jobs* (New York: Simon and Schuster, 2011).

36. Jim Collins, *Good to Great: Why Some Companies Make the Leap – and Others Don't* (New York: Harper Business, 2001).

37. Stefan Tengblad, 'Is there a "New Managerial Work"? A comparison with Henry Mintzberg's classic study 30 years later,' *Journal of Management Studies* 43, 7 (2006): pp. 1437–61.

38. Bobby J. Calder, 'An attribution theory of leadership', in B.
     Staw and J. Salacik, eds., *New Directions in Organizational
     Behavior* (Chicago: St. Clair Press, 1977), pp. 179–204; Jim
     Meindl, 'The romance of leadership as a follower-centric
     theory: a social constructionist approach', *Leadership
     Quarterly* 6 (1995): 329–41; Jeffrey Pfeffer,'The ambiguity
     of leadership', *Academy of Management Review* 2, 1 (1997):
     pp. 104–12.
39. Markus A. Fitza, 'The use of variance decomposition in the
     investigation of CEO effects: How large must the CEO effect
     be to rule out chance?', *Strategic Management Journal* 35, 12
     (2014): pp. 1839–52.
40. Joanne B. Ciulla, 'Ethics and leadership effectiveness,' in John
     Antonakis, Anna Cianciolo and Robert Sternberg, eds., *The
     Nature of Leadership* (Thousand Oaks, CA: Sage Publication,
     2004), pp. 302–27.
41. Francis J. Flynn and Barry M. Staw, 'Lend me your wallets:
     The effect of charismatic leadership on external support for
     an organization', *Strategic Management Journal* 25, 4 (2004):
     pp. 309–30.
42. Stefan Sveningsson and Mats Alvesson, *Managerial Life*
     (Cambridge: Cambridge University Press, 2016).
43. Abraham Zaleznik, 'Real work', *Harvard Business Review* 75, 6
     (1997), pp. 53–9.
44. Mats Alvesson, Martin Blom and Stefan Sveningsson, *Reflexive
     Leadership* (London: Sage, 2016).
45. André Spicer, 'Shooting the shit: The role of bullshit in
     organizations', *M@n@gement* 16(5) (2013): pp. 653–66.

5 Structure-Induced Stupidity

1.   Mats Alveson and Susanne Lundholm, *'Personalchefers arbete
     och identiet. Strategi och strul'* ('Personnel managers' work and
     identity. Strategy and Mess), Lund: Studentlitteratur, 2014.

2. David Graeber, *The Utopia of Rules: On Technology, Stupidity, and the Secret Joys of Bureaucracy* (London: Melville House, 2015); Brendan McSweeney, 'Are we living in a post-bureaucratic epoch?', *Journal of Organizational Change Management* 19, 1 (2006): pp. 22–37.

3. Kathleen M. Eisenhardt and Donald N. Sull, 'Strategy as simple rules', *Harvard Business Review* 79.1 (2001) pp. 106–19.

4. Harry Braverman (1974); cf. Paul Attewell, 'The deskilling controversy', *Work and Occupations* 14, 3 (1987): pp. 323–46.

5. F. W. Taylor, *The Principles of Scientific Management* (New York: Harper, 1914).

6. Charles D. Wrege and Amadeo G. Perroni, 'Taylor's pig tale: a historical analysis of Frederick W. Taylor's pig-iron experiments', *Academy of Management Journal* 17 (Mar. 1974): pp. 6–27.

7. Drew A. R. Ross, 'Backstage with the knowledge boys and girls: Goffman and distributed agency in an organic online community', *Organization Studies* 28, 3 (2007): pp. 307–25.

8. Jana Costas and Dan Kärreman, 'The bored self in knowledge work', *Human Relations* 69, 1 (2016): pp. 61–83.

9. George Ritzer, *The McDonaldization of Society* (Sage, 2004)

10. Peter Fleming, '"Kindergarten Cop": Paternalism and resistance in a high-commitment workplace', *Journal of Management Studies* 42, 7 (2005): pp. 1469–89.

11. Roland Paulsen, *Empty Labour* (Cambridge: Cambridge University Press, 2014).

12. V. Ottati, E. Price, C. Wilson and N. Sumaktoyo, 'When self-perceptions of expertise increase closed-minded cognition: The earned dogmatism effect', *Journal of Experimental Social Psychology* 61 (2015): pp. 131–8.

13. Mats Alvesson and Jörgen Sandberg, 'Habitat and habitus: Boxed-in and box-breaking research', *Organization Studies* 35, 7 (2014): pp. 967–87.

14. Jacob Foster, Andrey Rzhetsky and James A. Evans, 'Tradition and innovation in scientists' research strategies', *American Sociological Review* 80, 5 (2015): pp. 875–908.

15. Mats Alvesson and Dan Karreman, 'Unraveling HRM. Identity, ceremony and control in a management consultancy firm', *Organization Science* 18, 4 (2007): pp. 711–23

16. Annemette Kjærgaard, Mette Morsing and Davide Ravasi, 'Mediating identity: A study of media influence on organizational identity construction in a celebrity firm', *Journal of Management Studies* 48, 3 (2011): pp. 514–43.

17. Tim Hallett, 'The myth incarnate: recoupling processes, turmoil, and inhabited institutions in an urban elementary school', *American Sociological Review* 75, 1 (2010): pp. 52–74.

18. Ibid.: p. 67.

19. Michael Power, *The Audit Society: Rituals of Verification* (Oxford: Oxford University Press, 1997).

20. Gerry McGivern and Michael Fischer, 'Medical regulation, spectacular transparency and the blame business', *Journal of Health Organization and Management* 24, 6 (2010): pp. 597–610.

21. Margaret Heffernan, *Wilful Blindness: Why We Ignore the Obvious at Our Peril* (New York: Simon & Schuster, 2011).

6 Imitation-Induced Stupidity

1. Alexander T. Nicolai, Ann-Christine Schulz and Thomas W. Thomas, 'What Wall Street wants – exploring the role of security analysts in the evolution and spread of management concepts', *Journal of Management Studies* 47, 1 (2010): pp. 162–89.

2. Simona Giorgi and Klaus Weber, 'Marks of distinction: Framing and audience appreciation in the context of investment advice', *Administrative Science Quarterly* 60, 2 (2015): pp. 333–67.

3. Barry M. Staw and Lisa D. Epstein, 'What bandwagons bring: effects of popular management techniques on corporate

performance, reputation, and CEO pay', *Administrative Science Quarterly* 45, 3 (2000): pp. 523–56.

4. David Deephouse and Mark Suchman, 'Legitimacy in organizational institutionalism', in R. Greenwood, C. Oliver, R. Suddaby, K. Sahlin Andersson, eds., *Sage Handbook of Organizational Institutionalism* (London: Sage, 2008).

5. Jan Wallander, *Decentralisation – Why and How to Make It Work* (Stockholm: SNS Forlag, 2003), p. 115.

6. James Westphal, Ranjay Gulati and Stephen M. Shortell, 'Customization or conformity? An institutional and network perspective on the content and consequences of TQM adoption', *Administrative Science Quarterly* (1997): pp. 366–94.

7. Paul DiMaggio and Walter W. Powell, 'The iron cage revisited: Collective rationality and institutional isomorphism in organizational fields', *American Sociological Review* 48, 2 (1983): pp. 147–60.

8. Paul DiMaggio and Walter W. Powell, 'Introduction', in P. DiMaggio and W. Powell, ed., *The New Institutionalism in Organizational Analysis* (Chicago: University of Chicago Press, 1991).

9. Jerker Denrell, 'Vicarious learning, undersampling of failure, and the myths of management', *Organization Science* 14, 3 (2003): pp. 227–43.

10. Karl Ydén, *'Kriget' och Karriärsystemet* (The war and the career system), (Göteborg: BAS, 2006).

11. John Meyer and Brian Rowan, *The Structure of Educational Organizations. Environments and Organizations* (New York: John Wiley & Sons, 1978).

12. John Meyer and Brian Rowan, 'Institutionalized organizations: formal structure as myth and ceremony', *American Journal of Sociology* (1977): pp. 340–63.

13. Charles Perrow, 'Demystifying organizations', in R. Sarri and Y. Heskenfeld, eds., *The Management of Human Services* (New York: Columbia University Press, 1978).

14. Anshuman Prasad, Pushkala Prasad and Raza Mir, '"One mirror in another": managing diversity and the discourse of fashion', *Human Relations* 64, 5 (2011): pp. 703–24.

15. Ibid.: p. 709.

16. Ibid.: p. 710.

17. Ibid.: p. 718.

7 Branding-Induced Stupidity

1. 'Ny försvarslogo för miljoner', (New defense logo for millions) *Svenska Dagbladet*, 13 Nov. 2005.

2. Mary Jo Hatch and Majken Schulz, 'The dynamics of organizational identity', *Human Relations* 55, 8 (2002): pp. 989–1018.

3. Don Watson, *Worst Words* (Sydney: Vintage, 2015), p. 50.

4. Karl Marx, *Capital*, vol. 1 (London: Penguin).

5. Katya Assaf, 'Brand fetishism', *Connecticut Law Review* 43 (2010): p. 83.

6. Wally Olins, 'How brands are taking over the corporation', in M. Schultz et al., eds., *The Expressive Organization* (Oxford: Oxford University Press, 2000), p. 61.

7. Quoted in Vance Packard, *The Hidden Persuaders* (Harmondsworth: Penguin, 1981), p. 46.

8. Angela Orend and Patricia Gagné, 'Corporate logo tattoos and the commodification of the body', *Journal of Contemporary Ethnography* 38, 4 (2009): pp. 493–517.

9. Jess Collen, 'How much to tattoo my trademark on your body?', *Forbes*, 4 May 2013.

10. Richard Sennett, *The Culture of the New Capitalism* (New Haven, CT: Yale University Press, 2006), p. 144.

11. *The Absolut Story*, advertising brochure (2004), p. 17.

12. Naomi Klein, *No Logo* (Knopf, 2000), p. 17.

13. Mats Alvesson, Dan Kärreman and Carys Egan-Wyer, 'Working in the twilight of branding: Living up to the brand in an imperfect world,' Lund University working paper (2016).

14. We have used a pseudonym here.

15. Mats Alvesson, *The Triumph of Emptiness. Consumption, Higher Education and Work Organization* (Oxford: Oxford University Press 2013).

16. Christopher Lasch, *The Culture of Narcissism* (New York: W. W. Norton, 1978) p. 72.

17. Stephen Fineman, 'The natural environment, organization and ethics', in M. Parker, ed., *Ethics & Organizations* (London: Sage, 1998), p. 243.

18. Linda McGuire, 'Prisoners as customers or clients?', *Australian Journal of Public Administration* 56, 3 (1997): pp. 149–51.

19. John Kenneth Galbraith, *The Affluent Society*. (Harmondsworth: Penguin, 1958).

20. Lokham Meho, 'The rise and rise of citation analysis', *Physics World* (2007) 20(1), pp. 32–6.

21. David Graeber, 'On the Phenomenon of Bullshit jobs', *Strike Magazine* (2013).

8 Culture-Induced Stupidity

1. Dan Karreman and Mats Alvesson, 'Making newsmakers: Conversational identity at work', *Organization Studies* 22, 1 (2001): pp. 59–89.

2. Clifford Geertz *The Interpretation of Culture* (New York: Basic Books, 1973), p. 145.

3. Gideon Kunda, *Engineering Culture: Control and Commitment in a High-Tech Corporation* (Philadelphia, PA: Temple University Press, 1992), p. 88.

4. Ibid., p. 155.

5. Timothy Morris and Laura Empson, 'Organisation and expertise: An exploration of knowledge bases and the management of accounting and consulting firms', *Accounting, Organizations and Society* 23, 5 (1998): p. 618.

6. Mats Alvesson, *Understanding Organizational Culture* (London: Sage, 2013).

7.   Manfred Kets de Vries and Danny Miller, *The Neurotic Organization* (San Francisco: Jossey-Bass, 1984).

8.   Timo O. Vuori and Quy N. Huy, 'Distributed attention and shared emotions in the innovation process. How Nokia lost the smartphone battle', *Administrative Science Quarterly* 61, 1 (2015): pp. 9–51.

9.   Mats Alvesson, *Management of Knowledge-Intensive Companies* (Berlin: de Gruyter, 1995).

10. O. Amundsen, 'Fortellinger om organisationsendringer', Ph.D. thesis, Norges teknisk- naturvetenskaplige Universitet, Trondheim (2003).

11. Eric Abrahamson, 'Avoiding repetitive change syndrome', *MIT Sloan Management Review* 45, 2 (2004): p. 93.

12. Mats Alvesson and Stefan Sveningsson, *Changing Organizational Culture* (London: Routledge, 2015).

13. Robert Jackall, *Moral Mazes* (Oxford: Oxford University Press, 1988) p. 84.

14. Ibid., p. 87.

15. Stefan Linski, 'Rikspolischef Dan Eliasson: Vill inte gräva i historien', *Dagen Nyheter*, 26 Jan. 2016.

9 How to Do Stupidity Management and How to Counter It

1.   Thomas H. Davenport and Laurence Prusak. *Working Knowledge: How Organizations Manage What They Know* (Boston: Harvard Business Press, 1998).

2.   Nils Brunsson, *The Irrational Organization: Irrationality As a Basis for Organizational Action and Change* (London: John Wiley & Sons, 1985).

3.   Gideon Kunda, *Engineering Culture* (Philadelphia: Temple University Press, 1992), p. 185.

4.   Mats Alvesson, *Management of Knowledge-Intensive Companies* (Berlin: de Gruyter, 1995).

5. Mats Alvesson, *The Triumph of Emptiness. Consumption, Higher Education and Work Organization* (Oxford: Oxford University Press 2013).

6. Robert French, '"Negative capability": managing the confusing uncertainties of change', *Journal of Organizational Change Management* 14, 5 (2001): pp. 480–92; Peter F. Simpson, Robert French and Charles E. Harvey. 'Leadership and negative capability', *Human Relations* 55, 10 (2002): pp. 1209–26.

7. K. Eisold, 'The rediscovery of the unknown: an inquiry into psychoanalytic praxis', *Contemporary Psychoanalysis* 36, 1 (2000): p. 65.

8. Roberto Unger, *False Necessity* (Cambridge: Cambridge University Press, 1987).

9. Luc Boltanski and Laurent Thévenot, *On Justification* (Princeton, NJ: Princeton University Press, 2005).

10. Gary Klein, 'Performing a project premortem', *Harvard Business Review* 85, 9 (2007): pp. 18–19.

11. David Courpasson, Françoise Dany and Stewart Clegg, 'Resisters at work: Generating productive resistance in the workplace', *Organization Science* 23, 3 (2012): pp. 801–19.

Acknowledgements

We are grateful for comments from Yvonne Billing, Robyn O'Sullivan, Roland Paulsen, Jukka Rintamaki, Stephan Schaefer and Clare Grist Taylor on a draft of this book. We acknowledge the financial support from the K & A Wallenberg foundation and the Tom Hedelius and Jan Wallander research foundation. We would also like to thank the people who helped to undertake the fieldwork reported in the book – they include Martin Blom, Carys Egan-Wyer, Dan Kärreman, Stephan Schaefer and Stefan Svenningsson. The ideas in this book were initially developed in an article published in the *Journal of Management Studies* in 2012. Finally, we would like to thank the dozens of people we have discussed the ideas in this book with over the past seven years. You are too numerous to name, but your help has been invaluable.

Index